CLASSICAL INDIA

CLASSICAL INDIA

Edited by

WILLIAM H. McNEILL

and

JEAN W. SEDLAR

New York

OXFORD UNIVERSITY PRESS

London   1969   Toronto

Copyright © 1969 by Oxford University Press, Inc.
Library of Congress Catalogue Card Number: 68-8409
Printed in the United States of America
This reprint, 1972

Preface

The greatest obstacle to the historical study of ancient India is the chronological mistiness surrounding the original sources. Most classical Indian texts were shaped and re-shaped through generations of oral recitation. They were transmitted by word of mouth from master to pupil through organized school systems that trained members of the upper classes in their religious and social duties; and they survived because their validity and relevance remained largely unchallenged. Although some literary works—especially those emanating from court circles, like the dramas of Kalidasa—may confidently be ascribed to known authors and reasonably precise dates, this is not the case with most. Those compositions of greatest significance in the evolution of Indian civilization can be dated only by allowing for one or more centuries' possible error; and their authors are either anonymous or of questionable historicity.

The chief examples of literary anonymity and oral editing are the classic religious texts—the four Vedas of the Hindus and the early Buddhist Sutras—and the two great Hindu epics known as the *Mahabharata* and the *Ramayana*. As the original contents of these works became older and progressively less intelligible, or as religious conceptions changed with time, explanatory passages—which often changed the original meaning—were added. Traditional verses were retained beside newer ones, even when their original function had disappeared; and relatively recent compositions were incorporated into ancient texts and ascribed to the sages of former times. While such editing of traditional materials is by no means unknown in other civilizations, the habit of oral transmission made it especially pronounced in India. The best-known texts were committed to writing centuries after they first took form; and their component strata are correspondingly difficult to identify. The annals of kings—which occupy so prominent a place in ancient Near Eastern or Chinese literature—are virtually non-existent in India; politics and warfare were not considered worthy of record. With their dearth of references to historically identifiable persons or events, Indian writings usually provide few clues as to date of composition. Modern philological techniques—which depend on the analysis of language development—are of similarly limited use in unscrambling the chronology of texts so lacking in fixed points of orientation. The most precise dates in Indian history have been established on the evidence of Greek, Chinese, and (at a later period) Muslim and European writers.

In the absence of reliable dating, it becomes tempting to treat the whole of Indian history as a single cultural landscape. But no competent observer regards this as the true state of affairs. History did not stand still south of the Himalayas, even if its development is difficult to trace. Still, Indian literature can more easily be handled systematically than chronologically. For the purpose of this volume we have borrowed a convenient scheme from the ancient Indian sages and classified our texts according to subject-matter under four heads: 1) *artha*, or the practical skills of public and private life; 2) *kama*, or sense-gratification; 3) *dharma*, or law and righteousness; and 4) *moksha*, the means of transcending the common-sense world of things.

The last of these four, *moksha*, is undoubtedly the special hallmark of Indian civilization. It was Indian religion which most impressed European scholars in the early decades of the nineteenth century, once they had ceased to marvel at the discovery that Sanskrit is etymologically related to most of the languages of Europe. Other aspects of Indian culture proved less appealing to Europeans, or even—like the sensuousness of much Indian art—positively offensive to their sensibilities. Indians themselves tended to emphasize the spirituality of their cultural inheritance in contrast to the materialism of the West. In this way they explained why India had fallen so far behind

Europe and America in wealth and power: its aims had simply
been different. Modern Indians could claim superiority of spiritual insight much as Westerners took pride in their material
and technical accomplishments. The upshot was to give foreigners a rather one-sided picture of India which tended to ignore the non-religious aspects of its cultural heritage.

Because the Indian thought-world is so different from our
own, its accomplishments must necessarily be approached with
care. The first requirement is to ascertain what the basic texts
actually meant to those who wrote and used them. This is by
no means simple; and variations of interpretation and style
among available translations compound the problem. We must
then ask how the divergent aspects of Indian tradition fit together to make a distinctive civilization having a style of its
own. This of course begs the question: conceivably there is no
link at all between the amoralism of the *Arthashastra* and the
ethical prescriptions of the *Laws of Manu*, or between the open
sensuality of the *Kama Sutra* and the bodily asceticism enjoined
by the *Yoga Sutra* or the Buddhist monastic vows. Because these
various works are the products of different periods and regions
of India, perhaps no all-inclusive pattern or harmonizing of
apparent contradictions can be expected. On the other hand,
Indian thinkers themselves believed that the divergencies
within their moral and speculative tradition reflected a divinely
ordained separation of human activities according to age and
social class. And contemporary psychology may at least suggest
that such opposites as sexual indulgence and ascetic discipline
are capable of complementing and even sustaining one another.

In previous volumes of this series, we have characterized
ancient Near Eastern civilization by two key concepts: bureaucratic empire and monotheism; and Hellenic civilization by the
institution of the polis and the idea of natural law. In similarly
oversimplified fashion, the principal components of Indian civilization might be given as caste—the organization of society
into rigid, hereditary social classes—and a transcendental reli-
giosity pervading every sphere of life. The two were closely
associated in theory: for the religious idea of *karma* (roughly:

"sin") was supposed to explain everyone's present and future social status. But while the significance of religion and social class in ancient India can scarcely be denied, the degree of their importance may well be questioned; and the theory can best be tested against the original sources. The juxtaposition in this volume of texts of *artha* and *kama* as well as of *dharma* and *moksha* will let the reader judge for himself as to the actual inter-relatedness and respective influence of the various elements of ancient Indian civilization.

Chicago, Illinois   W. H. M.
June 1969

Contents

C. THE VINAYA

Editorial Note

Generally speaking, the selections in this volume have been reproduced just as they appear in the sources cited, except for the cuts made necessary by limitations of space. However, the letters usually written as "š" or "ś" are rendered here as "sh" to correspond to their approximate sound in English; and the spelling of an occasional word has been modernized. All introductions and footnotes are the work of the present editors, though in many instances material supplied by the original editor or translator has been a valuable source of information. The omission of a paragraph or more is ordinarily indicated by four dots at the end of a sentence. But a full line of ellipses signifies a larger omission, usually accompanied by a break in continuity, or indicates that our excerpt does not coincide with the beginning or end of a chapter in the original text.

ON THE TERMS "INDIA," "HINDUISM," AND "BRAHMAN"

"India" in this volume refers to the historical India, i.e. the geographical unit bounded on the north by the Hindu Kush and Himalaya Mountains and on the west, south, and east by the Arabian Sea, the Indian Ocean, and the Bay of Bengal. It includes the territories which now comprise the states of India, Pakistan, Nepal, and part of Afghanistan.

"Hinduism" is the religious and social system which gives continuity to Indian history. It has endured from the second millennium B.C. down to the present time; and modern Hinduism is a direct descendant of the system embodied in the ancient

Vedas. Hindus are united by their belief in the divine status of the Vedas, their reverence for certain other ancient scriptures such as the *Mahabharata* and the *Ramayana*, and their worship of the gods of the Hindu pantheon, of which Vishnu and Shiva are today the chief representatives. In its social aspect, the dominant institution of Hinduism is caste.

Western scholars sometimes designate the Hinduism of the pre-Buddhistic period (before 500 B.C.) as "Brahmanism," to distinguish it from the later Hinduism which includes the religion of the *Bhagavad Gita*, and the Puranas and the philosophy of Vedanta. This distinction is not universally observed, however. The term "Hinduism" is also used to differentiate this principal Indian tradition from Buddhism, Jainism, or Islam.

The word "Brahman" may denote two quite different things: (a) the highest of the four social classes of Hinduism, or a member of this class; and (b) the underlying essence of the universe. In this book, except in copyrighted texts, the alternate spelling "Brahmin" is used for the social class, while "Brahman" is reserved for the philosophical concept. Neither term should be confused with "Brahma"—the creator god in Hindu mythology.

CLASSICAL INDIA

On Artha, Kama, Dharma, and Moksha

The thinkers of ancient India classified all human activity into four complementary spheres. Each represented a legitimate object of striving, and the cultivation of all four was regarded as desirable. Each of these aims was sanctioned by an abundance of traditional folk wisdom as well as by formal literature. *Artha, kama,* and *dharma* were the normal and proper objects of worldly ambition; *moksha* meant release from the fetters of earthly existence.

Artha connotes material wealth and power—the possessions which bring physical comfort and security and the means for their acquisition. The science of *artha* deals not only with the individual person's pursuit of wealth, but also with state government and economics. Texts on the subject of *artha* may be found in the earliest extant Indian literature. The hymns, prayers, and incantations of the Vedas include many requests to the gods for material and physical well-being, for victory in war and the defeat of enemies, for freedom from disease and for successful agriculture and trade. The animal fables of the *Panchatantra,* which have become part of the folklore of the world, give many instances of practical wisdom. Systematic treatises like Kautilya's *Arthashastra,* the product of a wealthy court society, teach the arts of economics and politics on a more sophisticated level.

Kama means sensual gratification. In Indian mythology *kama* is personified as the god of love who pierces the heart with his arrows. The science of *kama* deals with not only sexual and romantic love but also the regulation of marriage and the family. Vedic literature includes numerous spells and ritual formulas in which the worshipper seeks aid in the acquisition of a wife, a husband, or children. The principal systematic work on the art of *kama* is Vatsyayana's *Kama Sutra*—a rather technical treatise which may be regarded as a textbook for lovers, but which also offers much advice on the conduct proper to wives and courtesans. Love in its more romantic aspects was celebrated in the courtly dramas of the Sanskrit poets, of whom the best known is Kalidasa, author of the love-play *Shakuntala.*

Dharma, which denotes Law in the widest sense, encompasses the whole sphere of custom, morals, and religious duty. The concept of *dharma* presumably evolved from the Vedic notion of *rta,* which

3

stands for the recurrences of natural phenomena—days and nights, the four seasons, the life-cycles of living things. In Buddhist texts *dharma* has the general connotation of "righteousness"; it signifies a Law applicable to everyone. But in Hindu literature, the term usually means the behavior suitable to a person's hereditary position in life. Since, according to the theory of *karma*, one's present status is determined by the store of merits and demerits accumulated in previous existences, *dharma* also denotes the inborn character of an individual. The demands of *dharma* are supposed to take precedence over all other valid forms of law, such as formal contracts or royal edicts. Specific applications of the Hindu *dharma* were laid down in the treatises known as Dharma Sutras and Dharma Shastras—law books which served as texts for the various schools of the Veda. The earlier ones deal with relatively restricted areas of human activity; the great compendium known as the *Laws of Manu* (*Manava Dharma Shastra*) covers virtually the entire range of orthodox Hindu life.

Moksha, or release, stands in sharp contrast to the other three aims; for its object is not success in worldly life but liberation from the limitations of that life. By far the largest part of ancient Indian literature deals with this final goal of human existence. *Moksha* was the object not only of religious thought and practice, but also of philosophical speculation; for Indian philosophers nearly always regarded their intellectual affirmations as relevant to the practical goal of salvation. In the Vedic period, salvation consisted of entrance into one of the godly heavens, where the worshipper would reside forever after. The Upanishads, however, proclaim the more abstruse doctrine that the individual soul (*Atman*) is identical with the world-soul (*Brahman*), and define salvation as the knowledge and experience of this unity. Salvation through personal effort and knowledge, rather than by the favor or grace of God, is characteristic of the principal systems of classical Indian philosophy: Vedanta (which is based upon the Upanishads), Sankhya, and Yoga, as well as of early Buddhism. But such long and rigorous paths to *moksha* were meant for monks or holy men, who possessed the leisure and education to pursue them. The desire for salvation on the part of ordinary people was served by the numerous sects devoted to the gods Vishnu or Shiva, in which the requirement for salvation was faith (*bhakti*). Similarly, the Mahayana form of Buddhism evolved the ideal of the *bodhisattva*, who postponed his own liberation in order to help his fellow men toward that goal.

I
Artha

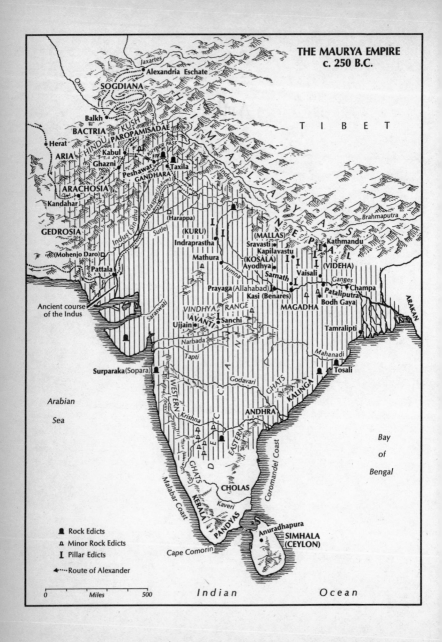

THE MAURYA EMPIRE
c. 250 B.C.

Jaxartes

● Alexandria Eschate
SOGDIANA

Oxus

● Balkh

BACTRIA   HINDU KUSH   PAROPAMISADAE

● Herat   ● Kabul
ARIA   ● Ghazni   Peshawar ●   ● Taxila
GANDHARA

ARACHOSIA   KHYBER PASS

● Kandahar

GEDROSIA   (Harappa)   (KURU)   I
    Indraprastha   (MALLAS)   Kathmandu
    Sravasti ●   N E P A L
(Mohenjo Daro) □   Mathura ●   Kapilavastu
    ● Pattala   (KOSALA)   I   I   I
    Sutlej   Ayodhya ●   Sarnath   Vaisali   (VIDEHA)
    Indus (Sindhu)   *Jumna*   Prayaga (Allahabad) ●   ● Champa
Ancient course   Kasi (Benares) ●   Pataliputra ●
of the Indus   *Saraswati*   VINDHYA   RANGE   MAGADHA   Bodh Gaya
    AVANTI   ● Sanchi   Tamralipti
    ● Ujjain   *Narbada*   *Mahanadi*
Hydaspes (Jhelum)

T I B E T

H I M A L A Y A S   *Brahmaputra*

Ganges

ARAKAN

Surparaka (Sopara) ▮   *Tapti*
    WESTERN   *Godavari*   ● Tosali
    Krishna   GHATS   KALINGA
Arabian   ANDHRA
    D E C C A N
Sea   EASTERN   GHATS
    Bay
    of
    Bengal
    CHOLAS
    GHATS   *Kaveri*
    KERALA   Coromandel Coast
    PANDYAS   Anuradhapura
    SIMHALA
Cape Comorin   (CEYLON)

Malabar Coast

▮ Rock Edicts
⌂ Minor Rock Edicts
I Pillar Edicts
◄···· Route of Alexander

├─────────┤
0   Miles   500

I n d i a n   O c e a n

Introduction to the Atharva Veda*

The hymns of the Vedas embody the religious ideas of the Aryan†
tribes who migrated into India from beyond the Himalayas between
about 1500 and 1000 B.C. Their religion—as yet scarcely influenced
by the remnants of the Indus civilization—shows many affinities
with the beliefs of other Indo-European peoples, particularly the
ancient Iranians. The Aryans worshipped many deities, most of
whom were male and in some way connected with the sky. The
focal point of Vedic worship was the sacrifice, a great public rite
presided over by Brahmin priests, employing a complicated ritual,
and involving the slaughter of many animals. The purpose of the
sacrifice was to please the gods through praise and offerings and
thereby gain such mundane favors as success in war, increase in
cattle, or progeny.

The *Atharva Veda*, youngest of the four Vedas, dates from a period (*ca.* 900-600 B.C.) when the sacrificial religion of the Brahmins
was in full flower. Its hymns rest upon a primitive, animistic view
of the universe, in which the powers of nature are personified as
deities and regarded with dread and awe. Consisting mainly of
spells and incantations aimed at avoiding harm or securing blessings to the worshipper, the *Atharva* in some respects represents a
decline from the cultural level of the three earlier Vedas. Still,
many of its hymns are undoubtedly very ancient. About one-seventh
of them may be found in the oldest of the Vedas, the *Rig*, sometimes
unchanged, sometimes with significant variations.

---

* For a general introduction to the Vedas, see Volume I of this series,
pp. 34-5.
† The word "Aryan" is a linguistic, not a racial term, referring either to the
entire Indo-European group of languages or to the Indo-Iranian branch of
that group. The invaders of India in the second millennium B.C. spoke an
Indo-European, or Aryan, tongue (Old Sanskrit); they are thus often de-
signated as Aryans to distinguish them from the peoples previously resident
in that country.

Although ancient Indian texts sometimes omit the *Atharva* from the list of canonical scriptures, later literature generally includes it as one of the Vedas, the sacred revelation of the gods. To the historian it offers a mine of information about the daily life and customs of the Aryans.

FROM THE ATHARVA VEDA

Against Enemies (Book I, Hymn 19)

1 Let not the piercers[1] find us, nor let the penetraters find [us]; far from us make the volleys fly, dispersing, O Indra.[2]

2 Dispersing from us let the shafts fly, those that are hurled and that are to be hurled; ye divine arrows of men, pierce my enemies.

3 Whether one of our own or whether a stranger, fellow or outsider, whoso assails us—let Rudra[3] with a volley pierce those my enemies.

4 Whatever rival, whatever non-rival, and whatever hater shall curse us, him let all the gods damage; incantation is my inner defense.[4]

For Safety and Increase of Kine (Book II, Hymn 26)

1 Hither let the cattle come that went away, whose companionship Vayu (the wind) enjoyed, whose form-givings Tvashtar[5] knows; in this cow-stall let Savitar[6] make them fast.

2 To this cow-stall let cattle stream together; let Brihaspati,[7]

From *Atharva-Veda Samhita*, trans. by William D. Whitney, rev. by Charles R. Lanman, Vol. 7 of the Harvard Oriental Series (Cambridge, Mass.: Harvard University Press, 1905). Notes in part adapted from Ralph T. H. Griffith, trans., *The Hymns of the Atharva Veda*, Vol. I (Benares: E. J. Lazarus & Co., 1916).

1. Hostile archers.
2. Chief of the gods.
3. A god of storm and thunder, father and leader of the Maruts (storm gods).
4. This last clause is a quotation from *Rig Veda* VI.75.
5. The craftsman-god who creates embryos.
6. The sun, especially the morning sun; its light drives away witches and evil spirits.
7. The god of prayer and priest of the gods, who intercedes with them on behalf of human beings.

foreknowing, lead them hither; let Sinivali[8] lead hither the van of them; make them fast when they have come, O Anumati.[9]

3 Together, together let cattle stream, together horses, and together men, together the fatness that is of grain; I offer with an oblation of confluence.

4 I pour together the milk of kine, together strength, sap,[10] with sacrificial butter[11]; poured together are our heroes; fixed are the kine with me [as] kine-lord.

5 I bring the milk of kine; I have brought the sap of grain; brought are our heroes, our wives, to this home.

Accompanying the Building of a House (Book III, Hymn 12)

1 Just here I fix [my] dwelling firm; may it stand in security, sprinkling ghee[12]; unto thee here, O dwelling, may we resort with all our heroes, with good heroes, with unharmed heroes.

2 Just here stand thou firm, O dwelling, rich in horses, in kine, in pleasantness, in refreshment, in ghee, in milk; erect thyself in order to (bring about) great good-fortune.

3 A garner art thou, O dwelling, of great roof, of cleansed grain; to thee may the calf come, may the boy, may the kine, streaming in at evening.

4 This dwelling let Savitar, Vayu,[13] Indra, Brihaspati fix, foreknowing; let the Maruts[14] sprinkle it with water, with ghee; let king Bhaga[15] deepen our ploughing.

5 O mistress of the building,[16] as sheltering, pleasant, hast thou, a goddess, been fixed by the gods in the beginning; clothing thyself in grass, mayest thou be well-willing; then mayest thou give us wealth together with heroes.

---

8. God of the new moon.
9. God of the full moon.
10. Perhaps a sort of beer, the "sap of grain" mentioned in verse 5.
11. Ghee, the melted butter used at the sacrifice.
12. Melted butter.
13. The god of the wind.
14. Storm-gods.
15. The protector-god and giver of wealth (the root of this word is the same as that of the Slavic Bog, "god").
16. The female deity who presides over house building.

6   With due order, O beam,[17] ascend the post; formidable, bearing rule, force away the foes; let not the attendants of thy houses be harmed, O dwelling; may we live a hundred autumns with all our heroes.

7   To it the tender boy, to it the calf, with moving creatures, to it the jar of *parishrut*,[18] with mugs of curd, have come.

8   Bring forward, O woman, this full jar, a stream of ghee combined with ambrosia; anoint these drinkers (?) with ambrosia; let what is offered-and-bestowed defend it (the dwelling?).

9   These waters I bring forward, free from *yakshma*,[19] *yakshma*-effacing; I set forth unto the houses, along with immortal fire.[20]

For Success in Trade (Book III, Hymn 15)

1   I stir up the trader Indra[21]; let him come to us, be our forerunner; thrusting [away] the niggard, the waylaying wild animal, let him, having the power, be giver of riches to me.

2   The many roads, travelled by the gods, that go about between heaven-and-earth—let them enjoy me[22] with milk, with ghee, that dealing I may get riches.

3   With fuel, O Agni,[23] with ghee, I, desiring, offer the oblation, in order to energy, to strength;—revering with worship (*brahman*), so far as I am able—this divine prayer, in order to (obtain) hundred-fold winning.

4   This offense of ours mayest thou, O Agni, bear with, what distant road we have gone.[24] Successful for us be bargain and sale; let return-dealing make me fruitful; do ye two enjoy this oblation in concord; successful for us be our going about and rising.

17. Literally, bamboo: the crossbeam.
18. A foaming beverage.
19. A lung disease.
20. Water and fire are the chief necessities of life; with them the householder takes formal possession of his dwelling.
21. The god Indra is a trader because he demands prayer and sacrifice in return for favors.
22. I.e., may they be pleased with my sacrifices to them.
23. The fire-god.
24. This sentence is a quotation from the *Rig Veda*; it is out of place here.

5   With what riches I practise bargaining, seeking riches with
riches, ye gods—let that become more for me, not less; O Agni,
put down with the oblation[25] the gain-slaying gods.

6   With what riches I practise bargaining, seeking riches with
riches, ye gods—therein let Indra assign me pleasure, let Prajapati,[26] Savitar, Soma,[27] Agni.

7   Unto thee with homage do we, O priest Vaishvanara,[28] give
praise; do thou watch over our progeny, our selves, our kine,
our breaths.

8   Every day may we bring constantly for thee as for a standing horse,[29] O Jatavedas[30]; rejoicing together with abundance
of wealth, with food, may we thy neighbors, O Agni, take no
harm.

For Successful Agriculture (Book III, Hymn 17)

1   The poets[31] harness the plows, they extend severally the
yokes—they the wise ones, with desire of favor (?) toward the
gods.

2   Harness ye the plows, extend the yokes; scatter the seed
here in the prepared womb; may the bunch (?) of *viraj*[32] be
burdened for us; may the sickles draw in the ripe [grain] yet
closer.

3   Let the plow, lance-pointed, well-lying, with well-
smoothed handle, turn up cow, sheep, an on-going chariot-
frame, and a plump wench.

4   Let Indra[33] hold down the furrow; let Pushan[34] defend it;
let it, rich in milk,[35] yield to us each further summer.

25. I.e., with the sacrifice which I offer.
26. The creator-god from whose body the universe was produced.
27. A name for the moon; also the juice of the soma-plant, personified as a
god.
28. "Dear to all men," an epithet for the god Agni (god of fire).
29. I.e., just as one brings fodder to a horse which is not turned out to
pasture.
30. "The wise," a name for Agni.
31. Possibly: the skillful men.
32. Unintelligible.
33. Indra is the god who sends rain.
34. A god who protects and multiplies human possessions; a form of the sun.
35. I.e., plentiful food. This stanza is a solemn formula taken from *Rig Veda*
IV.57.

5   Successfully let the good plowshares thrust apart the earth; successfully let the plowmen follow the beasts of draft; O Shunasira,[36] do ye (two), dripping (?) with oblation, make the herbs rich in berries for this man.

6   Successfully let the draft-animals, successfully the men, successfully let the plow plow; successfully let the straps be bound; successfully do thou brandish the goad.

7   O Shunasira, do ye (two) enjoy me here; what milk ye have made in heaven, therewith pour ye upon this [furrow].

8   O furrow, we reverence thee; be [turned] hitherward, O fortunate one, that thou mayest be well-willing to us, that thou mayest become of good fruit for us.

9   With ghee, with honey [is] the furrow all anointed,[37] approved by all the gods, by the Maruts; do thou, O furrow, turn hither unto us with milk, rich in refreshment, swelling with fulness of ghee.

To Heal Serious Wounds: With an Herb (Book IV, Hymn 12)

1   Grower art thou, grower; grower of severed bone; make this grow, O *arundhati*.[38]

2   What of thee is torn, what of thee is inflamed, is crushed in thyself—may Dhatar[39] excellently put that together again, joint with joint.

3   Let thy marrow come together with marrow, and thy joint together with joint; together let what of thy flesh has fallen apart, together let thy bone grow over.

4   Let marrow be put together with marrow; let skin grow with skin; let thy blood, bone grow; let flesh grow with flesh.

5   Fit thou together hair with hair; fit together skin with skin; let thy blood, bone grow; put together what is severed, O herb.

---

36. Shunasira is the collective term for two gods closely connected with agriculture, Shuna and Sira. The words probably mean "plowshare" and "plow."
37. In order to secure a good crop.
38. A climbing plant, which will bind the injured limb just as it binds the tree around which it grows.
39. The god who fixes and preserves.

6 Do thou here stand up, go forth, run forth, a chariot well-wheeled, well-tired, well-naved; stand firm upright.

7 If, falling into a pit, he hath been crushed, or if a stone hurled hath smitten [him]—as a Rhbu[40] the parts of a chariot, may it put together joint with joint.

For Abundant Rain (Book IV, Hymn 15)

1 Let the directions, full of mist, fly up together; let clouds, wind-hurried, come together; let the lowing [cows] of the resounding misty great bull,[41] the waters, gratify the earth.

2 Let the mighty, liberal ones (Maruts) (show forth) together; let the juices of the waters attach themselves to the herbs; let gushes of rain gladden the earth; let herbs of all forms be born here and there.

3 Do thou make the singers to behold together the mists; let rushes of waters rush up here and there; let gushes of rain gladden the earth; let plants of all forms be born here and there.

4 Let the troops of Maruts sing unto thee, O Parjanya,[42] noisy here and there; let gushes of raining rain rain along the earth.

5 Send up, O Maruts, from the ocean; brilliant [is] the song; ye make the mist fly up; let the lowing [cows] of the resounding misty great bull, the waters, gratify the earth.

6 Roar on, thunder, excite the water-holder; anoint the earth, O Parjanya, with milk; by thee poured out, let abundant rain come; let him of lean kine, seeking refuge, go home.[43]

7 Let the liberal ones favor you, also the fountains, great serpents[44]; let the clouds, started forward by the Maruts, rain along the earth.

.   .   .   .

40. A skillful workman.
41. The god Parjanya. See following note.
42. The god of the rain-cloud; the generator and nourisher of plant and animal life.
43. I.e., since rain will make the grass grow, the owner of lean kine need no longer search for pasture.
44. Fountains of heaven, and serpent-shaped masses of cloud.

For the Success and Prosperity of a King (Book IV, Hymn 22)

1 Increase, O Indra, this Kshatriya for me; make thou this man sole chief of the clans; unman all his enemies; make them subject to him in the contests for pre-eminence.

2 Portion thou this man in village, in horses, in kine; unportion that man who is his enemy; let this king be the summit of authorities[45]; O Indra, make every foe subject to him.

3 Let this man be riches-lord of riches; let this king be people-lord of people; in him, O Indra, put great splendors; destitute of splendor make thou his foe.

4 For him, O heaven-and-earth, milk ye much that is pleasant, like two milch kine that yield the hot-draught; may this king be dear to Indra, dear to kine, herbs, cattle.

5 I join to thee[46] Indra who gives superiority, by whom men conquer, are not conquered; who shall make thee sole chief of people, also uppermost of kings descended from Manu.[47]

6 Superior [art] thou, inferior thy rivals, whosoever, O king, are thine opposing foes; sole chief, having Indra as companion, having conquered, bring thou in the enjoyments of them that play the foe.

7 Of lion-aspect, do thou devour all the clans; of tiger-aspect, do thou beat down the foes; sole chief, having Indra as companion, having conquered, seize thou on the enjoyments of them that play the foe.

Against Witchcraft: With a Plant (Book V, Hymn 14)

1 An eagle discovered thee[48]; a hog dug thee with his snout; seek thou to injure, O herb, him that seeks to injure; smite down the witchcraft-maker.

2 Smite down the sorcerers, smite down the witchcraft-maker; then, whoever seeks to injure us, him do thou smite, O herb.

45. I.e., head of the royal family.
46. To the king.
47. The supposed ancestor of the human race.
48. The efficacy of magical plants depends in large part upon the difficulty of finding them.

3 Having cut around out of [his] skin a strip, as it were of a stag, fasten, O gods, upon the witchcraft-maker the witchcraft, like a necklace.

4 Lead thou[49] away the witchcraft back to the witchcraft-maker, grasping its hand; set it straight before him, that it may smite the witchcraft-maker.

5 Be the witchcrafts for the witchcraft-maker, the curse for him that curses; like an easy chariot let the witchcraft roll back to the witchcraft-maker.

10 Go as a son to a father; like a constrictor trampled on, bite; go, O witchcraft, back to the witchcraft-maker, as it were treading down [thy] bond.

11 Up, like a she-antelope, a she-elephant, with leaping on, like a hind, let the witchcraft go to its maker.

12 Straighter than an arrow let it fly, O heaven-and-earth, to meet him; let it, the witchcraft, seize again him, the witchcraft-maker, like a deer.

13 Let it go like fire up-stream, like water down-stream; like an easy chariot let the witchcraft roll back to the witchcraft-maker.

49. The herb.

Introduction to the Arthashastra

The *Arthashastra* is the earliest and most important surviving Indian treatise on the art of statecraft. Traditionally it has been regarded as the work of Kautilya, the shadowy but supremely clever advisor to King Chandragupta Maurya (reigned *ca.* 322-298 B.C.); but in its present form it is probably several centuries later. The book treats virtually every imaginable aspect of autocratic government, from the upbringing of princes to the organization of taxation and espionage, the promotion of agriculture and trade, suppression of crime and rebellion, and the conduct of foreign affairs. The author does not pretend to originality, but claims merely to present

the collected political wisdom of the Aryans. Other ancient
texts do in fact confirm the existence of earlier *Arthashastras*,
now lost, which expressed opinions similar to those attributed to
Kautilya. Indeed, the sophistication, the subtle psychology, and the
analytical power of Kautilya's *Arthashastra* mark it unmistakably
as the product of a highly developed civilization and a long political
tradition.

Except for a few tribal republics, autocracy was the typical form
of government in ancient India. The ruler's power was unchecked by
any abstract body of law or by formal institutional checks and bal-
ances. His government was personal in nature and his edict was
law, restricted only by the necessary respect for custom and the fear
of rebellion. The king was expected to uphold the traditional class
divisions of society and pay due respect to Brahmins, who theoreti-
cally outranked him in the social hierarchy. Otherwise his freedom of
action was considerable. But if neither laws nor constitutional proc-
esses (e.g., an assembly of notables) limited his power, neither did
they support it. In the Indian view, kingship was a necessary con-
comitant of social order, but any specific king or dynasty was dis-
pensable. Successful rule was its own justification, and no moral
stigma attached to the usurper.

Under such circumstances, the acquisition and preservation of
political power required a high degree of skill and constant vigilance. The ideal government, as envisaged by the *Arthashastra*, ex-
ercised complete and unceasing control over every aspect of its
subjects' lives. The bureaucracy was ubiquitous and well organized.
A widespread network of espionage kept watch over the people's
activities. Punishment for deviance was swift and ruthless. The development of agriculture and trade and public works—essential elements of political power—could not be left to chance, but were
actively promoted by the state. In foreign affairs, the *Arthashastra*
presupposed a multiplicity of small states living in uneasy co-exist-
ence. Each was presumed ready and eager to subvert its neighbors
and utilize any show of weakness for its own territorial advantage.
Alliance and enmity were equally temporary, both being grounded
upon similar considerations of expediency.

Kautilya (also known as Chanakya), the reputed author of the
Arthashastra, was undoubtedly a historical personage. A high-caste
Brahmin, he received a theological education at Taxila, a center for
advanced studies in orthodox Hindu religion. Without doubt he
cherished the wisdom of the Vedas and the traditional order of In-

dian society as opposed to the newer doctrines of Buddhists and Jains which were widespread in north India in his time. For a while he held an administrative post in the state of Magadha under the last king of the Nanda dynasty. Various traditions support the view that the Nanda family was of low caste and professed either Buddhism or Jainism, both of which rejected caste distinctions. It is uncertain what induced Kautilya to rebel against his sovereign and employer; but quite possibly it was orthodox prejudice combined with the will to power. The final verse of the *Arthashastra* states cryptically that Kautilya, out of "intolerance," "rescued the scriptures . . . which had passed to the Nanda king." In any event, the wily Brahmin attached himself to the young prince Chandragupta, future founder of the Maurya dynasty. Together they engineered the rebellion which overthrew the Nanda family and establish Chandragupta in power. The extent to which Kautilya's advice was responsible for this feat can only be surmised;* but the cleverness of the Brahmin minister has become legendary in India. All accounts agree that he continued to advise Chandragupta throughout his reign, and possibly also served his son and successor, Bindusara.

Chandragupta himself may have been a son of the last Nanda king by a secondary wife, though this is uncertain. Unlike the Nandas, he appears to have been an orthodox Hindu, a worshipper of the god Shiva. At the time of Alexander of Macedon's invasion of India (326 B.C.) he was in exile; and Greek sources record that he met Alexander and even provided him with information. Shortly after the death of Alexander at Babylon (323 B.C.), Chandragupta led an army which destroyed the Macedonian garrisons left behind in the Indus basin. At about the same time—whether before or after is not certain—he fomented the rebellion which overthrew and exterminated the Nandas and established himself on the throne of Magadha. From this base in the northeast, he went on to conquer all of India from the Hindu Kush to the Narbada River. Chandragupta Maurya thus became the first known king in history to have ruled most of India; and the Maurya empire (*ca.* 322-185 B.C.) marks one of the high points of Indian civilization.

Tradition claims that the *Arthashastra* served as an official man-

---

* A drama of the sixth century A.D., *The Signet of Rakshasha*, treats Chandragupta as an insignificant young man, a pawn in the hands of the wily Kautilya. Though the piece may have some basis in historical fact, it should also be noted that Chandragupta was the father and grandfather of two very capable kings, Bindusara and Ashoka (for Ashoka see below, pp. 101-12).

ual of conduct for the Maurya kings. But its assumption of a multiplicity of small kingdoms proves that this cannot have been the
case. Various of its references to people and places—most notably to
China, which was not called by that name in the fourth century B.C.
—suggest a date intermediate between the Mauryas and the next
imperial dynasty, the Guptas (*ca.* 320-480 A.D.). But the present
Arthashastra may well be based upon an original work by the historical Kautilya. Several ancient Indian authors refer to a book
about politics by Chandragupta's minister, which perhaps forms the
nucleus of the present text. Personal authorship was little valued in
ancient India; and it was common for famous works to be supple-
mented and modified. Aphorisms on political subjects would naturally attach themselves to the name of the legendary Kautilya.

Despite the chronological difficulties, the *Arthashastra* may still
be regarded, with reservations, as an approximate guide to Mauryan
society and government. The system it describes more closely resembles that of the Mauryas—as attested from independent sources—
than that of any other Indian dynasty before or since. Mauryan administration was marked by a high degree of organization and an
all-pervading system of espionage. Chandragupta was a stern despot
who enforced his rule with severity and lived in daily fear of assas-
sination. Certainly the elaborate governmental machinery described
in the *Arthashastra* could not have been invented by Chandragupta
and Kautilya, though it is reasonable to suppose that they were
responsible for improvements. The kingdom of Magadha which they
inherited from the Nandas was already a highly civilized and well-
organized state, famous for its enormous army and fantastic wealth.
In extending the Magadhan system to most of India, Chandragupta
need not have altered its essential structure.

It is unlikely that any actual Indian government—not even the
Maurya despotism—ever approached the totality of control and completeness of organization envisaged by the *Arthashastra*. But the book
is clearly the fruit of a well-developed state system of long standing;
and its author was thoroughly acquainted with political realities.
The pedantry and precise classifications of the work suggest the hand
of the scholar rather than the man of action; but its precepts are not
the work of a philosopher concerned with duty or justice. The author
regards the pursuit of political power as its own justification and
makes only the slightest gestures in the direction of *dharma*.

The parallel has often been remarked between the *Arthashastra*
and Machiavelli's *The Prince*, written a millennium and a half

later in Renaissance Italy. Both works are in fact products of a
political situation in which numerous small states were ruled by
despots with boundless ambition but little claim to legitimate
status. Mauryan India, like Renaissance Italy, boasted of a
courtly culture marked by a high degree of sophistication and re-
finement. In their utter cynicism regarding men's motives and
their single-minded devotion to the ruler's self-aggrandizement, the
two books no doubt reflect this milieu. Efficiency and expediency are
the authors' guiding principles, uninhibited by moral scruples except where respect for popular prejudice is necessary to prevent disorder. Their purpose is not to imagine an ideal state system, but to
describe the art of statecraft as actually practiced. Nonetheless, their
advice is not restricted to the specific conditions prevailing in their
own country and time. Both the *Arthashastra* and *The Prince* set
forth general principles, derived through rationalist analysis, which
they regard as applicable to any situation in which certain defined
conditions are present. In their somewhat different ways, both works
present a science of politics claiming universal validity.

FROM THE ARTHASHASTRA OF KAUTILYA

Chapter 6: Control of Senses

By conquering the six enemies of living (lust, anger, greed,
vanity, haughtiness and exuberance) he (the ruler) shall acquire balanced wisdom. He shall keep company with the
learned. He shall get information through his spies. By his
actions, he shall set up safety and security. By enforcing his
authority, he shall keep his subjects observing their duties and
obligations. He shall exercise control over himself by learning
sciences. He shall help his subjects to acquire wealth and do
good to them.

In this manner, with control over his impulses, he shall abstain from hurting the women and the property of others. He

From *Essentials of Indian Statecraft. Kautilya's Arthasastra for Contemporary Readers,* trans. by T. N. Ramaswamy (Bombay: Asia Publishing House,
1962). Reprinted by permission of Mrs. Ramaswamy and the Asia Publishing House.

shall avoid lust, falsehood, hauteur and evil inclinations. He shall keep away from wrong and wasteful transactions.

He shall enjoy his lawful desires in conformity with the right and the economic. He shall pursue the three merits of living: charity, wealth and desire.[1] Any one of these merits carried to excess not only hurts the other two, but itself.

Wealth is the foundation of the other two because charity and desire depend upon it for their fulfilment.

Teachers and ministers should keep the ruler away from dangers and warn him of time-schedules even in private.[2] Such teachers and ministers are always respected.

Authority is possible only with assistance. A single wheel cannot move by itself. The ruler, therefore, shall employ ministers and hear their advice.

Chapter 10: On Spies

Advised and assisted by a tried council of officers, the ruler should proceed to institute spies.

Spies are in the guise of pseudo-student, priest, householder, trader, saint practising renunciation, classmate or colleague, desperado, poisoner and woman mendicant.

An artful person, capable of reading human nature, is a pseudo-student. Such a person should be encouraged with presents and purse and be told by the officer: "Sworn to the ruler and myself you shall inform us what wickedness you find in others."

One initiated in scripture and of pure character is a priest-spy. This spy should carry on farming, cattle culture and commerce with resources given to him. Out of the produce and profit accrued, he should encourage other priests to live with him and send them on espionage work. The other priests also should send their followers on similar errands.

---

1. I.e., *dharma, artha, kama.*
2. This refers to a later chapter (18) which directs the ruler to set an example of energy and activity and assign his various functions to specific parts of the day. Here he is directed to maintain his schedule even when unobserved by others.

A householder-spy is a farmer fallen in his profession but pure in character. This spy should do as the priest.[3]

A trader-spy is a merchant in distress but generally trust-worthy. This spy should carry on espionage, in addition to his profession.

A person with proper appearance and accomplishments as an ascetic is a saint-spy. He surrounds himself with followers and may settle down in the suburb of a big city and may pretend prayer and fasting in public. Trader-spies may associate with this class of spies. He may practise fortune-telling, palmistry, and pretend supernatural and magical powers by predictions. The followers will adduce proof for the predictions of their saint. He may even foretell official rewards and official changes, which the officers concerned may substantiate by reciprocating.

Rewarded by the rulers with money and titles, these five in-stitutions of espionage should maintain the integrity of the country's officers.

Chapter 12: Home and Opposition Parties

Having instituted spies over his chief officers, the ruler should spread his intelligence network over the citizens and the coun-try folk.

Social spies, forming into opposite camps, should carry propa-ganda into places of confluence of people, tourist centres, as-sociations and general congregations. . . .

Spies should also know all news current in the state. Special spies should collect news of joy or distress among those who professionalise in grains, cattle and gold of the ruler, among those who supply them to the ruler (or administration); among those who harbour a relative or restrain a troubled area and those who check a wild tribe or an invading enemy. The greater the contentment of such groups of people, the greater the re-wards given to them. Those who demur should be propitiated by presents or conciliation, or disputes may be created to break their alliance with each other, as from a neighbouring enemy, a wild tribe or a disputant to the ruler's position.

3. I.e., carry on farming, as in the previous paragraph.

Failing this measure, they must be commissioned to collect unpopular fines and taxes. Those in severe opposition may be quelled by punishment in secret, or by exposing them to the wrath of the people of the land. Or having hostaged their families, they may be sent to the mines to break contact with the enemies [of the state].

The enemies [of the state] employ as instruments those who are incensed, those who are ambitious, as well as those who despise the ruler. Special spies, parading as fortune tellers, should be instituted to spy on such persons in their relation with each other and with foreigners.

Thus, in his own state, the ruler should preserve parties and factions among the people, friendly or opposed, powerful or puerile, against the intrigues and machinations of the foreigners.

Chapter 14: Administrative Councils

After consolidating the attitude of both internal and external parties, both within and abroad, the ruler should consider administrative affairs.

Deliberation in well-constituted councils precedes administrative measures. The proceedings of a council should be in camera and deliberations made top secret so that not even a bird can whisper. The ruler should be guarded against disclosure.

Whoever divulges secret deliberations should be destroyed. Such guilt can be detected by physical and attitudinal changes of ambassadors, ministers and heads.

Secrecy of proceedings in the council and guarding of officers participating in the council must be organised.

The causes of divulgence of counsels are recklessness, drink, talking in one's sleep and infatuation with women which assail councillors.

He of secretive nature or who is not regarded well will divulge council matters. Disclosure of council secrets is of advantage to persons other than the ruler and his high officers. Steps should be taken to safeguard deliberations.

Chapter 16: Protection of Princes

. . . .

The prince should be protected from wicked influences. He should be taught properly, since he is at an age of trust. He should be told about right, but not of non-right; he should be told of wealth, but not of non-wealth. He should be scared of drink and women by a process of making him drunk and of confronting him with blackmailing women. If fond of gambling, he should be blackmailed by tricksters. If fond of hunting, by forest brigands. If he shows proclivities for rebelling, he should be scared by narration of hardships and even ignominious death attending such ventures.

When a prince is of commendable disposition, he should be made commander-in-chief or nominated successor.

Princes are of three categories: those of dynamic intelligence; those of stagnant intelligence; and those who are mentally deficient.

He who carries out mandates of right and leading to wealth is of dynamic intelligence. He who never carries out good instructions is of stagnant intelligence. He who entangles himself in avoidable dangers leading to wickedness and poverty is mentally incompetent.

If a ruler has a deficient son, attempt should be made to beget a grandson by him. Or to get sons from his daughters.

If a ruler is too old or diseased to beget children, he may mandate a close relation or any neighbouring ruler of high qualities to beget a son for him through his queen.

Never should a mentally deficient son be made to sit on the seat of power.

Unless in times of grave danger, the eldest son should succeed the ruler. Sometimes sovereignty may reside in a corporation. Corporate sovereignty is the most invincible form of authority in the world.[4]

4. Because each member acts as a check on the others.

Chapter 20: Personal Security

.   .   .   .

The ruler should employ as his security staff only such persons as have noble and proven ancestry and are closely related to him and are well trained and loyal. No foreigners, or anonymous persons, or persons with clouded antecedents are to be employed as security staff for the ruler.

In a securely guarded chamber, the chief should supervise the ruler's food arrangements.

Special precautions are to be taken against contaminated and poisoned food. The following reveal poison: rice sending out deep blue vapour; unnaturally coloured and artificially dried-up and hard vegetables; unusually bright and dull vessels; foamy vessels; streaky soups, milk and liquor; white streaked honey; strange-tempered food; carpets and curtains stained with dark spots and threadbare; polishless and lustreless metallic vessels and gems.

The poisoner reveals himself by parched and dry mouth, hesitating talk, perspiration, tremour, yawning, evasive demeanour and nervous behaviour.

Experts in poison detection should be in attendance on the ruler. The physicians attending the ruler should satisfy themselves personally as to the purity of the drugs which they administer to the ruler. The same precaution is indicated for liquor and beverages which the ruler uses. Scrupulous cleanliness should be insisted on in persons in charge of the ruler's dress and toilet requisites. This should be ensured by seals. . . .

In any entertainment meant for the amusement of the ruler, the actors should not use weapons, fire and poison. Musical instruments and accoutrements for horses, elephants and vehicles should be secured in the palace.

The ruler should mount beasts and vehicles only after the traditional rider or driver has done so. If he has to travel in a boat, the pilot should be trustworthy and the boat itself secured to another boat. There should be a proper convoy on land or water guarding the ruler. He should swim only in rivers which

are free of larger fishes and crocodiles and hunt in forests free
from snakes, man-eaters and brigands.

He should give private audience only attended by his security
guards. He should receive foreign ambassadors in his full min-
isterial council. While reviewing his militia, the ruler should
also attend in full battle uniform and be on horseback or on the
back of an elephant. When he enters or exits from the capital
city, the path of the ruler should be guarded by staffed officers
and cleared of armed men, mendicants and the suspicious. He
should attend public performances, festivals, processions or religious gatherings accompanied by trained bodyguards. The
ruler should guard his own person with the same care with
which he secures the safety of those around him through espionage arrangements.

Chapter 21: Building of Villages

The ruler may form villages either on new sites or on old sites,
either by shifting population from heavily populated areas in
his own state or by causing population to immigrate into his
state.

Villages should consist of not less than a hundred and not
more than five hundred families of cultivators of the service
classes. The villages should extend from about one and a half
miles to three miles each [in circumference] and should be
capable of defending each other. Village boundaries may consist of rivers, hills, forests, hedges, caves, bridges and trees.

Each eight hundred villages should have a major fort. There
should be a capital city for every four hundred villages, a
market town for every two hundred villages, and an urban
cluster for every ten villages.

The frontiers of the state should have fortifications protected
by internal guards, manning the entrances to the state. The
interior of the state should be guarded by huntsmen, armed
guards, forest tribes, fierce tribes and frontier men.

Those who do social service by sacrifices, the clergy, and the
intellectuals should be settled in the villages on tax-free farms.

Officers, scribes, cattlemen, guards, cattle doctors, physicians, horse-trainers and news purveyors should be given life interest in lands.

Lands fit for cultivation should be given to tenants only for life. Land prepared for cultivation by tenants should not be taken away from them.

Lands not cultivated by the landholders may be confiscated and given to cultivators. Or they may be cultivated through hired labourers or traders to avoid loss to the state. If cultivators pay their taxes promptly, they may be supplied with grains, cattle and money.

The ruler should give to cultivators only such farms and concessions as will replenish the treasury and avoid denuding it.

A denuded exchequer is a grave threat to the security of the state. Only on rare occasions like settlement of new areas or in grave emergencies should tax-remissions be granted. The ruler should be benevolent to those who have conquered the crisis by remission of taxes.

He should facilitate mining operations. He should encourage manufacturers. He should help exploitation of forest wealth. He should provide amenities for cattle breeding and commerce. He should construct highways both on land and on water. He should plan markets.

He should build dikes for water either perennial or from other sources. He should assist with resources and communications those who build reservoirs or construct works of communal comfort and public parks.

All should share in corporate work, sharing the expenditure but not claiming profit.

The ruler should have suzerainty over all fishing, transport and grain trade, reservoirs and bridges.

Those who do not recognise the rights of their servants, hirelings and relatives should be made to do so.

The ruler should maintain adolescents, the aged, the diseased and the orphans. He should also provide livelihood to deserted women with prenatal care and protection for the children born to them.

Veterans of the village should improve the property of orphaned minors till they attain their majority. So also the property of the shrines.

When an earning person—man or woman—fails to maintain his or her child, wife, mother, father, minor brothers, sisters or young widows, he or she should be punished with a fine.

Similarly no man shall become an ascetic without making provision for the sustenance of his dependents. So, too, a person who attempts to seduce women into ascetism renders himself liable to punishment.

The villages are out of bounds for any but forest-resident ascetics, local finance companies and local corporate guilds. There shall be no actors, musicians, drummers, orators or poets sponging on the resources, labour and drinks of the villagers. Villagers live on their fields.

The ruler should abstain from taking over any area which is open to attack by enemies and wild tribes and which is visited by frequent famines and pests. He should also abstain from extravagant sports.

He should protect cultivation from heavy taxes, slave labour and severe penalties, herds of cattle from cattle lifters, wild animals, venomous creatures and diseases.

He should clear highways of the visitation of petty officials, workmen, brigands and guards. He should not only conserve existing forests, buildings and mines, but also develop new ones.

Chapter 26: Collection of Revenue

The collector collects dues from forts and other areas of the state, mines, buildings, and bridges, forests, settlements and commercial routes.

Dues from urban areas or forts comprise: tolls, fines, taxes on weights and measures, urban dues, dues from coinage, from seals and passports, from warehouses, from courtesans, from gambling, from selling sites, from work and engineering guilds and from immigrants.

Dues from other areas include produce from cultivated lands, government dues from farming lands, sacrificial dues, money taxes, dues from merchants, river-taxes, fees for ferries, dues from ships and boats, levy from towns, pasture levies, road cesses, taxes on land and prison taxes.

Dues from mines cover those from gold, silver, diamonds, precious stones, pearls, corals, ocean products, metals, salt and other minerals.

Dues from buildings and bridges include those from flower-gardens, orchards, vegetable-gardens, wet fields and seed-gardens.

Dues from forests are derived from game forests, timber forests and elephant forests.

Dues from settlements come from cattle-settlements, goats, sheep, asses, camels, horses and mules.

Dues from commercial routes arise from land and waterways.

All these form the receipt structure.

Several forms of receipt can be distinguished: capital receipts, share receipts, interest receipts, fine receipts, licenses, profits on coinage, penalties.

The structure of expenditure consists of:

Ceremonial expenditure on shrines and ancestors, gifts and endowments, domestic expenditure, intelligence service, stores, armaments, warehousing, stock filling, manufacturing, labour maintenance, defence expenditure, cattle farming, maintenance of museums, bird and beast sanctuaries and sustenance stores.

.   .   .   .

Chapter 29: Government Servants

Those who have administrative qualifications should, according to individual merit, be posted as principal officers of state departments. They should be constantly kept under vigilance in their duties, as men are by nature fickle and temperamental. Proper assessment must always be made of the procedure and method, the venue and time schedule, precise pattern, expenditure and result which they employ in carrying on their administrative duties.

They should perform their state duties without either dispute or unity among themselves, as directed.

When in unity they consume state revenues.

When in discord they damage the work.

Except with regard to remedial action in emergencies, they should do nothing without knowledge of their officer.

The officer who brings in as much as or much more than the fixed amount of revenue should be rewarded with advancement and honours.

He who reduces the revenue consumes state wealth. If the reduction is bona fide, the officer should be caused to make it up.

The officer who doubles the revenue consumes the vitality of the nation. Such an officer should be suitably punished. The officer who spends the revenue in fruitless ventures consumes the labour of artisans. He should be punished proportionately to the value of work involved, the number of days spent, the amount of investment made and the wages expended.

The head of each department should carefully inspect the amount of departmental work, revenues collected, and expenditure incurred both in detail and in the aggregate. He should also control extravagance, parsimony and exhibitionism. . . .

Every department should be manned by several tenure heads. This should be observed as a safeguard against fraud by a state official. It is as difficult to discover misappropriation among state officials as it is to find out when the fish drinks water.

Fraudulent administrators should not only be deprived of their ill-earned wealth, but also transferred from one office to another to prevent further misappropriation of state funds.

Administrators who enhance state revenues should be ensured of their tenure of service.

Chapter 31: Director of Trade

The director of trade should estimate the demand or absence of demand for and fluctuations in price of various kinds of goods which may be the products of land and water and which may have been conveyed either by land or water. He should also survey the time suitable for their distribution, conservation, purchase and sale.

Merchandise whose sources of supply are widely distributed should be centralised and the price enhanced. When the price becomes effective, another price should be promulgated.

State stores of local manufacture should be centralised. Imported goods should be distributed over wide markets for sale. All goods should be sold to the people at favourable prices.

The director should not charge such prices as will harm the people.

There should be no barrier to the time for sale of those articles for which the demand is recurring, nor should they be exposed to stock-piling.

Or dealers may sell state goods at fixed price at different markets covering their losses by subsidy. . . .

The director should allow facilities for importers of foreign goods. Shippers and traders dealing in foreign goods should be given tax exemptions to aid them in making profits.

Foreigners, except corporations and partnerships of local origin, should have exemptions from debt suits. State goods must be sold under regulations governing daily sale of such goods and accounting.

With regard to state-trading in foreign countries, the director should get an estimate of the value of the local commodities which can be bartered for foreign articles, and estimate the margin of profit left to cover charges payable in the foreign land like duties, road cesses and transport charges, military levies, ferry charges, working expenses for the merchant and his retinue and the share to be given to foreign government. If no profit can be realised, the director should ascertain if any local produce can be exchanged for any foreign produce. He may so arrange as to send one quarter of the valuable merchandise by safe routes to different land-markets. He may make valuable trade and diplomatic contacts with guards, city and rural officers. He should save his wealth and life from danger. If he faces any barrier to this destination, he may sell his merchandise in any market *en route*. Or he may divert his merchandise to other markets through waterways.

The merchant should obtain information *en route* as to market conditions in trading centres and divert his merchandise to profitable markets, avoiding unprofitable ones.

Chapter 35: The Director of Farming

With expert knowledge of the science of farming concerning shrubs and trees or with the assistance of those possessing expert knowledge of these sciences, the director of farming should conserve, in time, seeds of all varieties of grains, flowers, fruits, vegetables, bulbous roots, edible roots, greens, fibres and cotton.

He should cultivate state lands with the help of slaves, labourers and prisoners. They should be supplied with farming implements and farm cattle. They should be assisted by ironsmiths, carpenters, rope makers and persons who capture pests. All losses from the aforesaid persons should carry fines equal to the loss.

Uncultivated lands should be cultivated by share croppers, or by farm labourers for a quarter of the produce or by those who pay a reasonable tithe to the state.

Where irrigation is done by manual labour, 20 per cent of the produce will constitute water-rate; where water is borne on shoulders, 25 per cent; where irrigation is by lift 33 per cent; where irrigation is by rivers or lakes from 33 per cent to 25 per cent of produce should be water-rates.

The director should grow wet, winter and dry crops on suitable lands where labour and irrigation are available.

Chapter 37: Controller of Courtesans

. . . .

The controller should estimate the earnings, the property, income and expenses of every courtesan. He should control their extravagant expenses.

No person, other than the mother, should receive the moveable property of a courtesan. If any one does, he shall be liable to penalty. No courtesan can sell or mortgage her property. Such a transaction will carry penalty.

If a courtesan defames, she must pay penalty. Double penalty for causing hurt and more for disfiguring any one.

No man can have intercourse with a courtesan against her consent or with a nymphet [under age]. Such crimes carry capital punishment.

When a courtesan does not obey the ruler's order to entertain anyone, she will be whipped or be made to pay a prohibitive penalty. If a courtesan does not entertain a client after receiving fees, she should pay penalty of double the amount of fees received. If a courtesan murders a client, she will be burnt alive or drowned.

When a client steals a courtesan's jewellry, he will be fined eight times the value of the goods stolen. Every courtesan must supply to the controller information about the daily earnings, her estimated income and the name of her client. Every courtesan should pay to the state two days' earnings every month.

The state should maintain those who teach courtesans, female slaves and actresses the arts of singing, instrumental music, reading, dancing, acting, writing, painting, mind reading, perfumery and garland making, massaging, and arts of entertainment.

The teachers should train sons of courtesans as stage actors.

Wives of actors and persons of that category, trained in various languages and symbols, should be appointed to seduce and liquidate foreign spies.

Chapter 41: Decay, Stabilisation, and Progress of States

Every state can be said to have a sixfold policy as against any other state.

Ancient thinkers hold that armistice, war, neutrality, invasion, alliance and peace are the six principal policy-relations. Sixfold policy can be reduced into peace, which means concord supported by pacts; war, implying armed aggression; neutrality involving nonchalance; armed invasion against another power; alliance involving appeal for assistance to another power; bilateral policy involving making war with one and suing for peace with another.

Any power inferior to another should sue for peace; any power superior in might to another should launch into war; any power which fears no external attack and which has no strength to wage war should remain neutral; any power with high war-potential should indulge in invasion; any debilitated power should seek new alliances; any power which tries to play for time in mounting an offensive should indulge in a bilateral policy of making war with one and suing for peace with another.

A state should always observe such a policy as will help it strengthen its defensive fortifications and life-lines of communications, build plantations, construct villages, and exploit the mineral and forest wealth of the country, while at the same time preventing fulfilment of similar programmes in the rival state.

Whoever estimates that the rate of growth of the state's potential is higher than that of the enemy can afford to ignore such an enemy.

Any two states hostile to each other, finding that neither has an advantage over the other in fulfilment of their respective programmes, should make peace with each other.

No state should pursue a policy which, while not enabling it to have means to fulfil its own programmes, does not impose a similar handicap on its neighbour: this is the path to reversion.

When any state evaluates that its loss over time would be much less than its acquisition as compared with its rivals, it can afford to ignore its present recession.

When any two states which are rivals expect to acquire equal possessions over the same span of time, they should keep peace with each other.

Stagnation occurs when there is neither progression nor regression. When a temporary stagnation is expected to lead to greater rate of growth than that of the rival, the stagnation can be ignored.

A state can augment its resources by observing peaceful pacts with an enemy in the following situations:

Where, maintaining peace, productive operations of strategic importance can be planned and executed, preventing the rival state at the same time from fulfilling similar programmes;

When under the terms of the peace pact, the state can enjoy the resources created by the productive projects of its enemy in addition to its own resources;

When the state can plan works of sabotage through espionage on the plans and projects of its enemy;

Where under powerful incentives of happy settlements, immigration concessions, tax exemptions, pleasant work-conditions, large profits and high wages, immigration can be induced of strategic workers from an enemy state;

Where because of a prior pact, the enemy can harass another state which is also hostile;

Where because of invasion of the enemy state by another power, the workers of the enemy state immigrate and settle down in the state;

Where because of damage to the productive sectors of the enemy, his potential for offensive is reduced;

Where the state can, by pacts with other states, increase its own resources;

Where a sphere of alliance is formed of which an enemy state is a member, the alliance can be broken by forming fresh alliances.

A state can increase its own resources by preserving hostility with another state in the following situations:

Where the state is composed of military races and war-like corporations;

Where the state has natural defensive fortifications like mountains, woods, rivers and forts and is capable of liquidating the enemy's offensive;

Where harassing operations can be launched on an attacking enemy from powerful fortifications in the states;

Where internal disorders sabotage the war potential of the enemy;

Where invasion of the enemy by another hostile power can be expected to create strategic immigration of skilled workers into the state.

A policy of neutrality can be sustained in the following situations:

Where the balance of power between states is even: as when neither state can immobilise the other;

Where, in the event of an attack, the state can intensify the tribulations of the enemy without loss of its own strategic power.

A state can indulge in armed invasion only:

Where, by invasion, it can reduce the power of an enemy without in any way reducing its own potential, by making suitable arrangements for protection of its own strategic works.

A state should form an alliance with a powerful power where its potential is strong neither to harass its enemy nor to withstand its offensive. It should also attempt reconstruction of its potential from the stage of regression to that of stabilisation and from that of stabilisation to that of progress.

A state can pursue a bilateral policy where it can benefit in resources by maintaining peace with one enemy, and waging war with another.

The central aim of inter-state sixfold policy is to enable a state to advance from a condition of regression to progress through the intermediary state of stabilisation or balance of the forces of advance.

Chapter 54: Restoration of Lost Balance of Power

When an invader is assailed by an alliance of his enemies, he should try to purchase the leader of the alliance with offers of gold and his own alliance and by diplomatic camouflage of the threat of treachery from the alliance of powers. He should instigate the leader of the allied enemies to break up his alliance.

The invader should also attempt to break the allied enemies' formation by setting up the leader of the alliance against the weaker of his enemies, or attempt to forge a combination of the weaker allies against their leader. He may also form a pact with the leader through intrigue, or offer of resources. When the confederation is shattered, he may form alliances with any of his former enemies.

If the allied enemies have no leader, the invader can form a pact with the most influential member of the confederated allies. Or with a powerful member, or with a popular member or with a designing member or with a transient ally, bent on protecting and advancing his own self-interest.

If a state is weak in treasury or in striking power, attention should be directed to strengthen both through stabilisation of authority. Irrigational projects are a source of agricultural prosperity. Good highways should be constructed to facilitate movements of armed might and merchandise. Mines should be developed, as they supply ammunition. Forests should be conserved, as they supply material for defence, communication and vehicles. Pasture lands are the source of cattle wealth.

Thus, a state should build up its striking power through development of the exchequer, the army and wise counsel; and, till the proper time, should conduct itself as a weak power towards its neighbours, to evade conflict or envy from enemy or allied states. If the state is deficient in resources, it should acquire them from related or allied states. It should attract to itself capable men from corporations, from wild and ferocious tribes, and foreigners, and organise espionage that will damage hostile powers.

Introduction to the Panchatantra

The *Panchatantra* ("Five Looms") is one of two surviving collections of animal fables from ancient India (the *Hitopadesa* is the other). The book in its present form was probably put together between about A.D. 100 and 500; but the tales it contains must have circulated by word of mouth for many centuries previously. Variants of some of the stories appear also in the *Jatakas*—accounts of the former existences of the Buddha—indicating that they belonged to the common stock of Indian folklore.

The tone of the stories is purely secular and worldly-wise. Though certainly designed to amuse, they were also regarded in

India as texts of *artha*. The animal protagonists represent very human characteristics—arrogance and greed, fear and vengefulness. With a gentle irony, the fables make fun of stupidity and relate the downfall of the proud and the foolish. Invariably, cleverness proves superior to brute strength. The import of the *Panchatantra* is to glorify shrewdness and trickery; its ethics are approximately those of the *Arthashastra*, from which it frequently quotes.

In form the *Panchatantra* is divided into five books, each consisting of a frame story into which several other tales are incorporated. Most of the fables are introduced by a proverbial aphorism summing up the "moral," which is then repeated at the end of the episode. The book begins with the lament of a wise king that his three sons are ignorant fools. The king's advisors, reflecting that traditional methods of study are strenuous even for the intelligent, suggest summoning a certain learned Brahmin, who is reputed to know everything knowable about political science. The Brahmin undertakes to instruct the dull-minded princes in such a way that even they cannot fail to master the art of politics. His teaching is embodied in the animal fables which follow.

The *Panchatantra* has attained an extraordinarily wide diffusion throughout the world. Since its first known translation into a non-Indian tongue (Pahlavi—Middle Iranian) in the sixth century A.D., it has been rendered into more than two hundred different versions in over fifty languages. About A.D. 750 it was translated into Arabic, and by the eleventh century it had reached Europe. In India today it is known throughout the peninsula in both verse and prose, in ancient and modern vernaculars. Many of the *Panchatantra* stories undoubtedly also spread by word of mouth, carried by traders and missionaries. Any number of fables that seem to be part of the indigenous folklore in lands from Iceland to Jave can be traced to *Panchatantra* originals, often through several intermediate versions. Only the Indian habitats and characteristics of the animals concerned prevent the assumption of an independent origin. In their delineation of basic human traits, their humor and sympathy for the underdog, as well as their practical advice, the fables of the *Panchatantra* have a nearly universal appeal. Probably no other product of the Indian imagination has had so great an influence upon the literature of the world.

FROM THE PANCHATANTRA

Lion and Hare

In a certain forest-region there was a lion named Haughty. And he kept up a continuous slaughter of the beasts. Then all the beasts came together and humbly addressed the king of beasts: "Sire, what profit is there in this pitiless and purposeless slaughtering of all the beasts, which endangers your lordship's prospects in the next world? It is evident that we are utterly undone (by it), and you also will fail of sustenance, so that it is fatal to both parties. So grant us this favour. We ourselves will send to your lordship for your food one wild creature every day, from each tribe in turn." The lion said: "Agreed." From that time on they sent him a single beast each day, and he continually ate the same. Now once upon a time as the lot passed from tribe to tribe it came the turn of a hare. But he, when all the beasts sent him forth, reflected: "This means the end of me; I am entering the jaws of death. What now would be a timely thing for me to do? Yet after all, is anything impossible for the clever? So I will kill the *lion* by craft." Thereupon he proceeded very slowly, so that he arrived too late for dinner-time. But the lion, his throat lean with hunger, was filled with rage and said to him furiously: "No matter how angry one is, killing is the worst thing one can do! You are a dead creature this day. Tell me, why this delay on your part?" Then the hare bowed and said courteously: "My lord, it is not my fault. As I was coming along another lion stopped me on the road and was going to eat me. And I said: 'I am going to our lord the lion Haughty, to serve as his dinner.' Then he said: 'That Haughty is a thief. So go and call him and return quickly, that whichever of us two shall prove himself king by his prowess may eat all of these beasts.' So I have come to report this to my lord." Hearing this the lion said angrily: "How can there be another lion here in

From *The Panchatantra*, trans. by Franklin Edgerton (London: George Allen and Unwin, 1965). Reprinted by permission of George Allen & Unwin, Ltd.

this wood ruled by my right arm! Go and show me the scoun-
drel quickly!" The hare said: "In that case come, my lord, and
I will show him to you." But he, the hare, took him and
showed him a deep well full of clear water, saying: "Look
there! There he is!" Then that fool of a lion saw his own image
in the water, and thought: "This is that rival of mine," and
was furiously angry. And he roared his lion's roar. Thereupon
a roar of redoubled strength came back out of the well, because
of the echo from it. And when the lion heard this roar, he
thought: "He must be exceedingly strong!" And he hurled himself upon him and perished. But the hare, being overjoyed himself and having brought joy to all the beasts, received their
grateful thanks and dwelt in that wood in peace.

Therefore I say: "Whosoever has wit has power; but as for
the foolish, how can he be powerful? Behold how the lion
Haughty was destroyed by the hare!"

Brahman and Rogues

Once a brahman who had got a goat from another village to
make an animal-sacrifice was going to his own home with the
goat on his shoulder, when he was seen on the way by rogues.
They thought: "Let us get this brahman to let go the goat!" So
they came to a decision, and they divided themselves into
groups of one, two, and three, and came in the opposite direction along the road before him. But the first of them said to the
brahman: "Why are you carrying this dog on your shoulder?
Or is it because he is good at killing animals?" So saying he
departed. The brahman thought: "What does this villain mean?
The idea of my carrying a dog on my shoulder!" As soon as
the next two rogues met him, they also said to the brahman:
"Brahman, what is this unseemly thing that you are doing?
The sacred cord, the rosary, the holy water-pot, and the sect-
mark on your forehead, and a dog on your shoulder—it does
not fit at all! But no doubt it must be a clever dog at killing
hares, deer, and boars." So saying they went past. But the
brahman in wonderment put the goat on the ground, and felt
of the parts of its body all over, its ears, horns, privy parts, tail,

and other members, and thought: "They are fools; how can they imagine that this is a dog?" and put it on his shoulder again and went on. After this the other three said to the brahman: "Touch us not! Go to one side of us! For you are pure in outward appearance alone, brahman; you are handling a dog, and so you must surely be a hunter!"[1] So saying they departed. Then that brahman thought: "Can I have taken leave of my senses? And yet the majority must be right. Unnatural things are indeed found to occur in the world; perhaps this is an ogre that has taken the form of a dog. After all an ogre would be capable of assuming a dog's form." So thinking he turned the goat loose, and bathed[2] and went home. And the rogues took the goat and ate it.

Therefore I say: "Many powerless adversaries, opening hostilities, can succeed in tricking (their enemy) by their wits, as happened to the brahman in the case of the goat."

Brahman, Thief, and Ogre

Once a certain poor brahman received a present of a pair of cows, which had been brought up from young calves by feeding with ghee, oil, salt, grass, and (other) wholesome foods, so that they were very fat. And a certain thief saw them, and he thought as follows: "This very day I shall steal them." So he started out in the early evening, and as he went along some unknown person touched him on the shoulder. Whereupon he asked in alarm: "Who are you?" And he spoke truthfully: "I am a night-roaming brahman-ogre.[3] You also tell me who you are." Said he: "I am a thief." And when the other asked again: "Where are you going?" he said: "I intend to steal a pair of cows from a certain brahman. But where are you going?" Then being reassured by this information the brahman-ogre also said: "I too have started out to seize that same brahman." Then

1. Hunters in India belong to one of the lowest and most despised orders of society.
2. In order to purify himself from the touch of the dog, regarded as an unclean animal.
3. A brahman who, because of his evil deeds in some previous existence, was reborn as an ogre (*rakshasa*)—a monster who eats human flesh.

they went thither both together and stayed at one side, waiting for the proper time. And when the brahman had gone to sleep the brahman-ogre was creeping up to seize him first; when the thief said to him: "This is not the right way. After I have stolen his two cows, then you may seize him." Said the other: "That too would be wrong. Perchance the noise of the cows might wake him, and then I should have come in vain." The thief said: "If when you seize him he gets up and makes an outcry, then everybody will be roused; and then I cannot steal his two cows. So I will steal the cows first, and afterwards you may eat the brahman." As they were thus disputing with one another they got angry, and with their rivalry they straightway woke up the brahman. Thereupon the thief said: "Brahman, this brahman-ogre wants to seize you." But the brahman-ogre said: "This thief wants to steal your two cows." Hearing this the brahman got up and being put on his guard saved himself from the ogre by reciting the mantra[4] of his sect's deity, and saved his two cows from the thief by brandishing his cudgel. So both the thief and the ogre ran away.

Therefore I say: "Even enemies may be useful when they fall out with each other. The thief saved (the brahman's) life, while the ogre (saved) his two cows."

The Barber Who Killed the Monks

There was in a certain city a merchant's son of old, who had lost his wealth, his kinsfolk, and his fortune, and was ground down by poverty. Attended by his old nurse he had lived since childhood in a part of a broken-down house, and he had been brought up by his old nurse, a slave-woman. (Once) early in the evening he meditated, sighing a long and earnest sigh: "Alas, when will there be an end to this (my) poverty?" As he pondered thus he slept during the night. And towards morning he saw a dream. Three monks came and woke him and said to him: "Friend, tomorrow we shall come to visit you in this same form. For (we are) three heaps of treasure stored away by your forefathers, and when you slay us with a cudgel we shall turn

4. Sacred hymn.

into dinars. And you must show no mercy in doing this." So in the morning he awoke, still pondering on this dream, and said to the nurse: "Today, mother, you must be well prepared all day for a solemn rite. Make the house ceremonially pure by smearing on cow-dung and so forth, and we will feed three brahmans to the best of our ability. I for my part am going to get a barber." So it was done, and the barber came to trim his beard and nails. When his beard had been trimmed in proper fashion, the figures which he had seen in the dream came in. And as soon as the merchant's son saw these monks, he dealt with them as he had been commanded. And they became piles of money. And as he took in this mass of wealth, the merchant's son gave the barber three hundred dinars as a fee, and in order to keep the secret. But the barber, having seen him (do this), went home and drew a hasty conclusion from what he had seen, and thought: "I too will kill three monks with a cudgel and turn them into three heaps of treasure." So he took a cudgel and stood in readiness; and presently three monks, impelled by their previous deeds, came a-begging. Thereupon the barber smote them with the cudgel and killed them. And he got no treasure. Straightway the king's officers came and arrested the barber and took him away and impaled him.

Therefore I say: "What is imperfectly seen, imperfectly understood, imperfectly heard, and imperfectly investigated, should not be done by any man—as was done by the barber. So you also are just such a fool. Therefore wise men must not perform any action until it has been carefully considered."

Introduction to the Harsha-carita

The *Harsha-carita* is a historical romance based upon the life of King Harsha (reigned A.D. 606-47). Although it is a paean to the king by Bana, a court poet, it also provides a valuable eyewitness report about one of the principal figures in Indian history.

Harsha inherited a small kingdom conquered by his father, the

Raja of Thanesar. For nearly six years the son fought uninterruptedly in order to confirm the recently acquired territories in their allegiance. In subsequent campaigns he added to this patrimony, until he ruled the greater part of northern India from his capital at Kanauj. The Chinese Buddhist pilgrim Hsüan Tsang, who resided for a time at his court, reports that the king's conquests were achieved with 5,000 elephants, 20,000 cavalry, and 50,000 infantry. The following brief description of his army breaking camp gives an indication of the manner in which Indian campaigns were conducted. The poet Bana may well have been present on such occasions; for his descriptions are detailed and vivid, though overly elaborate in style and doubtless embroidered for effect.

FROM THE HARSHA-CARITA OF BANA

Chapter VII

Some days having passed, on a day with care calculated and approved by a troop of astronomers numbering hundreds, was fixed an hour of marching suitable for the subjugation of all the four quarters. The king had bathed in golden and silvern vessels, like autumn clouds which were skilled in pouring water; had with deep devotion offered worship to the adorable Nilalohita;[1] fed the up-flaming fire, whose masses of blaze formed a rightward whorl; bestowed upon Brahmans sesamum vessels of precious stones, silver, and gold in thousands, myriads also of cows having hoofs and horn tips adorned with creepers of gold-work; sat upon a throne with a coverlet of tiger skin; duly anointed first his bow and then his body down to the feet with sandal bright as his own fame; put on two seemly robes of bark silk marked with pairs of flamingos; formed about his head a chaplet of white flowers to be, like the moon's digit, a sign of the supreme. . . . Finally with all good omens pressing forward officiously, like devoted servants, in the van, amid a clamourous cry of "Victory!" from the delighted people, he

From *The Harsa-carita of Bana*, trans. by E. B. Cowell and F. W. Thomas (Delhi: Motilal Benarsidass, 1961). Reprinted by permission of the Royal Asiatic Society, London.
1. The god Rudra (Shiva).

issued forth from his house, like the Golden Foetus from Brahma's egg,[2] to set on foot an age of gold.

The starting place was fixed at a large temple built of reeds not far from the city and close to the Sarasvati.[3] It displayed a lofty pillared gateway, an altar supporting a golden cup adorned with sprays, affixed chaplets of wild flowers, wreaths of white banners, strolling white-robed people, and muttering Brahmans. During the king's stay there the village notary appeared with his whole retinue of clerks, and saying, "Let his majesty, whose edicts are never void, even now bestow upon us his commands for the day," so presented a new-made golden seal with a bull for its emblem. The king took it. As soon however as a ball of earth was produced, the seal slipped from the king's hand and fell face downwards upon the ground, and the lines of the letters were distinctly marked upon the nearly dry mud and soft earth of the Sarasvati's bank. Apprehensive of an evil omen, the courtiers were depressed, but the king thought in his heart: "The minds of the dull are indeed blind to reality. The omen signifies that the earth shall be stamped with the single seal of my sole command: but the rustics interpret otherwise." Having thus mentally welcomed the omen, he bestowed upon the Brahmans a hundred villages delimited by a thousand ploughs. That day he spent in the same place, and when night arrived, complimented all the kings and retired to rest.

At the close of the third watch, when all creatures slept and all was still, the marching drum was beaten with a boom deep as the gaping roar of the sky elephants. Then, after first a moment's pause, eight sharp strokes were distinctly given anew upon the drum, making up the number of the leagues in the day's march.

Straightway the drums rattled, the *nandis*[4] rang out joyously, the trumpets brayed, the *kahalas* hummed, the horns blared; the noise of the camp gradually increased. Officers occupied

---

2. This refers to the mythological account of the creation of the world by the god Brahma.

3. A river north of Delhi. Its exact course is now unknown.

4. A drum beaten as a good omen.

themselves in arousing the courtiers. The heavens were con-
founded by a confused noise of drumsticks added to a rapid
tapping of mallets. Commanders mustered crowds of barrack
superintendents. Thousands of torches lighted by the people
made inroads upon the darkness of night with their glare. Loving pairs were roused from sleep by the tramp of the women
of the watch. Shrill words of command from the marshals dispelled the slumbers of blinking riders. Awakened elephant
herds vacated their sleeping stalls. There was a shaking of
manes from troops of horses risen from sleep. The noisy camp
resounded with mattocks uprooting ground fastenings. Elephant
hobbles rattled as their pins were extracted. Rearing horses
curved their hoofs at the clear low noise of chain-keys brought
towards them. A clanking sound of halter fetters filled the ten
regions to overflowing, as the foragers loosed the rutting elephants. Leathern bags, bursting with fullness, were extended
upon the dusty backs of elephants, which had been rubbed down
by strokes from wisps of hay. Servants of house-builders rolled
up awnings and cloth screens belonging to tents and marquees.
Leathern sacks were filled to roundness with bundles of pegs.
Store-room stewards collected stores of platters. Many elephant
attendants were pressed to convey the stores. The houses of the
neighbourhood were blocked with clusters of cups and vessels,
which were lifted upon numerous elephants, while the riders
kept the animals steady. Wicked elephants were loaded with a
cargo of utensils hurriedly tossed upon them by travel-practised
domestics. Amid the laughter of the crowd helpless corpulent
bawds lagged as they were with difficulty dragged along with
hands and legs sprawling sideways. Many huge and savage
elephants trumpeted as the free play of their limbs was checked
by the tightening of the girth-bands of their gaudy housings.
A jangling of bells taking place in the elephant troop inflamed
all ears with fever. Camels, as sacks were set on their backs,
bellowed at the outrage. The carriages of the high-born nobles'
wives were thronged with roguish emissaries sent by princes of
rank. Elephant riders, deceived as to the time of starting,
searched for new servants. Highly honoured footmen led the
fine horses of the king's favourites. . . . The low people of the

neighbourhood, running up as the elephants and horses started, looted heaps of abandoned grain. Donkeys ridden by throngs of boys accompanied the march. Crowds of carts with creaking wheels occupied the trampled roads. Oxen were laden with utensils momentarily put upon them. Stout steers, driven on in advance, lagged out of greed for fodder lying near them. In front were carried the kitchen appliances of the great feudatories. First ran banner-bearers. Hundreds of friends were spectators of the men's exits from the interior of their somewhat contracted huts. Elephant keepers, assaulted with clods by people starting from hovels which had been crushed by the animals' feet, called the bystanders to witness the assaults. Wretched families fled from grass cabins ruined by collisions. Despairing merchants saw the oxen bearing their wealth flee before the onset of the tumult. A troop of seraglio elephants advanced where the press of people gave way before the glare of their runners' torches. Horsemen shouted to dogs tied behind them. Old people sang the praises of tall Tangana horses which by the steady motion of their quick footfalls provided a comfortable seat. Deccan[5] riders disconsolately contended with fallen mules. The whole world was swallowed up in dust.

. . . .

5. The Deccan is the central Indian plateau lying between the Narbada River and the Tamil-speaking region of the far south.

II
Kama

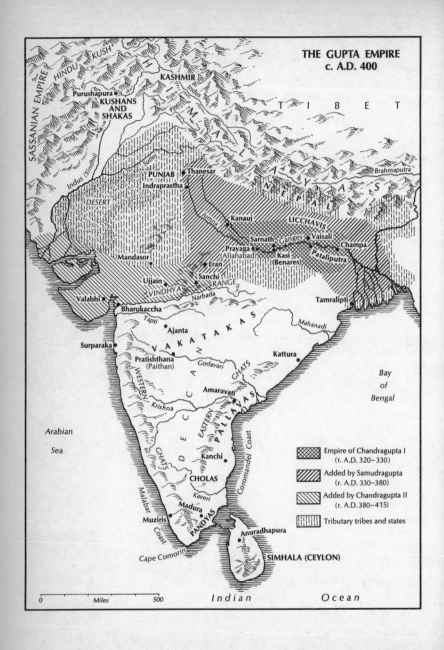

**THE GUPTA EMPIRE
c. A.D. 400**

SASSANIAN EMPIRE

HINDU KUSH

KUSH

KASHMIR

Purushapura •
KUSHANS
AND
SHAKAS

Indus (Sindhu)

HIMALAYAS

TIBET

NEPAL

Brahmaputra

Sutlej

PUNJAB • Thanesar
Indraprastha

DESERT

Kanauj •
LICCHAVIS

Sarnath • Vaisali
Prayaga • Ganges
(Allahabad)   Champa
Kasi   Pataliputra
(Benares)

Mandasor •

Ujjain • VINDHYA
        Eran •
        Sanchi
RANGE

Valabhi •
Bharukaccha •   Narbada   Tamralipti

Tapti   VAKATAKAS   Mahanadi

Ajanta •

Surparaka •   Kattura •

Pratishthana   Godavari
(Paithan)   GHATS   Bay
        of
WESTERN   Bengal

Amaravati •

Krishna

Arabian

Sea   EASTERN
        PALLAVAS

Kanchi •

CHOLAS   Coromandel Coast

        Empire of Chandragupta I
        (r. A.D. 320–330)

        Added by Samudragupta
        (r. A.D. 330–380)

Kaveri   Added by Chandragupta II
Madura   (r. A.D. 380–415)
Muziris •
PANDYAS   Tributary tribes and states

Malabar   Anuradhapura •
Coast
Cape Comorin   SIMHALA (CEYLON)

0   Miles   500   Indian   Ocean

FROM THE ATHARVA VEDA*

A Love-Spell: With a Sweet Herb (Book I, Hymn 34)

1   This plant is honey-born; with honey we dig thee; forth from honey art thou engendered; [so] do thou make us possessed of honey.

2   At the tip of my tongue honey, at the root of my tongue honeyedness; mayest thou be altogether in my power, mayest thou come unto my intent.

3   Honeyed [is] my in-stepping, honeyed my forth-going; with my voice I speak what is honeyed; may I be of honey-aspect.

4.   Than honey am I sweeter, than the honey-plant more honeyed; of me verily shalt thou be fond, as of a honeyed branch.

5   About thee with an encompassing sugar-cane have I gone, in order to (obtain) absence of mutual hatred; that thou mayest be one loving me, that thou mayest be one not going away from me.

To Get a Husband for a Woman (Book II, Hymn 36)

1   Unto our favor, O Agni,[1] may a wooer come, to this girl, along with our fortune. Enjoyable [is she] to suitors, agreeable at festivals; be there quickly good-fortune for her with a husband.

* For Introduction to the Atharva Veda, see above, pp. 7-8.
From *Atharva-veda Samhita*, trans. by William D. Whitney, rev. by Charles R. Lanman, Vol. 7 of the Harvard Oriental Series (Cambridge, Mass.: Harvard University Press, 1905). Notes in part adapted from Ralph T. H. Griffith, trans., *The Hymns of the Atharva Veda*, Vol. I (Benares: E. J. Lazarus & Co., 1916).
   1. The fire god.

2   Fortune enjoyed by Soma,[2] enjoyed by Brahman,[3] brought together by Aryaman[4]; with the truth of divine Dhatar,[5] the husband-finder I perform.

3   May this woman, O Agni, find a husband; for king Soma maketh her of good-fortune; giving birth to sons, she shall become chief consort; having gone to a husband, let her, having good-fortune, bear rule.[6]

4   As, O bounteous one,[7] this pleasant covert hath been dear to the well-settled wild beasts, so let this woman be dear to Bhaga,[8] mutually dear, not disagreeing with her husband.

5   Ascend thou the boat of Bhaga,[9] full, unfailing; with that cause to cross over hither a suitor who is according to thy wish.

6   Shout to [him], O lord of riches[10]; make a suitor hither-minded; turn the right side[11] to every one who is a suitor according to thy wish.

7   Here [is] gold, bdellium[12]; here [is] *auksha*,[13] likewise fortune; these have given thee unto husbands, in order to find one according to thy wish.

8   Hither let Savitar[14] conduct for thee, conduct a husband that is according to thy wish; do thou assign [him] to her, O herb.

Against a Rival Wife: With a Plant (Book III, Hymn 18)

1   I dig (up) this herb, of plants the strongest, with which one

2. The young bride belongs to the god Soma, who in Vedic mythology was the husband of Surya, the typical bride.
3. The priest; or prayer.
4. A name for the god Agni. This is a pun on the word *aryaman*, meaning "companion," i.e., the companion who arranges a marriage for his friend.
5. The god who upholds the marriage sacrament.
6. I.e., as the principal wife of a king.
7. Indra, chief of the gods.
8. The god who brings wealth and blesses married love.
9. This seems to refer to some custom whereby the girl attempts to discover who will be a proper husband for her.
10. Indra.
11. I.e., the place of honor.
12. A fragrant gum used to make perfume.
13. Probably a sweet-smelling unguent.
14. The sun-god, the universal life-giver.

drives off her rival; with which one wins completely her husband.

2 O thou of outstretched leaves, fortunate, god-quickened, powerful, do thou thrust away my rival, make my husband wholly mine.

3 Since he has not named thy name, thou also stayest not with him as husband; unto distant distance make we my rival go.

4 Superior [am] I, O superior one; superior, indeed, to them that are superior; below [is] she that is my rival; lower [is] she than they that are lower.

5 I am overpowering; likewise art thou very powerful; we both, becoming full of power, will overpower my rival.

6 I have put on for thee[15] the overpowering one; I have put (beneath) thee the very powerful one; after me let thy mind run forth as a cow after her calf, run as water on its track.

For Fecundity (Book III, Hymn 23)

1 By what thou hast become barren, that we make disappear from thee; that now we set down elsewhere, far away from thee.

2 Unto thy womb let a foetus come, a male one, as an arrow to a quiver; let a hero be born unto thee here, a ten-months' son.[16]

3 Give birth to a male, a son; after him let a male be born; mayest thou be mother of sons, of those born and whom thou shalt bear.

4 And what excellent seeds the bulls generate, with them do thou acquire a son; become thou a productive milch-cow.

5 I perform for thee the [ceremony] of Prajapati; let a foetus come to thy womb; acquire thou a son, O woman, who shall be weal for thee; weal also for him do thou become.

6 The plants of which heaven has been the father, earth the mother, ocean the root—let those herbs of the gods favor thee, (for the) acquisition of a son.

15. The husband.
16. I.e., born in the tenth lunar month.

To Command a Woman's Love (Book III, Hymn 25)

1   Let the up-thruster[17] thrust thee up; do not abide in thine own lair; the arrow of love that is terrible, therewith I pierce thee in the heart.

2   The arrow feathered with longing, tipped with love, necked with resolve—having made that well-straightened, let love pierce thee in the heart.

3   The well-straightened arrow of love which dries the spleen,[18] forward-winged, consuming—therewith I pierce thee in the heart.

4   Pierced with consuming pain, dry-mouthed, do thou come creeping to me, gentle, with fury allayed, entirely [mine], pleasant-spoken, submissive.

5   I goad thee hither with a goad, away from mother, likewise from father, that thou mayest be in my power, mayest come unto my intent.

6   Do ye, O Mitra-and-Varuna,[19] cast out the intents from her heart; then, making her powerless, make her [to be] in my own control.

17. The impeller: Kama, the god of love.
18. The spleen and liver were regarded as the seat of the passions.
19. Mitra and Varuna regarded as a single deity.

Introduction to the Kama Sutra

The *Kama Sutra* is the oldest and most important Indian treatise now extant on the art of love. Its reputed author is Vatsyayana, of whom nothing whatever is known except that his personal name was Mallanaga and that he belonged to the Vatsyayana sect. Textual evidence establishes that he lived sometime between the first and fourth centuries A.D. Unquestionably he was the product of a wealthy and refined milieu, though we do not know at what place or what his own station in life may have been. In any event, he knew and drew upon a considerable existing literature on the subject of love; and he seems to have been rather a compiler and arranger than an original thinker.

As one of the recognized aims of earthly life in the Indian scheme of things, *kama* was a perfectly legitimate pursuit, free of many of the inhibitions which surround discussion of the subject in modern Western countries. In the widest sense of the term, *kama* meant pleasure of every sort—all the amenities which wealth and culture provide—though generally it bore an erotic connotation. The society to which Vatsyayana belonged obviously thought that love should be studied like any other art. The *Kama Sutra,* in fact, has all the earmarks of a textbook, including elaborate scholarly classifications and a dry, pedantic style. Obviously it was intended for the instruction of the urbanized upper classes, or perhaps for the retinue of a princely court. It assumes a high level of material comfort and the leisure to engage in polite amusements. Its tolerance of seduction for financial or political advantage likewise bespeaks a close relationship to the centers of power.

The *Kama Sutra* offers a wealth of information about the social customs of ancient upper-class India, and especially about the position of women. Its description of the virtuous wife as a paragon of submissiveness to her husband is one frequently encountered in Indian literature; and this certainly represented the ideal, if not always the fact. Polygamy was taken for granted, at least among those who could afford it, and produced the inevitable ill-will among rival wives. Courtesans occupied a recognized place in society; and those of the higher type—educated in at least some of the recommended sixty-four feminine arts—were highly honored. But the adulteress was an utter outcast, whom any man might enjoy without shame, because she disturbed the social order.

From the Western, Christian viewpoint, the *Kama Sutra* is amoral or even immoral; but there is no reason to believe that it shocked its Indian contemporaries. It respects the traditional, religiously based class division of society which was the foundation of the Indian concept of *dharma.* The sort of intrigue it recommends—in which cleverness is valued above all—was no doubt widespread in the sophisticated urban society from which it sprang. But despite its frankness in sexual matters, the *Kama Sutra* is far from suggesting that love ought to be the chief preoccupation for anyone except a professional courtesan. *Kama* in ancient India was at best a religious duty resulting in the birth of sons, and at worst a permissible pleasure. As such, it was a fit subject for scientific study.

FROM THE KAMA SUTRA OF VATSYAYANA

PART I

Chapter II: On the Acquisition of Dharma, Artha, and Kama

Man, the period of whose life is one hundred years, should practice Dharma, Artha and Kama at different times and in such a
manner that they may harmonize together and not clash in any
way. He should acquire learning in his childhood, in his youth
and middle age he should attend to Artha and Kama, and in his
old age he should perform Dharma, and thus seek to gain Moksha, *i.e.*, release from further transmigration. Or, on account
of the uncertainty of life, he may practice them at times when
they are enjoined to be practised. But one thing is to be noted,
he should lead the life of a religious student until he finishes
his education.

Dharma is obedience to the command of the Shastra or Holy
Writ of the Hindoos to do certain things, such as the performance of sacrifices, which are not generally done, because they
do not belong to this world, and produce no visible effect; and
not to do other things, such as eating meat, which is often done
because it belongs to this world, and has visible effects.

Dharma should be learnt from the Shruti (Holy Writ), and
from those conversant with it.

Artha is the acquisition of arts, land, gold, cattle, wealth,
equipages and friends. It is, further, the protection of what is
acquired, and the increase of what is protected.

Artha should be learnt from the king's officers, and from
merchants who may be versed in the ways of commerce.

Kama is the enjoyment of appropriate objects by the five
senses of hearing, feeling, seeing, tasting and smelling, assisted
by the mind together with the soul. The ingredient in this is a
peculiar contact between the organ of sense and its object, and

From Vatsyayana, *The Kama Sutra*, trans. by Sir Richard Burton and
F. F. Arbuthnot (London: The Kama Shastra Society, 1883).

the consciousness of pleasure which arises from that contact is called Kama.

Kama is to be learnt from the Kama Sutra (aphorisms on love) and from the practice of citizens.

When all the three, viz., Dharma, Artha and Kama come together, the former is better than the one which follows it, *i.e.*, Dharma is better than Artha, and Artha is better than Kama. But Artha should always be first practised by the king, for the livelihood of men is to be obtained from it only. Again, Kama being the occupation of public women, they should prefer it to the other two, and these are exceptions to the general rule.

Objection 1. Some learned men say that as Dharma is connected with things not belonging to this world, it is appropriately treated of in a book; and so also is Artha, because it is practised only by the application of proper means, and a knowledge of those means can only be obtained by study and from books. But Kama being a thing which is practised even by the brute creation, and which is to be found everywhere, does not want any work on the subject.

Answer. This is not so. Sexual intercourse being a thing dependent on man and woman requires the application of proper means by them, and those means are to be learnt from the Kama Shastra.[1] The non-application of proper means, which we see in the brute creation, is caused by their being unrestrained, and by the females among them only being fit for sexual intercourse at certain seasons and no more, and by their intercourse not being preceded by thought of any kind.

Objection 2. The Lokayatikas[2] say: Religious ordinances should not be observed, for they bear a future fruit, and at the same time it is also doubtful whether they will bear any fruit at all. What foolish person will give away that which is in his own hands into the hands of another? Moreover, it is better to have a pigeon to-day than a peacock to-morrow; and a copper

---

1. *Shastra* means "scripture" or "treatise"; it is a broader term than *sutra*, which signifies "thread" or "aphorism." Here Vatsyayana may be referring to writings on love in general rather than to his own book specifically.

2. The Lokayatikas (Lokayatas) were a philosophical school with a materialist viewpoint.

coin which we have the certainty of obtaining, is better than a gold coin, the possession of which is doubtful.

Answer. It is not so. 1st. Holy Writ, which ordains the practice of Dharma, does not admit of a doubt.

2nd. Sacrifices such as those made for the destruction of enemies, or for the fall of rain, are seen to bear fruit.

3rd. The sun, moon, stars, planets and other heavenly bodies appear to work intentionally for the good of the world.

4th. The existence of this world is effected by the observance of the rules respecting the four classes of men and their four stages of life.[3]

5th. We see that seed is thrown into the ground with the hope of future crops.

Vatsyayana is therefore of opinion that the ordinances of religion must be obeyed.

Objection 3. Those who believe that destiny is the prime mover of all things say:—We should not exert ourselves to acquire wealth for sometimes it is not acquired although we strive to get it, while at other times it comes to us of itself without any exertion on our part. Everything is therefore in the power of destiny, who is the lord of gain and loss, of success and defeat, of pleasure and pain. Thus we see that Bali[4] was raised to the throne of Indra by destiny, and was also put down by the same power, and it is destiny only that can re-instate him.

Answer. It is not right to say so. As the acquisition of every object pre-supposes at all events some exertion on the part of man, the application of proper means may be said to be the cause of gaining all our ends, and this application of proper means being thus necessary (even where a thing is destined to happen), it follows that a person who does nothing will enjoy no happiness.

Objection 4. Those who are inclined to think that Artha is the chief object to be obtained argue thus. Pleasures should not be

3. The four classes are: Brahmins (priests), Kshatriyas (warriors), Vaishyas (merchants or farmers), and Shudras (servants). The four stages of life are: student, householder, forest hermit, and wandering ascetic. For the various regulations governing the classes and life-stages, see below, pp. 137-57.

4. In Hindu mythology, Bali was a demon who conquered Indra, chief of the gods, but was in turn conquered by the god Vishnu.

sought for, because they are obstacles to the practice of Dharma and Artha, which are both superior to them, and are also disliked by meritorious persons. Pleasures also bring a man into distress, and into contact with low persons; they cause him to commit unrighteous deeds, and produce impurity in him; they make him regardless of the future, and encourage carelessness and levity. And lastly, they cause him to be disbelieved by all, received by none, and despised by everybody, including himself. It is notorious, moreover, that many men who have given themselves up to pleasure alone, have been ruined along with their families and relations. . . .

[Several examples from popular mythology are cited.]

Answer. This objection cannot be sustained, for pleasures, being as necessary for the existence and well being of the body as food, are consequently equally required. They are, moreover, the results of Dharma and Artha. Pleasures are, therefore, to be followed with moderation and caution. No one refrains from cooking food because there are beggars to ask for it, or from sowing seed because there are deer to destroy the corn when it is grown up.

Thus a man practising Dharma, Artha and Kama enjoys happiness both in this world and in the world to come. The good perform those actions in which there is no fear as to what is to result from them in the next world, and in which there is no danger to their welfare. Any action which conduces to the practice of Dharma, Artha and Kama together, or of any two, or even one of them, should be performed, but an action which conduces to the practice of one of them at the expense of the remaining two should not be performed.

Chapter III: On the Arts and Sciences To Be Studied

Man should study the Kama Sutra and the arts and sciences subordinate thereto, in addition to the study of the arts and sciences contained in Dharma and Artha. Even young maids should study this Kama Sutra along with its arts and sciences before marriage, and after it they could continue to do so with the consent of their husbands.

Here some learned men object, and say that females, not being allowed to study any science, should not study the Kama Sutra.

But Vatsyayana is of opinion that this objection does not hold good, for women already know the practice of Kama Sutra, and that practice is derived from the Kama Shastra, or the science of Kama itself. Moreover, it is not only in this but in many other cases that though the practice of a science is known to all, only a few persons are acquainted with the rules and laws on which the science is based. Thus the Yadnikas or sacrificers, though ignorant of grammar, make use of appropriate words when addressing the different Deities, and do not know how these words are framed. Again, persons do the duties required of them on auspicious days, which are fixed by astrology, though they are not acquainted with the science of astrology. In a like manner riders of horses and elephants train these animals without knowing the science of training animals, but from practice only. And similarly the people of the most distant provinces obey the laws of the kingdom from practice, and because there is a king over them, and without further reason. And from experience we find that some women, such as daughters of princes and their ministers, and public women, are actually versed in the Kama Shastra.

A female, therefore, should learn the Kama Shastra, or at least part of it, by studying its practice from some confidential friend. She should study alone in private the sixty-four practices that form a part of the Kama Shastra. Her teacher should be one of the following persons, viz., the daughter of a nurse brought up with her and already married,[5] or a female friend who can be trusted in everything, or the sister of her mother (*i.e.*, her aunt), or an old female servant, or a female beggar who may have formerly lived in the family, or her own sister, who can always be trusted.

The following are the arts to be studied, together with the Kama Sutra:—

1. Singing.

5. All of the approved teachers must be married.

2. Playing on musical instruments.

3. Dancing.

4. Union of dancing, singing, and playing instrumental music.

5. Writing and drawing.

6. Tattooing.

7. Arraying and adorning an idol with rice and flowers.

8. Spreading and arranging beds or couches of flowers, or flowers upon the ground.

9. Colouring the teeth, garments, hair, nails and bodies, *i.e.*, staining, dyeing, colouring and painting the same.

10. Fixing stained glass into a floor.

11. The art of making beds, and spreading out carpets and cushions for reclining.

12. Playing on musical glasses filled with water.

13. Storing and accumulating water in aqueducts, cisterns and reservoirs.

14. Picture making, trimming and decorating.

15. Stringing of rosaries, necklaces, garlands and wreaths.

16. Binding of turbans and chaplets, and making crests and top-knots of flowers.

17. Scenic representations. Stags playing.

18. Art of making ear ornaments.

19. Art of preparing perfumes and odours.

20. Proper disposition of jewels and decorations, and adornment in dress.

21. Magic or sorcery.

22. Quickness of hand or manual skill.

23. Culinary art, *i.e.*, cooking and cookery.

24. Making lemonades, sherbets, acidulated drinks, and spirituous extracts with proper flavour and colour.

25. Tailor's work and sewing.

26. Making parrots, flowers, tufts, tassels, bunches, bosses, knobs, &c., out of yarn or thread.

27. Solution of riddles, enigmas, covert speeches, verbal puzzles and enigmatical questions.

[In all, sixty-four skills are enumerated.]

A public woman, endowed with a good disposition, beauty and other winning qualities, and also versed in the above arts, obtains the name of a Ganika, or public woman of high quality, and receives a seat of honour in an assemblage of men. She is, moreover, always respected by the king, and praised by learned men, and her favour being sought for by all, she becomes an object of universal regard. The daughter of a king too, as well as the daughter of a minister, being learned in the above arts, can make their husbands favourable to them, even though these may have thousands of other wives besides themselves. And in the same manner, if a wife becomes separated from her husband, and falls into distress, she can support herself easily, even in a foreign country, by means of her knowledge of these arts. Even the bare knowledge of them gives attractiveness to a woman, though the practice of them may be only possible or otherwise according to the circumstances of each case. A man who is versed in these arts, who is loquacious and acquainted with the arts of gallantry, gains very soon the hearts of women, even though he is only acquainted with them for a short time.

Chapter V:
About the Kinds of Women Resorted to by the Citizens

When Kama is practised by men of the four castes according to the rules of the Holy Writ (*i.e.*, by lawful marriage) with virgins of their own caste, it then becomes a means of acquiring lawful progeny and good fame, and it is not also opposed to the customs of the world. On the contrary the practice of Kama with women of the higher castes, and with those previously enjoyed by others, even though they be of the same caste, is prohibited. But the practice of Kama with women of the lower castes, with women excommunicated from their own caste, with public women, and with women twice married,[6] is neither enjoined nor prohibited. The object of practising Kama with such women is pleasure only.

6. This term applies not to a remarried widow, but to a woman who has left her husband and is living with another man. Then as now in India, widow remarriage was generally not permitted.

Nayikas,[7] therefore, are of three kinds, viz., maids, women twice married, and public women. Gonikaputra[8] has expressed an opinion that there is a fourth kind of Nayika, viz., a woman who is resorted to on some special occasion even though she be previously married to another. These special occasions are when a man thinks thus:—

(a) This woman is self-willed, and has been previously enjoyed by many others besides myself. I may, therefore, safely resort to her as a public woman though she belongs to a higher caste than mine, and, in so doing I shall not be violating the ordinances of Dharma.

Or thus:—

(b) This is a twice-married woman and has been enjoyed by others before me, there is, therefore, no objection to my resorting to her.

Or thus:—

(c) This woman has gained the heart of her great and powerful husband, and exercises a mastery over him, who is a friend of my enemy; if, therefore, she becomes united with me she will cause her husband to abandon my enemy.

Or thus:—

(d) This woman will turn the mind of her husband, who is very powerful, in my favour, he being at present disaffected towards me, and intent on doing me some harm.

Or thus:—

(e) By making this woman my friend I shall gain the object of some friend of mine, or shall be able to effect the ruin of some enemy, or shall accomplish some other difficult purpose.

Or thus:—

(f) By being united with this woman, I shall kill her husband, and so obtain his vast riches which I covet.

7. *Nayika* is a technical term designating any woman who may be resorted to legitimately, without sin.

8. An ancient authority on the art of love. His works are now lost.

Or thus:—
(g)   The union of this woman with me is not attended with
      any danger, and will bring me wealth, of which, on ac-
      count of my poverty and inability to support myself, I
      am very much in need. I shall, therefore obtain her vast
      riches in this way without any difficulty.

Or thus:—
(h)   This woman loves me ardently, and knows all my weak
      points, if therefore, I am unwilling to be united with her,
      she will make my faults public, and thus tarnish my char-
      acter and reputation. Or she will bring some gross accu-
      sation against me, of which it may be hard to clear my-
      self, and I shall be ruined. Or perhaps she will detach
      from me her husband who is powerful, and yet under her
      control, and will unite him to my enemy, or will herself
      join the latter.

Or thus:—
(i)   The husband of this woman has violated the chastity of
      my wives, I shall therefore return that injury by seduc-
      ing his wives. . . .

    For these and similar other reasons the wives of other men
may be resorted to, but it must be distinctly understood that is
only allowed for special reasons, and not for mere carnal desire.

.   .   .   .

PART III

Chapter 1: On Marriage

When a girl of the same caste, and a virgin, is married in accordance with the precepts of Holy Writ, the results of such an
union are: the acquisition of Dharma and Artha, offspring, af-
finity, increase of friends, and untarnished love. For this reason
a man should fix his affections upon a girl who is of good family, whose parents are alive, and who is three years or more

younger than himself. She should be born of a highly respectable family, possessed of wealth, well connected, and with many relations and friends. She should also be beautiful, of a good disposition, with lucky marks on her body, and with good hair, nails, teeth, ears, eyes, and breasts, neither more nor less than they ought to be, and no one of them entirely wanting, and not troubled with a sickly body. The man should, of course, also possess these qualities himself. But at all events, says Ghotakamukha,[9] a girl who has been already joined with others (*i.e.*, no longer a maiden) should never be loved, for it would be reproachable to do such a thing.

Now in order to bring about a marriage with such a girl as described above, the parents and relations of the man should exert themselves, as also such friends on both sides as may be desired to assist in the matter. These friends should bring to the notice of the girl's parents, the faults, both present and future, of all the other men that may wish to marry her, and should at the same time extol even to exaggeration all the excellencies, ancestral, and paternal, of their friend, so as to endear him to them, and particularly to those that may be liked by the girl's mother. One of the friends should also disguise himself as an astrologer, and declare the future good fortune and wealth of his friend by showing the existence of all the lucky omens and signs, the good influence of planets, the auspicious entrance of the sun into a sign of the Zodiac, propitious stars and fortunate marks on his body. Others again should rouse the jealousy of the girl's mother by telling her that their friend has a chance of getting from some other quarter even a better girl than hers.

A girl should be taken as a wife, as also given in marriage, when fortune, signs, omens, and the words of others are favourable,[10] for, says Ghotakamukha, a man should not marry at any time he likes. A girl who is asleep, crying, or gone out

9. Another ancient writer on love.
10. According to old custom, before undertaking anything of importance a person went to a neighbor's house to overhear the conversation in the family. If the first words heard were lucky, success in the undertaking was predicted; if unlucky, failure.

of the house when sought in marriage, or who is betrothed to
another, should not be married. . . .

When a girl becomes marriageable her parents should dress
her smartly, and should place her where she can be easily seen
by all. Every afternoon, having dressed her and decorated her
in a becoming manner, they should send her with her female
companions to sports, sacrifices, and marriage ceremonies, and
thus show her to advantage in society, because she is a kind
of merchandise. They should also receive with kind words and
signs of friendliness those of an auspicious appearance who may
come accompanied by their friends and relations for the purpose
of marrying their daughter, and under some pretext or other
having first dressed her becomingly, should then present her to
them. After this they should await the pleasure of fortune, and
with this object should appoint a future day on which a de-
termination could be come to with regard to their daughter's
marriage. On this occasion when the persons have come, the
parents of the girl should ask them to bathe and dine, and
should say "Everything will take place at the proper time," and
should not then comply with the request, but should settle the
matter later.

When a girl is thus acquired, either according to the custom
of the country, or according to his own desire, the man should
marry her in accordance with the precepts of the Holy Writ,
according to one of the four kinds of marriage.[11]

Thus ends marriage.

There are also some verses on the subject as follows:—

Amusement in society, such as completing verses begun by
others, marriages, and auspicious ceremonies should be carried
on neither with superiors, nor inferiors, but with our equals.
That should be known as a high connection when a man, after
marrying a girl, has to serve her and her relations afterwards
like a servant, and such a connection is censured by the good.
On the other hand, that reproachable connection, where a man
together with his relations, lords it over his wife, is called a

11. I.e., union with the four kinds of *Nayikas*, as enumerated above: maids,
women twice married, public women, and women enjoyed for some special
purpose.

low connection by the wise. But when both the man and the woman afford mutual pleasure to each other, and when the relatives on both sides pay respect to one another, such is called a connection in the proper sense of the word. Therefore a man should contract neither a high connection by which he is obliged to bow down afterwards to his kinsmen, nor a low connection, which is universally reprehended by all.

PART IV

Chapter I
On the Manner of Living of a Virtuous Woman

A virtuous woman, who has affection for her husband, should act in conformity with his wishes as if he were a divine being, and with his consent should take upon herself the whole care of his family. She should keep the whole house well cleaned, and arrange flowers of various kinds in different parts of it, and make the floor smooth and polished so as to give the whole a neat and becoming appearance. She should surround the house with a garden, and place ready in it all the materials required for the morning, noon and evening sacrifices. Moreover she should herself revere the sanctuary of the Household Gods, for says Gonardiya,[12] "nothing so much attracts the heart of a householder to his wife as a careful observance of the things mentioned above."

Towards the parents, relations, friends, sisters, and servants of her husband she should behave as they deserve. In the garden she should plant beds of green vegetables, bunches of the sugar cane, and clumps of the fig tree, the mustard plant, the parsley plant, . . . clusters of various flowers such as the . . . jasmine, . . . the yellow amaranth, the wild jasmine, . . . the china rose and others. . . . She should also have seats and arbours made in the garden, in the middle of which a well, tank, or pool should be dug.

The wife should always avoid the company of female beggars, female Buddhist mendicants, unchaste and roguish women,

12. An ancient writer on love.

female fortune tellers and witches. As regards meals she should always consider what her husband likes and dislikes, and what things are good for him, and what are injurious to him. When she hears the sounds of his footsteps coming home she should at once get up, and be ready to do whatever he may command her, and either order her female servant to wash his feet, or wash them herself. When going anywhere with her husband, she should put on her ornaments, and without his consent she should not either give or accept invitations, or attend marriages and sacrifices, or sit in the company of female friends, or visit the temples of the Gods. And if she wants to engage in any kind of games or sports, she should not do it against his will. In the same way she should always sit down after him, and get up before him, and should never awaken him when he is asleep. The kitchen should be situated in a quiet and retired place, so as not to be accessible to strangers, and should always look clean.

In the event of any misconduct on the part of her husband, she should not blame him excessively, though she be a little displeased. She should not use abusive language towards him, but rebuke him with conciliatory words, whether he be in the company of friends or alone. Moreover, she should not be a scold, for says Gonardiya, "there is no cause of dislike on the part of a husband so great as this characteristic in a wife." Lastly she should avoid bad expressions, sulky looks, speaking aside, standing in the doorway, and looking at passers-by, conversing in the pleasure groves, and remaining in a lonely place for a long time; and finally she should always keep her body, her teeth, her hair and everything belonging to her tidy, sweet, and clean.

. . . .

Chapter II: On the Conduct of the Elder Wife towards the Other Wives of Her Husband, and on that of a Younger Wife towards the Elder Ones . . . and on the Conduct of a Husband towards Many Wives

The causes of re-marrying during the lifetime of the wife are as follows:

(1) The folly or ill temper of the wife.
(2) Her husband's dislike of her.
(3) The want of offspring.
(4) The continual birth of daughters.
(5) The incontinence of the husband.

From the very beginning a wife should endeavour to attract the heart of her husband, by showing to him continually her devotion, her good temper, and her wisdom. If however she bears him no children, she should herself tell her husband to marry another woman. And when the second wife is married, and brought to the house, the first wife should give her a position superior to her own, and look upon her as a sister. In the morning the elder wife should forcibly make the younger one decorate herself in the presence of their husband, and should not mind all the husband's favour being given to her. If the younger wife does anything to displease her husband the elder one should not neglect her, but should always be ready to give her most careful advice, and should teach her to do various things in the presence of her husband. Her children she should treat as her own, her attendants she should look upon with more regard, even than on her own servants, her friends she should cherish with love and kindness, and her relations with great honour.

When there are many other wives besides herself, the elder wife should associate with the one who is immediately next to her in rank and age, and should instigate the wife who has recently enjoyed her husband's favour to quarrel with the present favourite. After this she should sympathize with the former, and having collected all the other wives together, should get them to denounce the favourite as a scheming and wicked woman, without however committing herself in any way. If the favourite wife happens to quarrel with the husband, then the elder wife should take her part and give her false encouragement, and thus cause the quarrel to be increased. If there be only a little quarrel between the two, the elder wife should do all she can to work it up into a large quarrel. But if after all this she finds the husband still continues to love his favourite wife she should then change her tactics, and endeavour to bring about a conciliation between them, so as to avoid her husband's displeasure.

Thus ends the conduct of the elder wife.

The younger wife should regard the elder wife of her husband as her mother, and should not give anything away, even to her own relations, without her knowledge. She should tell her everything about herself, and not approach her husband without her permission. Whatever is told to her by the elder wife she should not reveal to others, and she should take care of the children of the senior even more than of her own. When alone with her husband she should serve him well, but should not tell him of the pain she suffers from the existence of a rival wife. She may also obtain secretly from her husband some marks of his particular regard for her, and may tell him that she lives only for him, and for the regard that he has for her. She should never reveal her love for her husband, nor her husband's love for her to any person, either in pride or in anger, for a wife that reveals the secrets of her husband is despised by him. As for seeking to obtain the regard of her husband, Gonardiya says, that it should always be done in private, for fear of the elder wife. If the elder wife be disliked by her husband, or be childless, she should sympathize with her, and should ask her husband to do the same, but should surpass her in leading the life of a chaste woman.

Thus ends the conduct of the younger wife towards the elder.

. . . .

A man marrying many wives should act fairly towards them all. He should neither disregard nor pass over their faults, and should not reveal to one wife the love, passion, bodily blemishes, and confidential reproaches of the other. No opportunity should be given to any one of them of speaking to him about their rivals, and if one of them should begin to speak ill of another, he should chide her and tell her that she has exactly the same blemishes in her character. One of them should please by secret confidence, another by secret respect, and another by secret flattery, and he should please them all by going to gardens, by amusements, by presents, by honouring their relations, by telling them secrets, and lastly by loving unions. A young woman who is of a good temper, and who conducts herself according to the precepts of the Holy Writ, wins her husband's attachment, and obtains a superiority over her rivals.

Thus ends the conduct of a husband towards many wives.

PART VII

Chapter II: Concluding Remarks

.   .   .   .

There are also some verses in conclusion:

"Thus have I written in a few words the "Science of love," after reading the texts of ancient authors, and following the ways of enjoyment mentioned in them."

"He who is acquainted with the true principles of this science pays regard to Dharma, Artha, Kama, and to his own experiences, as well as to the teachings of others, and does not act simply on the dictates of his own desire. As for the errors in the science of love which I have mentioned in this work, on my own authority as an author, I have, immediately after mentioning them, carefully censured and prohibited them."

"An act is never looked upon with indulgence for the simple reason that it is authorised by the science, because it ought to be remembered that it is the intention of the science, that the rules which it contains should only be acted upon in particular cases. After reading and considering the works of Babhravya and other ancient authors, and thinking over the meaning of the rules given by them, the Kama Sutra was composed, according to the precepts of Holy Writ, for the benefit of the world, by Vatsyayana, while leading the life of a religious student, and wholly engaged in the contemplation of the Deity."

"This work is not intended to be used merely as an instrument for satisfying our desires. A person acquainted with the true principles of this science, and who preserves his Dharma, Artha, and Kama, and has regard for the practices of the people, is sure to obtain the mastery over his senses."

"In short, an intelligent and prudent person, attending to Dharma and Artha, and attending to Kama also, without becoming the slave of his passions, obtains success in everything that he may undertake."

Introduction to Shakuntala

Kalidasa is by common consent the greatest poet and dramatist of classical India. Virtually nothing is known of his life history, though chronologically he can be placed in the early fifth century A.D. Quite probably he was one of the literary figures connected with the court of Ujjain—then the chief cultural and commercial center of western India—for he refers to that city frequently and in a familiar way. Legend associates him with a ruler of Ujjain called Vikramaditya ("Sun of Valor"), who was probably Chandragupta II of the Gupta dynasty.* The Gupta empire, which covered most of northern India between about A.D. 320 and 480, marked a period of extraordinary cultural flourishing. Toward the end of the fourth century A.D., Chandragupta II conquered Ujjain; and one of his court poets may well have been the famous Kalidasa.

Kalidasa was clearly a man of extensive education. He had mastered the traditional Hindu sciences of rhetoric and drama and was well versed in philosophy, religion, and astrology. He possessed a superbly exact knowledge of Sanskrit at a time when Sanskrit was already to some degree an artificial tongue. As far as we know, seven compositions represent his complete life's work: three plays and four long poems. Successful literary work in Kalidasa's day demanded the most careful craftsmanship and minute attention to the rules of grammar as laid down in the textbooks. The greatest names in classical Sanskrit literature produced astonishingly little.

The story of *Shakuntala* was taken by Kalidasa from an episode in the *Mahabharata*—that voluminous compendium of legend and history which is one of the two chief epics of Indian literature. But the poet has modified the original plot to suit his dramatic purposes. In the epic, King Dushyanta is a rather contemptible person who seduces the hermit-maid Shakuntala and then abandons her; Kalidasa has transformed him into a figure of dignity and nobility. In the play the king is the epitome of royal virtue: he shows elab-

* Not to be confused with the earlier Chandragupta (reigned *c*. 322-298 B.C.) who founded the Maurya dynasty.

orate respect for Brahmins and ascetics, refuses to hunt the animals of the hermitage, treats his servants kindly, and prior to every action contemplates the requirements of *dharma*. It would not occur to him to touch a hermit-maiden, which he at first takes Shakuntala to be. The mere fact that he is attracted to her suggests to him that she cannot be what she seems—for a man like himself could not entertain thoughts of love toward a girl vowed to chastity. Indeed, her friends soon reveal that the maiden is actually the daughter of a king and a nymph, and therefore fit to be a royal bride.

Shakuntala is a similarly idealized figure. Physically beautiful, tender-hearted, devoted to her foster-father and her girl companions, exquisitely sensitive to the animals and flowers of the hermitage grounds, she responds to the king's first approaches with suitable shyness and reserve. So fragile is she that—in the style of certain European literary heroines of the nineteenth century—her very life is endangered by love-pangs. Preoccupied with her feelings, she in all innocence fails to notice the presence of the worthy ascetic Durvasas and thus neglects to pay him appropriate respect. This is a fault which cannot be overlooked; for according to the Indian theory of *karma*, actions must bear their proper consequences. The ill-tempered Durvasas calls down upon Shakuntala a terrible curse, which causes the noble-minded king to forget that he ever married her. Shakuntala, large with child, journeys to the royal palace only to be rejected with pious discourse by the virtuous king, who fears to touch another man's wife. Shakuntala is borne away by gods; ultimately the king remembers her and they finally live happily ever after.

The happy ending was a standard feature of the classical drama. Sanskrit plays were often melodramatic, filled with pathos; but dramatic convention forbade a tragic conclusion. No actions regarded as unpleasant or crude—such as violence or kissing—were permitted on stage; at most they might be described in the dialogue. The purpose of drama, according to the textbooks, was to arouse a kind of aesthetic tranquillity or sublimated emotion. The texts enumerated eight "flavors" which produced the desired state—love, courage, repugnance, anger, laughter, terror, pity, and surprise.

The classical drama was designed for a highly select, well-educated audience. There were no public theaters: plays were performed at court or in the homes of rich persons, or in temple courtyards on feast-days. No scenery and few properties were employed: highly stylized, conventionalized dance-movements conveyed the appropriate emotions. The plays were written in prose, interspersed by frequent poetic interludes. They contained an assortment of stock characters, e.g., the hero, the villain, the comic fool, each with his standard characteristics. Ornamentation—simile and metaphor, punning and alliteration—was much in evidence; where possible, words were chosen for their multiple meanings, suggesting several different ideas at once. Plots were often borrowed from mythology, though religious feeling was usually absent; the gods were merely human-like figures with superhuman powers.

Kalidasa's treatment of love is as far removed from that of Vatsyayana in the *Kama Sutra* as Romanticism has been from Rationalism in every age. Both authors were the product of similar milieus, and may even have been contemporaries. But the tender passion idealized by Kalidasa has little in common with the "pleasure" of Vatsyayana. Love for Kalidasa was, to be sure, physical; but it was a delicate emotion indulged in for its own sake and untouched by rational calculation or obvious motives of self-interest. As a feeling spontaneously arising, perhaps even decreed by fate, it could hardly be the subject for the sort of hard-headed practical advice offered by Vatsyayana. Kalidasa's characters are of noble birth and manifest the high-mindedness and sublime emotions proper to their station in life. His audience could rest assured that the demands of *dharma* had been perfectly complied with, sin duly expiated, and virtue properly rewarded.

FROM SHAKUNTALA BY KALIDASA

Act II: The Secret

(Enter the clown.)

Clown (*sighing*). Damn! Damn! Damn! I'm tired of being friends with this sporting king. "There's a deer!" he shouts, "There's a boar!" And off he chases on a summer noon through woods where shade is few and far between. We drink hot, stinking water from the mountain streams, flavoured with leaves—nasty! At odd times we get a little tepid meat to eat.

From the book *Shakuntala and Other Writings by Kalidasa*, trans. by Arthur W. Ryder (London: J. M. Dent & Sons; New York: E. P. Dutton & Co., 1912). Reprinted by permission of J. M. Dent & Sons and E. P. Dutton & Co., Inc.

And the horses and the elephants make such a noise that I can't even be comfortable at night. Then the hunters and the bird-chasers—damn 'em—wake me up bright and early. They do make an ear-splitting rumpus when they start for the woods. But even that isn't the whole misery. There's a new pimple growing on the old boil. He left us behind and went hunting a deer. And there in a hermitage they say he found—oh, dear! oh, dear! he found a hermit-girl named Shakuntala. Since then he hasn't a thought of going back to town. I lay awake all night, thinking about it. What can I do? Well, I'll see my friend when he is dressed and beautified. (*He walks and looks about.*) Hello! Here he comes, with his bow in his hand, and his girl in his heart. He is wearing a wreath of wild flowers! I'll pretend to be all knocked up. Perhaps I can get a rest that way. (*He stands, leaning on his staff. Enter the king, as described.*)

King (*to himself*).

> Although my darling is not lightly won,
>   She seemed to love me, and my hopes are bright;
> Though love be balked ere joy be well begun,
>   A common longing is itself delight.

(*Smiling.*) Thus does a lover deceive himself. He judges his love's feelings by his own desires.

> Her glance was loving—but 'twas not for me;
> Her step was slow—'twas grace, not coquetry;
> Her speech was short—to her detaining friend.
> In things like these love reads a selfish end!

Clown (*standing as before*). Well, king, I can't move my hand. I can only greet you with my voice.

King (*looking and smiling*). What makes you lame?

Clown. Good! You hit a man in the eye, and then ask him why the tears come.

King. I do not understand you. Speak plainly.

Clown. When a reed bends over like a hunchback, do you blame the reed or the river-current?

King. The river-current, of course.

Clown. And you are to blame for my troubles.

King. How so?

Clown. It's a fine thing for you to neglect your royal duties and such a sure job—to live in the woods! What's the good of talking? Here I am, a Brahman, and my joints are all shaken up by this eternal running after wild animals, so that I can't move. Please be good to me. Let us have a rest for just one day.

King (*to himself*). He says this. And I too, when I remember Kanva's daughter, have little desire for the chase. For

> The bow is strung, its arrow near;
> And yet I cannot bend
> That bow against the fawns who share
> Soft glances with their friend.

Clown (*observing the king*). He means more than he says. I might as well weep in the woods.

King (*smiling*). What more could I mean? I have been thinking that I ought to take my friend's advice.

Clown (*cheerfully*). Long life to you, then. (*He unstiffens.*)

King. Wait. Hear me out.

Clown. Well, sir?

King. When you are rested, you must be my companion in another task—an easy one.

Clown. Crushing a few sweetmeats?

King. I will tell you presently.

Clown. Pray command my leisure.

King. Who stands without? (*Enter the door-keeper.*)

Door-keeper. I await your Majesty's commands.

King. Raivataka, summon the general.

Door-keeper. Yes, your Majesty. (*He goes out, then returns with the general.*) Follow me, sir. There is his Majesty, listening to our conversation. Draw near, sir.

General (*observing the king, to himself*). Hunting is declared to be a sin, yet it brings nothing but good to the king. See!

> He does not heed the cruel sting
> Of his recoiling, twanging string;
> The mid-day sun, the dripping sweat
> Affect him not, nor make him fret;

His form, though sinewy and spare,
Is most symmetrically fair;
No mountain-elephant could be
More filled with vital strength than he.

(*He approaches.*) Victory to your Majesty! The forest is full
of deer-tracks, and beasts of prey cannot be far off. What better
occupation could we have?

King. Bhadrasena, my enthusiasm is broken. Madhavya has
been preaching against hunting.

General (*aside to the clown*). Stick to it, friend Madhavya.
I will humour the king a moment. (*Aloud.*) Your Majesty, he
is a chattering idiot. Your Majesty may judge by his own case
whether hunting is an evil. Consider:

The hunter's form grows sinewy, strong, and light;
He learns, from beasts of prey, how wrath and fright
Affect the mind; his skill he loves to measure
With moving targets. 'Tis life's chiefest pleasure.

Clown (*angrily*). Get out! Get out with your strenuous life!
The king has come to his senses. But you, you son of a slave-
wench, can go chasing from forest to forest, till you fall into
the jaws of some old bear that is looking for a deer or a jackal.

King. Bhadrasena, I cannot take your advice, because I am
in the vicinity of a hermitage. So for to-day

The hornèd buffalo may shake
The turbid water of the lake;
Shade-seeking deer may chew the cud,
Boars trample swamp-grass in the mud;
The bow I bend in hunting, may
Enjoy a listless holiday.

General. Yes, your Majesty.

King. Send back the archers who have gone ahead. And
forbid the soldiers to vex the hermitage, or even to approach it.
Remember:

There lurks a hidden fire in each
Religious hermit-bower;

Cool sun-stones kindle if assailed
   By any foreign power.

General. Yes, your Majesty.

Clown. Now will you get out with your strenuous life? (*Exit general.*)

King (*to his attendants*). Lay aside your hunting dress. And you, Raivataka, return to your post of duty.

Raivataka. Yes, your Majesty. (*Exit.*)

Clown. You have got rid of the vermin. Now be seated on this flat stone, over which the trees spread their canopy of shade. I can't sit down till you do.

King. Lead the way.

Clown. Follow me. (*They walk about and sit down.*)

King. Friend Madhavya, you do not know what vision is. You have not seen the fairest of all objects.

Clown. I see you, right in front of me.

King. Yes, every one thinks himself beautiful. But I was speaking of Shakuntala, the ornament of the hermitage.

Clown (*to himself*). I mustn't add fuel to the flame. (*Aloud.*) But you can't have her because she is a hermit-girl. What is the use of seeing her?

King. Fool!

And is it selfish longing then,
   That draws our souls on high
Through eyes that have forgot to wink,
   As the new moon climbs the sky?

Besides, Dushyanta's thoughts dwell on no forbidden object.

Clown. Well, tell me about her.

King. Sprung from a nymph of heaven
      Wanton and gay,
   Who spurned the blessing given,
      Going her way;

By the stern hermit taken
   In her most need:
So fell the blossom shaken,
   Flower on a weed.

Clown (*laughing*). You are like a man who gets tired of good dates and longs for sour tamarind. All the pearls of the palace are yours, and you want this girl!

King. My friend, you have not seen her, or you could not talk so.

Clown. She must be charming if she surprises *you.*

King. Oh, my friend, she needs not many words.

> She is God's vision, of pure thought
>   Composed in His creative mind;
> His reveries of beauty wrought
>   The peerless pearl of womankind.
> So plays my fancy when I see
> How great is God, how lovely she.

Clown. How the women must hate her!

King. This too is in my thought.

> She seems a flower whose fragrance none has tasted,
>   A gem uncut by workman's tool,
> A branch no desecrating hands have wasted,
>   Fresh honey, beautifully cool.
>
> No man on earth deserves to taste her beauty,
>   Her blameless loveliness and worth,
> Unless he has fulfilled man's perfect duty—
>   And is there such a one on earth?

Clown. Marry her quick, then, before the poor girl falls into the hands of some oily-headed hermit.

King. She is dependent on her father, and he is not here.

Clown. But how does she feel toward you?

King. My friend, hermit-girls are by their very nature timid. And yet

> When I was near, she could not look at me;
>   She smiled—but not to me—and half denied it;
> She would not show her love for modesty,
>   Yet did not try so very hard to hide it.

Clown. Did you want her to climb into your lap the first time she saw you?

King. But when she went away with her friends, she almost showed that she loved me.

> When she had hardly left my side,
> "I cannot walk," the maiden cried,
> And turned her face, and feigned to free
> The dress not caught upon the tree.

Clown. She has given you some memories to chew on. I suppose that is why you are so in love with the pious grove.

King. My friend, think of some pretext under which we may return to the hermitage.

Clown. What pretext do you need? Aren't you the king?

King. What of that?

Clown. Collect the taxes on the hermits' rice.

King. Fool! It is a very different tax which these hermits pay —one that outweighs heaps of gems.

> The wealth we take from common men,
>   Wastes while we cherish;
> These share with us such holiness
>   As ne'er can perish.

Voices behind the scenes. Ah, we have found him.

King (listening). The voices are grave and tranquil. These must be hermits. (*Enter the door-keeper.*)

Door-keeper. Victory, O King. There are two hermit-youths at the gate.

King. Bid them enter at once.

Door-keeper. Yes, your Majesty. (*He goes out, then returns with the youths.*) Follow me.

First youth (looking at the king). A majestic presence, yet it inspires confidence. Nor is this wonderful in a king who is half a saint. For to him

> The splendid palace serves as hermitage;
> His royal government, courageous, sage,
> Adds daily to his merit; it is given
> To him to win applause from choirs of heaven
> Whose anthems to his glory rise and swell,
> Proclaiming him a king, and saint as well.

Second youth. My friend, is this Dushyanta, friend of Indra?
First youth. It is.
Second youth.

> Nor is it wonderful that one whose arm
> Might bolt a city gate, should keep from harm
>   The whole broad earth dark-belted by the sea;
> For when the gods in heaven with demons fight,
> Dushyanta's bow and Indra's weapon bright
>   Are their reliance for the victory.

The two youths (*approaching*). Victory, O King!
King (*rising*). I salute you.
The two youths. All hail! (*They offer fruit.*)
King (*receiving it and bowing low*). May I know the reason of your coming?
The two youths. The hermits have learned that you are here, and they request——
King. They command rather.
The two youths. The powers of evil disturb our pious life in the absence of the hermit-father. We therefore ask that you will remain a few nights with your charioteer to protect the hermitage.
King. I shall be most happy to do so.
Clown (to the king). You rather seem to like being collared this way.
King. Raivataka, tell my charioteer to drive up, and to bring the bow and arrows.
Raivataka. Yes, your Majesty. (*Exit.*)
The two youths.

> Thou art a worthy scion of
>   The kings who ruled our nation
> And found, defending those in need,
>   Their truest consecration.

King. Pray go before. And I will follow straightway.
The two youths. Victory, O King! (*Exeunt.*)
King. Madhavya, have you no curiosity to see Shakuntala?

Clown. I *did* have an unending curiosity, but this talk about the powers of evil has put an end to it.

King. Do not fear. You will be with me.

Clown. I'll stick close to your chariot-wheel. (*Enter the door-keeper.*)

Door-keeper. Your Majesty, the chariot is ready, and awaits your departure to victory. But one Karabhaka has come from the city, a messenger from the queen-mother.

King (respectfully). Sent by my mother?

Door-keeper. Yes.

King. Let him enter.

Door-keeper (goes out and returns with KARABHAKA). Karabhaka, here is his Majesty. You may draw near.

Karabhaka (approaching and bowing low). Victory to your Majesty. The queen-mother sends her commands——

King. What are her commands?

Karabhaka. She plans to end a fasting ceremony on the fourth day from to-day. And on that occasion her dear son must not fail to wait upon her.

King. On the one side is my duty to the hermits, on the other my mother's command. Neither may be disregarded. What is to be done?

Clown (laughing). Stay half-way between, like Trishanku.

King. In truth, I am perplexed.

> Two inconsistent duties sever
>   My mind with cruel shock,
> As when the current of a river
>   Is split upon a rock.

(*He reflects.*) My friend, the queen-mother has always felt to-ward you as toward a son. Do you return, tell her what duty keeps me here, and yourself perform the offices of a son.

Clown. You don't think I am afraid of the devils?

King (smiling). O mighty Brahman, who could suspect it?

Clown. But I want to travel like a prince.

King. I will send all the soldiers with you, for the pious grove must not be disturbed.

Clown (strutting). Aha! Look at the heir-apparent!

King (*to himself*). The fellow is a chatterbox. He might
betray my longing to the ladies of the palace. Good, then! (*He
takes the clown by the hand. Aloud.*) Friend Madhavya, my
reverence for the hermits draws me to the hermitage. Do not
think that I am really in love with the hermit-girl. Just think:

> A king, and a girl of the calm hermit-grove,
> Bred with the fawns, and a stranger to love!
> Then do not imagine a serious quest;
> The light words I uttered were spoken in jest.

Clown. Oh, I understand that well enough.

(Exeunt ambo.)

III

Dharma

Introduction to the Bhagavad Gita

The *Bhagavad Gita* is probably the best-known and best-loved document in all Indian religious literature. As it has come down to us, it forms part of Book VI of the great folk-epic called the *Mahabharata*. At an early date the *Mahabharata* came to be regarded as sacred tradition, second only to the Vedas in holiness; but it is undoubtedly secular in origin. It recounts the history of a legendary great war between two branches of the same family—the Kauravas and the Pandavas—for control of a kingdom in north India. The tales of the heroes' exploits were recited at religious sacrifices presided over by Brahmin priests; and over the centuries they underwent much priestly editing. As it stands today, the *Mahabharata* is a vast collection of loosely related episodes interspersed with discussions on statecraft, religion, and morals.

Possibly the narrative core of the *Mahabharata* had a basis in historical fact, going back to the period when Aryan herdsmen from the Iranian tableland invaded north India, subjugated the native population, and established their own kingdoms (*ca.* 1500-1000 B.C.). But the poem is the product of many centuries of development and exhibits a wide variety of attitudes. In part, it is the story of lusty barbarian warriors rejoicing in their physical prowess and imbued with the sheer joy of combat. Other portions, certainly of later date, present the heroes as much concerned with religious duties. The poem is full of supernatural elements—heroes are transformed into gods, weapons have magical potency, and armies reach fantastic numbers. Various episodes having little connection with the history of the Kauravas and Pandavas have been included, forming some four-fifths of the whole. Probably the entire *Mahabharata* was substantially complete in its present form by the second century B.C., though certain revisions were undoubtedly made afterward. Today it exists in both a northern version and a southern version.

Within the space of eighteen brief chapters, the *Bhagavad Gita* ("The Lord's Song") brings together the major strands of orthodox* Hindu religion and applies them to the solution of a characteristic human dilemma. The episode which provokes the diverse teachings of the *Gita* occurs just prior to the great eighteen-day battle on the plain of Kurukshetra ("field of the Kurus"), in which most of the combatants will perish. The hero Arjuna, leader of the Pandava forces, foresees that this battle, if allowed to proceed, will prove disastrous for both sides. But Arjuna is also a Kshatriya—a member of the hereditary warrior class—and as such is duty-bound to fight bravely. He is forced to resolve the conflict between two apparently conflicting *dharmas*—the duty of the family member to respect his relatives and teachers, and the no less stringent duty of the warrior to fight. Discussion of this question between Arjuna and his charioteer, Krishna, gives formal structure to the *Gita*.

Within its brief compass, the *Gita* incorporates a variety of doctrines which are logically incompatible. A dualist philosophy stands beside a monistic one; good works receive praise, but so does ascetic withdrawal from the world; submission to a personal redeemer-god and absorption into the impersonal world-spirit are both proclaimed as the supreme goal. But to Indian readers, it is precisely these divergencies which give the *Gita* its value. Unlike many other Hindu religious works, which are revered only by a particular sect and dedicated to a specific deity, the *Gita* has an almost universal appeal. Instead of rejecting apparently contradictory doctrines, it incorporates them and seeks to minimize their differences. In this harmonizing process, one system of thought may be set forth as a preparatory discipline for another; or both may be described as equally valid paths to salvation. Nonetheless, the *Gita* lacks any systematic, over-all plan. Many passages show only the most tenuous relation to what precedes or follows; and only the slenderest of threads connects many of them with the dilemma faced by Arjuna at Kurukshetra.

Those scholars, both Indian and Western, who revere the *Gita* as a religious document generally prefer to regard it as the creation of a unique, inspired poet. According to this view, the entire poem was inserted into the *Mahabharata* as a finished composition. But internal evidence suggests that the *Gita*, like the *Mahabharata* of

* Orthodox Hindu doctrines are those which regard the four Vedas as the direct revelations of the Deity. The principal non-orthodox systems are Buddhism and Jainism.

which it forms a part, represents various strata of development. The assumption of a single author makes it difficult to explain the contradictions, the unnecessary repetitions, and the evident irrelevance of most of the dialogue to the hero's actual situation. Moreover, sophisticated theological speculation seems strangely out of place in the midst of a heroic saga. The narrative core of the *Gita* (as opposed to its religious teaching) easily fits into the basic framework of the *Mahabharata*. Arjuna's dilemma, the incarnation of the god Vishnu in the form of the charioteer Krishna, and the appearance of the god in his terrible supernatural form, are events perfectly in keeping with the general character of the epic. Until quite recently in India it was standard practice for anonymous poets to add their verses to an already existing composition, preferring the dignity of association with an established work to the doubtful fame of personal authorship. From a historical standpoint it seems reasonable to believe that diverse religious statements were gradually added to the original *Gita* narrative—each author seeking to interpret existing passages in the light of his own convictions by showing that there was no important difference between them.

The following extracts from the *Gita* tell its basic story. Krishna appears here not as a savior preaching redemption after death, but as the ever-present deity who controls events in this world. He, Krishna, has already determined the outcome of the battle of Kurukshetra; Arjuna cannot influence a result decreed by God. Moreover, Arjuna's freedom to decide between alternative actions is illusory. He is a warrior not merely by accident of birth into a Kshatriya family, but in his fundamental, inborn character: his own warrior nature will force him to fight. The culmination of the story comes in Chapter XI, when Krishna assumes his superhuman aspect. Overwhelmed by this vision, Arjuna agrees to worship the god and thereafter to be merely his instrument. Freed from his dejection, he arises to fight the great battle.

The entire *Gita* is cast in the form of a report by the charioteer Sanjaya to Dhritarashtra, the blind father of the Kauravas. As the narrative begins, Dhritarashtra asks for an account of the preliminaries to the battle. His son Duryodhana, a leader of the Kaurava army, has a presentiment that his forces, though numerically larger than those of the Pandavas, will prove to be the weaker in battle. In typical epic style, he proceeds to review the names of the principal warriors on each side.

FROM THE BHAGAVAD GITA:
THE EPIC NARRATIVE

Chapter I

[Sanjaya said:]

20   Then, O Lord of the Earth![1] the son of Pandu (Arjuna), whose ensign was the monkey, seeing Dhritarashtra's army arrayed and the throwing of weapons about to begin, raised his bow and spoke the following words to Krishna:

Arjuna said:

21-23   O Achyuta (changeless, Krishna), place my chariot between the two armies desirous of battle, so that I may see with whom I have to fight in this outbreak of war, for I desire to observe those who are assembled here for battle wishing to please the evil-minded son of Dhritarashtra[2] by taking his side.

Sanjaya said:

24-25   O King! Requested thus by Gudakesha[3] (Arjuna), Krishna, having placed the war chariot between the two armies in front of Bhishma,[4] Drona[5] and all the rulers of the earth, spoke thus: O son of Pritha[6] (Arjuna), behold all the Kuru[7] forces gathered together.

From *Srimad Bhagavad Gita, or The Blessed Lord's Song*, trans. by Swami Paramananda (Boston: The Vedanta Center, 1913). Identification of passages from the epic core of the *Gita* according to Rudolf Otto, *The Original Gita* (London: George Allen & Unwin, Ltd., 1939), trans. from the German by J. E. Turner.

1. Dhritarashtra.
2. Duryodhana is meant. The Pandavas believed that he was the Kaurava most responsible for depriving them of what they considered their rightful inheritance.
3. One possible translation of this epithet is "thick-haired"; another is "conqueror of sloth."
4. Bhishma was the commander-in-chief of the Kauravas.
5. Drona was the revered teacher of both the Kaurava and the Pandava brothers, who had been brought up together at Dhritarashtra's court.
6. Pritha was Arjuna's mother.
7. I.e., Kaurava.

26 Then Partha[8] (Arjuna) saw there in both armies arrayed grandfathers, fathers-in-law, uncles, brothers and cousins, his own sons and their sons and grandsons, comrades, teachers and friends.

27 Then he, the son of Kunti[9] (Arjuna), seeing all his kinsmen stationed in their ranks, spoke thus sorrowfully, overwhelmed with deep compassion:

Arjuna said:

28 O Krishna, seeing these my kinsmen, gathered here desirous to fight, my limbs fail me, my mouth is parched;

29 My body shivers, my hair stands on end, my Gandiva (bow) slips from my hand, my skin is burning.

30 O Keshava (Krishna, the slayer of Keshi[10]), I am not able to stand upright, my mind is in a whirl and I see adverse omens.

31 O Krishna, neither do I see any good in slaying my own people in this strife. I desire neither victory, nor kingdom, nor pleasures.

32-34 Teachers, uncles, sons and grandsons, grandfathers, fathers-in-law, brothers-in-law, besides other kinsmen, for whose sake empire, enjoyment and pleasures are desired, they themselves stand here in battle, forsaking life and wealth. What avail, then, is kingdom, enjoyment, or even life, O Govinda[11] (Krishna)?

35 These warriors I do not wish to kill, even though I am killed by them, not even for the dominion over the three worlds, how much less for the sake of this earth, O slayer of Madhu.[12]

36 O Janardana[13] (giver of prosperity and salvation, Krishna), what pleasure could there be for us by killing the sons of Dhritarashtra?[14] Sin alone would take possession of us by slaying these evil-doers.

8. Partha means "son of Pritha."
9. Another name for Arjuna's mother.
10. Keshi was the name of a demon.
11. Govinda was an epithet for Krishna; it means "protector of cows."
12. Madhu was a demon.
13. Janardana literally means "destroyer of (the demon) Jana."
14. Dhritarashtra was the elder brother of Pandu, the deceased father of the Pandava brothers. Thus Dhritarashtra's sons are Arjuna's cousins.

37   Therefore we ought not to kill these sons of Dhritarashtra who are our relations; for how can we, O Madhava (Krishna), obtain happiness by destroying our own kinsmen?

38   Although these (my enemies), their understanding being overpowered by greed, see no evil from extinction of families and no sin in hostility to friends.

39   But, O Janardana, why should not we turn away from this sin, seeing clearly the evil in destruction of family?

40   From the destruction of a family the immemorial religious rites[15] of that family perish. Spirituality[15] being destroyed, that whole family is overpowered by unrighteousness.[16]

41   O Krishna, from the predominance of unrighteousness the women of that family become corrupt[17]; and women being corrupted, there arises intermingling of castes.[18]

42   This intermingling of castes leads the destroyers of the family to hell, as also the family itself; for their ancestors fall,[19] being deprived of the offerings of rice-ball and water.[20]

43   By these misdeeds of the slayers of the family, bringing about confusion of caste, the immemorial religious rites of family and caste are destroyed.

44   O Janardana, we have heard that for such men, whose household religious rites have been destroyed, the dwelling in hell is inevitable.

45   Alas! what a great sin we are resolved to incur, being

15. *Dharma*, which may mean rites and ceremonies as well as religious duty in the larger sense.

16. *Adharma*, or non-*dharma*. *Dharma* is destroyed when the guardians of the family tradition perish.

17. Because men are the guardians of women, and the number of men is reduced.

18. In the absence of sufficient men, women will disregard the caste rules regarding marriage. Marriage outside of one's caste is forbidden in most instances by Hindu law.

19. They fall from the heaven called *Pitri-loka* ("world of the Fathers"), where their residence depends upon the offerings of their earthly descendants.

20. Rice-balls and water were employed in the ceremony offered by the eldest son for the soul of his deceased father. Deprived of this ceremony, the soul of the dead goes to Hell. The rites can be performed only by the sons of legitimate marriages, i.e., marriages between members of the same caste.

prepared to slay our kinsmen, actuated by greed of kingdom and pleasure.[21]

46   Verily, it would be better for me if the sons of Dhritarashtra, weapons in hand, should slay me in the battle, unresisting and unarmed.

Sanjaya said:

47   Speaking thus in the midst of the battlefield, Arjuna sank down on the seat of his war chariot, casting aside his bow and arrows, his mind overwhelmed with sorrow.

Chapter II

Sanjaya said:

1   To him (Arjuna) whose mind was thus overpowered by pity and grief and eyes dimmed with tears, Madhusudana[22] (Krishna) spoke these words:

The Blessed Lord said:

2   O Arjuna, whence comes upon thee in this critical moment this depression unworthy of an Aryan, disgraceful, and contrary to the attainment of heaven?[23]

3   O son of Pritha, yield not to unmanliness[24]; it does not befit thee. Casting off this mean faint-heartedness, arise, O terror of thy foes!

Arjuna said:

4   O destroyer of enemies and slayer of Madhu (Krishna), how can I fight with arrows in battle against Bhishma and Drona,[25] who are worthy to be worshipped (by me).

5   Instead of slaying these great-souled masters, it would be

21. The origin of the entire war is that the Pandavas are attempting to regain a kingdom they regard as rightfully theirs, and which the Kauravas have usurped.
22. Slayer of (the demon) Madhu.
23. For the warrior, courage in battle is the pathway to heaven.
24. I.e., conduct unbecoming a warrior.
25. Bhishma was Arjuna's grandfather; Drona his teacher.

better even to live in this life by begging; but killing them, all our enjoyments of wealth and desires, even in this world,[26] will be stained with blood.

6   Indeed I know not which of the two is better for us, whether we should conquer them or they should conquer us. For those very sons of Dhritarashtra stand before us, after slaying whom we should not care to live.

7   With my nature overpowered by pity and depression and mind confused about duty,[27] I implore Thee (O Krishna) tell me with certainty what is good for me. I am Thy disciple,[28] instruct me, who have taken refuge in Thee.

8   For I see not what can remove this grief which withers my senses, even if I should obtain unrivalled and flourishing dominion over the earth and rulership over the gods.

Sanjaya said:

9   Gudakesha[29] (Arjuna), the conqueror of his foes, having thus spoken to the Lord of the senses[30] (Krishna), said: "I shall not fight, O Govinda!" and became silent.

10   O descendant of King Bharata,[31] Hrishikesha (Krishna), as if smilingly, spoke these words to him (Arjuna), who was thus grief-stricken in the midst of the two armies.

The Blessed Lord said:

11   Thou hast been mourning for those who should not be mourned for and yet thou speakest (apparent) words of wisdom; but the truly wise mourn not either for the dead or for the living.

12   It is not that I have never existed before, nor thou, nor all

26. Not to mention the other world.
27. *Dharma.*
28. Until the questioner acknowledges himself to be a disciple, the teacher may not impart the highest knowledge.
29. See note 3, above.
30. Hrishikesha (as in the following verse). Here translated as "Lord of the senses," it may actually mean "curly-haired."
31. Dhritarashtra, to whom Sanjaya is speaking. Bharata was the ancestor of both the Kauravas and the Pandavas (thus: *Maha-Bharata*, or "Great Bharatas").

these kings. Nor is it that all of us shall cease to exist hereafter.

13   As in this body the embodied soul[32] passes through child-hood, youth and old age, in the same manner it goes from one body to another; therefore the wise are never deluded regard-ing it (the soul).

20   This (Self)[33] is never born, nor does It die, not after once having been, does It go into non-being. This (Self) is unborn, eternal, changeless, ancient. It is never destroyed even when the body is destroyed.

22   As man casts off worn-out garments and puts on others which are new, similarly the embodied soul, casting off worn-out bodies, enters into others which are new.

29   Some look upon It (Self) with wonder, some speak about It with wonder, some hear about It with wonder and yet others, even after hearing about It, know It not.

30   The dweller in the body of everyone is ever indestructible; therefore, O Bharata,[34] thou shouldst not grieve over any crea-ture.

31   Looking upon it even from the standpoint of thine own Dharma, thou shouldst not waver, for nothing is higher for a Kshatriya (warrior) than a righteous war.

32   O son of Pritha, fortunate indeed are Kshatriyas to whom comes unsought,[35] as an open gate to heaven, such a war.

33   But if thou shouldst not take part in this righteous war, then forfeiting thine own duty and honor, thou shalt incur sin.

34   People will ever speak ill of thee; for the esteemed, dis-honor is even worse than death.

35   These great car-warriors[36] will think that thou hast with-drawn from the battle through fear. And thou shalt be thought of lightly by those who once honored thee highly.

36   Thine enemies will speak unutterably disgraceful things against thee and blame thy valor. What can be more painful than this?

32. *Atman*, also translated as "Self."
33. *Atman*.
34. Arjuna, here addressed by the name of his ancestor.
35. Krishna takes the standpoint that Arjuna's enemies had precipitated the war.
36. Charioteers, i.e., the Kauravas.

37   If thou fallest in battle, thou shalt obtain heaven; if thou conquerest, thou shalt enjoy the earth. Therefore, O son of Kunti, arise and be resolved to fight.

.   .   .   .

Chapter X

The Blessed Lord said:

1   O mighty-armed, again do thou listen to My Supreme Word,[37] which I, wishing thy welfare, declare unto thee who art rejoiced (to hear Me).

2   All the Devas[38] know not My origin, nor do the great Rishis[39] (Seers); for I am the Source of all the Devas and the great Rishis.

3   He who knows Me as birthless and beginningless, the Supreme Lord of the universe, he among mortals is undeluded and is freed from all sins.[40]

4   Intelligence, wisdom, non-delusion, forgiveness, truth, control of the senses, serenity of the heart, pleasure and pain, birth and death, fear and fearlessness.

5   Non-injury, equanimity, contentment, austerity, benevolence, fame and infamy; these different states of beings arise from Me alone.

6   The seven great Rishis, the elder four as well as the Manus,[41] were born of My mind and endowed with My nature, from whom (are generated) all these creatures in the world.

7   He who comprehends in reality these My various manifestations and My Yoga power,[42] he becomes well-established in unshakable Yoga. There is no doubt in this.

37. The "words" concerning the indestructibility of the soul and the honor of the warrior are subordinate to the third "word," namely that God (Krishna) is the Creator and demands Arjuna's reverent devotion.
38. Literally, "shining ones," gods. Human beings who have lived virtuous lives on earth may become Devas after death and occupy a temporary position in one of the lower heavens.
39. The Rishis were holy wise men.
40. I.e., the cause of sin is ignorance.
41. In Hindu popular mythology, the seven Rishis and four Manus were among the first beings to be created.
42. Through various meditational practices, Yogis attained extraordinary powers; God's power is described as that of a Yogi.

8   I am the Origin of all, everything evolves from Me.[43]
Knowing this, the wise worship Me with loving ecstasy.

.   .   .   .

Chapter XI

Arjuna said:

1   The supremely profound word regarding Self-knowledge,
spoken by Thee out of compassion for me, has dispelled this my
delusion.[44]

2   O Lotus-Eyed (Krishna), I have heard at length from
Thee of the creation and dissolution of beings, as well as of
Thine inexhaustible glory.

3   O Great Lord, as Thou hast declared Thyself, so it is. O
Supreme Being, I desire to see Thy Godly Form.

4   O Lord, if Thou thinkest me able (worthy) to see that
(Form), then, O Lord of Yogis,[45] show me Thine Infinite Self.

The Blessed Lord said:

5   Behold, O Partha, My various celestial Forms, of different
colors and shapes, by hundreds and by thousands.

6   O descendant of Bharata, behold the Adityas, the Rudras,
the Vasus, the twin Asvins and the Maruts.[46] Behold many
wonders that were not seen before.

8   But with these eyes of thine thou canst not see Me; therefore I give thee Divine sight. Behold my Supreme Yoga power!

Sanjaya said:

9   O King,[47] having spoken thus, the great Lord of Yoga,
Hari[48] (Krishna), then showed to Partha His Supreme Godly
Form.

43. I.e., I determine all events.
44. The delusion that Arjuna must bear responsibility for the slaying of his
relatives.
45. I.e., God is the supreme Yogi.
46. Various Hindu deities.
47. Dhritarashtra.
48. Krishna was a member of the Hari clan.

10   With many faces and eyes, with many wondrous sights, with many celestial ornaments and with many celestial weapons uplifted,

11   Wearing celestial garlands and garments, anointed with celestial fragrant perfumes; the all-wonderful Deity, infinite, facing the universe everywhere.

12   If the effulgence of a thousand suns were to shine at once in the sky, that might resemble the splendor of that great Being.

14   Then Dhananjaya,[49] overpowered with wonder, and his hair standing on end, bending down his head in awe to the Deity, spoke with folded hands:

Arjuna said:

17   I see Thee with diadems, maces, discus, shiningly effulgent everywhere, blazing all around like the burning fire and the sun, dazzling to the sight and immeasurable.

19   I see Thee without beginning, middle or end, with infinite power, with numberless arms, the sun and moon as Thine eyes, Thy mouth as the blazing fire, heating this universe with Thine own radiance.

20   By Thee alone the space between heaven and earth and all the quarters is pervaded. O Great Soul, seeing this, Thy wonderful and terrifying Form, the three worlds are stricken with fear.

21   Verily, these hosts of Devas are entering into Thee; some in fear, praising Thee with folded hands. The host of great Rishis and Siddhas,[50] saying "Svasti" (peace, may it be well), are singing Thy glory in beautiful hymns.

22   The Rudras, Adityas, Vasus, Sadhyas, the Visvas, the Asvins, the Maruts, the Ushmapas, the host of Gandharvas, Yakshas, Asuras, Siddhas,[51] they are all looking at Thee wonderstruck.

23   O Mighty-armed, seeing Thine immeasurable form, with many mouths and eyes, with many arms, thighs and feet, with

49. Arjuna, "subduer of foes."
50. Siddhas were semi-divine beings known for their purity and holiness.
51. Various Hindu deities representing the powers of the universe.

many loins, and fearful with many large teeth, the worlds and
I, as well, are agitated with terror.

24   O Vishnu,[52] seeing Thee touching the sky, shining in
many colors, with mouths wide open, and with large blazing
eyes, my heart is terrified and I find neither peace nor tranquillity.

25   O Lord of gods! seeing Thy mouths, terrible with long
teeth blazing like the fires of destruction, I know not the four
quarters, nor do I find any peace. Have mercy, O Abode of the
universe!

26   All these sons of Dhritarashtra, with the multitude of
monarchs, Bhishma, Drona and Sutaputra (Karna),[53] as well
as our own principal warriors,

27   Enter rushingly into Thy mouths, terrible with long
teeth and fearful to look at. Some are seen hanging between
Thy teeth, with their heads crushed to powder.

28   As the many torrents of rivers rush towards the ocean,
similarly do these heroes amongst men enter into Thy mouths,
blazing fiercely on all sides.

29   As the moths rush into the burning fire with headlong
speed for destruction, in the same manner do these creatures
rush into Thy mouths with headlong speed, only to perish.

30   O Vishnu! swallowing all the worlds with Thy blazing
flames, Thou art licking all around. Thy fierce, radiant rays,
filling the whole universe, are burning.

31   Tell me, who art Thou, in this terrible Form? Salutation
to Thee! O Supreme Deity, have mercy! O Primeval One, I
desire to know Thee, for indeed I know not Thy purpose.

The Blessed Lord said:

32   I am eternal, world-destroying Time,[54] manifested here
for the destruction of these people. Even without Thee, none
of these warriors, arrayed here in the hostile armies, shall live.

33   Therefore, do thou arise and acquire glory. Conquering

52. Krishna now appears in his true nature as the god Vishnu.
53. Fighters on the Kaurava side.
54. Time (which destroys all earthly creatures) is regarded as a manifesta-
tion of the god, sometimes also as the destroyer-god Rudra.

the enemies, enjoy the unrivalled kingdom. By Me alone have
they already been slain; be thou merely an instrumental cause,
O Savyasachin[55] (Arjuna).

34   Drona, Bhishma, Jayadratha, Karna, as well as the other
brave warriors, are already slain by Me. Do thou kill and be
not distressed by fear. Fight! and thou shalt conquer thine
enemies in battle.

Sanjaya said:

35   Having heard these words of Keshava (Krishna), (Arjuna) the diadem-wearer, with folded hands, trembling, prostrating himself, again spoke to Krishna in a choked voice, bowing down, overwhelmed with fear.[56]

Arjuna said:

36   O Lord of the senses (Krishna), it is right that the world
delights and rejoices in Thy glory. The Rakshasas (demonic
creatures) fly with fear in all directions and the host of Siddhas
bow down to Thee in adoration.

41   Not knowing this Thy glory and regarding Thee merely
as a friend, whatever I may have said presumptuously, out of
either carelessness or fondness, addressing Thee as "O Krishna,"
"O Yadava,"[57] "O Friend";

42   O Changeless One, in whatever manner I may have been
disrespectful to Thee, in jesting, in walking, in reposing, sitting,
or at meals, alone, or in the presence of others; O Unfathom-
able One, I implore Thee to forgive all that.

43   Thou art the Father of the moving and unmoving world,
and its object of worship; greater than the great, O Incomparable Power, no one in the three worlds exists equal to Thee.
How can, then, anyone excel Thee?

44   O Adorable Lord! prostrating my body in adoration, I beg
Thy forgiveness. O God, as a father forgives his son, a friend

55. Arjuna received this epithet because of his dexterity in shooting arrows
with both his right and his left hand.
56. Sanjaya's words are probably intended to persuade Dhritarashtra to con-
clude peace with the Pandavas and thereby avoid certain destruction.
57. Krishna belonged to the Yadu tribe.

his dear friend, a beloved one his love, even so do Thou forgive me!

45 O God, joyous am I to have seen (Thy form) which I never saw before; yet my heart is agitated with terror, therefore show me that Form of Thine. O God of gods! O Abode of the universe, have mercy!

46 I desire to see Thee as before, with diadem, mace and discus. O Universal Form of thousand arms, do Thou manifest Thyself in that same Four-armed Form (form of Vishnu).[58]

The Blessed Lord said:

47 O Arjuna, mercifully have I shown thee this Supreme Form by My own Yoga power. This effulgent, infinite, primeval, great universal Form of Mine, which has not been seen by anyone else before thee.

48 O great hero of the Kurus, not by the study of the sacred Vedas or by sacrifice, not by charity or rituals, nor by severe austerities, am I visible in such Form in this world of men to any other than thee.

49 Be not frightened nor bewildered, having seen this terrific Form of Mine, getting rid of thy fear and with gladdened heart, behold thou again this My former Form.[59]

Sanjaya said:

50 Vasudeva (Krishna), having thus spoken to Arjuna, showed again His own Form. The Great-souled One, having assumed again His gentle Form,[60] pacified him (Arjuna) who was terrified.

Arjuna said:

51 O Janardana, seeing this, Thy gentle human Form, now my thoughts are collected and I have recovered myself.

.   .   .   .

58. The god Vishnu in his divine form was supposed to have four arms, holding a conch, a discus, a mace, and a lotus. In this form he occasionally appeared to his devotees.
59. I.e., as the four-armed Vishnu (not as Krishna, the charioteer).
60. As four-armed Vishnu.

Chapter XVIII

The Blessed Lord said:

58   Fixing thy heart on Me, thou shalt, by My grace, overcome all obstacles; but if, through egoism, thou wilt not hear
Me, thou shalt perish.

59   If, actuated by egoism, thou thinkest: "I will not fight,"
in vain is this thy resolve. Thine own nature[61] will impell thee.

60   O son of Kunti, being bound by thine own Karma,[62] born
of thine own nature, thou shalt be helplessly led to do that
which from delusion thou desirest not to do.

61   O Arjuna, the Lord dwells in the heart of all beings, causing all beings to revolve, as if mounted on a wheel.

66   Giving up all Dharmas (righteous and unrighteous actions), come unto Me alone for refuge. I shall free thee from
all sins; grieve not.

72   O son of Pritha, has this been heard by thee with an attentive mind? O Dhananjaya, has the delusion of thine ignorance been destroyed?

Arjuna said:

73   My delusion is destroyed and I have regained my memory, through Thy grace, O Changeless One. I stand firm with
doubts dispelled; I will do Thy Word.

61. I.e., his warrior nature.
62. Karma is the force or energy accumulated in previous lifetimes which
determines a person's status in this life.

Introduction to the Edicts of Ashoka

Ashoka Maurya (reigned 273-232 B.C.) was the third king of the dynasty founded by Chandragupta and Kautilya,* and one of the few men until modern times to rule nearly the whole of India. He inherited an established empire extending from the Himalayas to the Deccan, and ruled effectively for a period of forty years. But his chief fame derives from his propagation of Buddhism, which largely through his efforts was transformed from a local sect into an international religion practiced throughout a major part of Eastern Asia.

The capital of the Maurya empire was at Pataliputra (Patna) in the region where the Buddha himself had preached and where Buddhist tradition was strongest. We may suppose that Ashoka was familiar with Buddhist doctrines long before his actual conversion, though in his early years he seems to have followed the sacrificial religion of the Brahmins. He tells us himself, in the remarkable stone edicts which provide most of our information about his reign, that in those days he led the ordinary life of a Hindu noble, fond of hunting and feasting. In the common fashion of kings, he began an aggressive war against a neighboring state, the Kalingas, which he conquered and added to his empire. This conquest proved to be the turning point of his career. Revulsion at the suffering which accompanied this war prompted him radically to change his entire concept of kingship. He became first a Buddhist layman, then a monk, and devoted himself thereafter to preaching and propagating the Buddhist faith.

The traditional Indian concept of *dharma* was that the fulfillment of one's own hereditary role in life, even imperfectly, was preferable to assuming the role of someone else. But Buddhist ideas of *dharma* stressed ethical conduct rather than social conformity; and Ashoka seems successfully to have combined the roles of king and monk. No evidence suggests that, having taken the vows, he

* See Introduction to the *Arthashastra of Kautilya*, pp. 15-19 above.

neglected his royal duties in any way. He was the able and autocratic sovereign of an empire which, deprived of his firm hand, crumbled into fragments within a half-century of his death. His zeal for the faith is likewise beyond question. No political necessity prompted his conversion; for even on its home ground of Magadha, Buddhism was but one of several influential sects in his day. Ashoka freely employed his imperial power and wealth for religious ends. He endowed many Buddhist monasteries and shrines, and used the Maurya bureaucratic machine to enforce his humane edicts. In public places throughout the empire he set up enormous sandstone pillars bearing pious inscriptions in vernacular languages, which any literate person might read; in more remote spots, where sandstone was unavailable, he had Buddhist sermons incised into great rocks.

Ashoka organized an immensely ambitious missionary effort having the evident aim of converting the entire known world. Buddhist missions were dispatched not only to neighboring lands, but to such faraway kingdoms as Egypt, Macedonia, and Cyrene. It it not recorded that the emperor's efforts bore any fruit in such distant places; but the effect of his missions closer to home can scarcely be overestimated. The impetus given by Ashoka transformed Buddhism from a sect of only local importance into the dominant religion of northern India. From there it spread, in subsequent centuries, through most of South and East Asia.

Ashoka's rock and pillar edicts—of which more than forty have been located to date—give a remarkable picture of the emperor's personality and faith. His expression of regret at his conquest of the Kalingas is probably unique in the annals of royalty. He liked to repeat the injunction that men must exert themselves—that *dharma* required constant and strenuous personal effort. *Dharma* ("the Law of Piety") in the larger sense could in fact be practiced by men of all religious persuasions, as Ashoka doubtless intended it to be. A number of his inscriptions inculcate the duty of reverence for parents, superiors, and elders, and respect for animal life—virtues also recognized in the teaching of the Brahmins, though given added emphasis by Buddhists. Other edicts stress almsgiving, toleration for other religions, and abstention from evil speech. Ashoka made no attempt to prove these precepts by argument. Generally he propounded them as self-evident, though in at least one case he cited the authority of the Buddha. Like Buddha, too, he refrained from discussing metaphysical questions or the existence or nonexistence of God. Moral conduct was his ultimate aim, rather than theological doctrine or ceremonial observance.

Though little is known about the history of the Maurya state under Ashoka's successors, it is conceivable that his efforts on behalf of Buddhism contributed to its downfall. The advance of Buddhism must have proved profoundly disturbing to the Brahmin priesthood, threatening not only its religious influence but also its hereditary social position. Ashoka himself held enlightened views on toleration, and endowed the foundations of various religions. But from the orthodox Hindu standpoint, Buddhism was a heresy which denied the sacred character of the Vedas, ignored traditional rites, and disregarded caste restrictions. Ashoka's edicts limiting the slaughter of animals interfered with the Brahmins' sacrifices, which many persons no doubt regarded as essential to salvation. Still, no native Indian religion ever exhibited the harsh antagonism and exclusiveness which would later characterize Christianity or Islam. Buddhism and Hinduism existed side by side in India for many centuries, competing also with several other sects. In the fourth or fifth century A.D.—perhaps because of the renaissance in Hindu religion—Buddhism began to decline. Today it is virtually extinct in India, though it remains the predominant faith in large areas of Eastern Asia.

FROM THE EDICTS OF ASHOKA

Minor Rock Edict I: The Fruit of Exertion

According to the words of the Prince and High officers of Suvarnagiri the High officers in Isila[1] are to be addressed with salutations and addressed in the manner following:—

"His Sacred Majesty gives these instructions:—

" 'For more than two-and-a-half years I was a lay disciple, without, however, exerting myself strenuously. But a year—in fact, more than a year ago—I entered the Order,[2] and since then have exerted myself strenuously.

Edicts trans. by Vincent A. Smith in *Asoka, The Buddhist Emperor of India,* 3rd ed. rev. and enl. (Oxford: At the Clarendon Press, 1920), pp. 149-50, 158, 160-61, 182-3, 185-7, 209-12.

1. Suvarnagiri and Isila were towns somewhere in southwestern India. The Prince referred to was apparently the viceroy of a region in the south.

2. The Order of Buddhist monks.

" 'During that time the men in India who had been unassociated with the gods became associated with them.[3] For this is the fruit of exertion. Nor is this to be attained by greatness only, because even by the small man who chooses to exert himself, immense heavenly bliss may be won.

" 'For that purpose has this proclamation been proclaimed:

" ' "Let [small] and great exert themselves to this end."

" 'My neighbours, too, should learn this lesson, and may this lesson long endure!

" 'And this purpose will increase—yea, it will increase vastly, at least half as much again[4] will it increase.'

"And this proclamation was proclaimed by the body of missionaries, [to wit], 256[5] [persons]."

Minor Rock Edict II: Summary of the Law of Piety or Duty

Thus saith His Sacred Majesty:—

"Father and mother must be hearkened to; similarly, respect for living creatures must be firmly established; truth must be spoken.

"These are the virtues of the Law which must be practised. Similarly, the teacher must be reverenced by the pupil, and fitting courtesy must be shown to relations."

This is the ancient nature of things—this leads to length of days, and according to this men must act.

Rock Edict I: The Sacredness of Life

This scripture of the Law of Duty has been written by command of His Sacred and Gracious Majesty the King:

"Here no animal may be slaughtered for sacrifice, nor shall any merry-making be held.[6] Because in merry-makings His

---

3. This sentence seems to mean that true teaching raises men to the level of gods.

4. Idiom meaning "in large measure."

5. Indians regarded 256 ($= 16^2 = 32 \times 8 = 64 \times 4$) as a perfect number.

6. The emperor apparently refers to a public feast held at the capital at which meat and wine were served. Perhaps this particular feast was especially riotous, since he does not object to "certain merry-makings." Ashoka's disapproval of the festival at the capital was probably owing to the slaughter of animals necessary to provide the meat.

Sacred and Gracious Majesty sees much offence, although certain merry-makings are excellent in the sight of His Sacred and Gracious Majesty the King. Formerly, in the kitchen of His Sacred and Gracious Majesty the King each day many hundred thousands of living creatures were slaughtered to make curries. But now, when this scripture of the Law is being written, only three living creatures are slaughtered for curry [daily], to wit, two peacocks and one antelope—the antelope, however, not invariably. Even those three living creatures shall not be slaughtered in future."

Rock Edict II: Provision of Comforts for Men and Animals

"Everywhere in the dominions of His Sacred and Gracious Majesty the King, as well as among his neighbors, the Cholas, Pandyas, the Satiyaputra, the Keralaputra, as far as the Tamraparni,[7] Antiochos the Greek king,[8] or even the kings the neighbours of that Antiochos—everywhere have been made the healing arrangements of His Sacred and Gracious Majesty the King in two kinds, [namely], healing arrangements for men and healing arrangements for beasts. Medicinal herbs also, both medicinal herbs for men and medicinal herbs for beasts, wheresoever lacking, have been everywhere both imported and planted. Roots also and fruits, wheresoever lacking, have been everywhere imported and planted. On the roads, too, wells have been dug and trees planted for the enjoyment of man and beast."

Rock Edict XII: Toleration

"His Sacred and Gracious Majesty the King does reverence to men of all sects, whether ascetics or householders, by gifts and various forms of reverence.

"His Sacred Majesty, however, cares not so much for gifts or external reverence as that there should be a growth of the essence of the matter[9] in all sects. The growth of the essence of

7. These peoples all lived in the extreme south of the peninsula, beyond the boundaries of Ashoka's empire. The Tamraparni was a river of that region.

8. Antiochos Theos, the Seleucid king of Western Asia.

9. I.e., the qualities essential to piety in all sects.

the matter assumes various forms, but the root of it is restraint of speech, to wit, a man must not do reverence to his own sect or disparage that of another without reason. Depreciation should be for specific reasons only, because the sects of other people all deserve reverence for one reason or another.

"By thus acting a man exalts his own sect, and at the same time does service to the sects of other people. By acting contrari-wise a man hurts his own sect, and does disservice to the sects of other people. For he who does reverence to his own sect while disparaging the sects of others wholly from attachment to his own, with intent to enhance the splendour of his own sect, in reality by such conduct inflicts the severest injury on his own sect.

"Concord, therefore, is meritorious, to wit, hearkening and hearkening willingly to the Law of Piety as accepted by other people. For this is the desire of His Sacred Majesty that all sects should hear much teaching and hold sound doctrine.

"Wherefore the adherents of all sects, whatever they may be, must be informed that His Sacred Majesty does not care so much for gifts or external reverence as that there should be growth in the essence of the matter and respect for all sects.

"For this very purpose are employed the Censors of the Law of Piety, the Censors of the Women, the (?) Superintendents of pastures,[10] and other [official] bodies. And this is the fruit thereof—the growth of one's own sect and the enhancement of the splendour of the Law of Piety."

Rock Edict XIII: True Conquest

"Kalinga[11] was conquered by His Sacred and Gracious Majesty the King when he had been consecrated eight years.[12] One hundred and fifty thousand persons were thence carried away captive, one hundred thousand were there slain, and many times that number died.

10. The duties of these various officials are uncertain. The women may be those belonging to the royal household.
11. Or "the Kalingas": a province on the eastern coast of India.
12. Ashoka's formal consecration as king occurred in the year 269 B.C. He actually succeeded his father on the throne in 273 B.C.

"Directly after the Kalingas had been annexed began His Sacred Majesty's zealous protection of the Law of Piety, his love of that Law, and his inculcation of that Law. Thence arises the remorse of His Sacred Majesty for having conquered the Kalingas, because the conquest of a country previously unconquered involves the slaughter, death, and carrying away captive of the people. That is a matter of profound sorrow and regret to His Sacred Majesty.

"There is, however, another reason for His Sacred Majesty feeling still more regret, inasmuch as the Brahmans and ascetics, or men of other denominations, or householders who dwell there, and among whom these duties are practised, [to wit], hearkening to superiors, hearkening to father and mother, hearkening to teachers (or 'elders'), and proper treatment (or 'courtesy to') of friends, acquaintances, comrades, relatives, slaves, and servants, with steadfastness of devotion—to these befalls violence (or 'injury'), or slaughter, or separation from their loved ones. Or violence happens to the friends, acquaintances, comrades, and relatives of those who are themselves well protected, while their affection [for those injured] continues undiminished. Thus for them also that is a mode of violence, and the share of this distributed among all men is a matter of regret to His Sacred Majesty, because it never is the case that faith in some one denomination or another does not exist.

"So that of all the people who were then slain, done to death, or carried away captive in Kalinga, if the hundredth part or the thousandth part were now to suffer the same fate, it would be matter of regret to His Sacred Majesty. Moreover, should any one do him wrong, that too must be borne with by His Sacred Majesty, so far as it can possibly be borne with. Even upon the forest folk in his dominions, His Sacred Majesty looks kindly, and he seeks to make them think [aright], for [otherwise] repentance would come upon His Sacred Majesty. They are bidden to turn from their [evil] ways that they be not chastised. Because His Sacred Majesty desires for all animate beings security, self-control, peace of mind, and joyousness.[13]

13. Buddhist doctrine stresses the joyousness obtained by the perfectly emancipated saint (*Arhat*).

"And this the chiefest conquest in the opinion of His Sacred Majesty, that conquest of the Law of Piety, which, again, has been won by His Sacred Majesty both here [in his own dominions] and among all his neighbours as far as six hundred leagues, where the king of the Greeks named Antiochos dwells, and to the north of that Antiochos [where dwell] the four (4) kings named severally Ptolemy, Antigonos, Magas, and Alexander—[14][likewise] in the south, the Cholas and Pandyas as far as the Tamraparni [river][15]—and here, too, in the King's dominions—among the Greeks,[16] Kambojas,[17] the Nabhapantis of Nabhaka,[18] among the Bhojas, Pitinikas,[19] Andhras, and Pulindas[20]—everywhere they follow the instruction of His Sacred Majesty in the Law of Piety.

"Even where the envoys of His Sacred Majesty do not penetrate, these people, too, hearing His Sacred Majesty's ordinance based upon the Law of Piety and his instruction in that Law, practise and will practise the Law.

"And, again, the conquest thereby won everywhere is everywhere a conquest full of delight. Delight is won in the conquests of the Law. A small matter, however, is that delight. His Sacred Majesty regards as bearing much fruit only that which concerns the other world.

"And for this purpose has this scripture of the Law been recorded, in order that my sons and grandsons, who may be, may not think it their duty to conquer a new conquest.

14. Ptolemy Philadelphos of Egypt (r. 285-247 B.C.); Antigonos Gonatas of Macedonia (r. 278-239 B.C.); Magas of Cyrene (Africa) (d. 258 B.C.); and Alexander of Epirus (r. 272-258 B.C.).
15. The kingdom of the Pandhyas occupied the extreme southern tip of the Indian peninsula; the Cholas were their immediate neighbors on the northeast, along the Coromandel coast. The Tamraparni was a river of the far south (not a name for Ceylon, as it is sometimes translated).
16. The Greeks referred to here (called Yonas or Yavanas) were persons of Greek descent who lived on the northwest frontier of India.
17. The Kambojas were a northern Himalayan nation, possibly Tibetans.
18. An unidentified people.
19. The Bhojas and Pitinikas lived in west central India, to the north of modern Bombay.
20. The Andhras were a powerful nation living in the basin of the Godavari River on the eastern coast; the Pulindas were wild tribes from the Vindhya hills.

"If, perchance, a conquest should please them (?)[21] they should take heed only of patience and gentleness, and regard as a conquest only that which is effected by the Law of Piety. That avails for both this world and the next. Let all their joy be that which lies in effort; that avails for both this world and the next."

Pillar Edict VII: Review of Ashoka's Measures for the Propagation of the Law of Piety in His Empire

1   Thus saith His Sacred and Gracious Majesty the King:—

"The kings who lived in times past desired that men might grow with the growth of the Law of Piety. Men, however, did not grow with the growth of the Law of Piety in due proportion."

2   Concerning this thus saith His Sacred and Gracious Majesty the King:—

"This [thought] occurred to me:—In times past kings desired that men might grow with the growth of the Law of Piety in due proportion; men, however, did not in due proportion grow with the growth of the Law.

"By what means, then, can men be induced to conform? by what means can men grow with the growth of the Law of Piety in due proportion? by what means can I lift up at least some of them through the growth of that Law?"

3   Concerning this thus saith His Sacred and Gracious Majesty the King:—

"This [thought] occurred to me:—

" 'Proclamation of the Law of Piety will I proclaim; with instruction in that Law will I instruct; so that men hearkening thereto may conform, lift themselves up, and mightily grow with the growth of the Law of Piety.'

"For this my purpose proclamations of the Law of Piety have been proclaimed; instructions in that Law of many kinds have been disseminated; my [?] missioners, likewise my Agents set over the multitude, will expound and expand my teaching.

"The Governors, also, set over many hundred thousands of

21. It is not clear whether this refers to a conquest by arms.

souls have received instructions—'In such and such a manner
expound my teaching to the body of subordinate officials of the
Law.' "

4   Thus saith His Sacred and Gracious Majesty:—

"Considering further the same purpose, I have set up pillars
of the Law, appointed Censors (High Officers) of the Law, and
made a proclamation of the Law."

5   Thus saith His Sacred and Gracious Majesty the King:—

"On the roads, too, I have had banyan-trees planted to give
shade to man and beast; groves (or 'gardens') of mango-trees
I have had planted; at every half-*kos*[22] I have had wells dug;
rest-houses, too, have been erected; and numerous watering-
places have been provided by me here and there for the enjoyment of man and beast.

"A small matter, however, is that so-called enjoyment.

"With various blessings has mankind been blessed by former kings, as by me also; by me, however, with the intent that
men may conform to the Law of Piety, has it been done even
as I thought."

6   Thus saith His Sacred and Gracious Majesty:—

"My Censors (or 'High Officers') of the Law of Piety,[23] too,
are employed on manifold objects of the royal favour affecting
both ascetics and householders, and are likewise employed
among all denominations. On the business of the Church,[24] too,
they are employed, as well as among the Brahmans and Jains[25]
are they employed. Similarly, they are employed among the
Jains; among miscellaneous sects, too, are they employed.

"The High Officers of various kinds shall severally superin-
tend their respective charges, whereas the High Officers of the
Law of Piety (Censors) are employed both on such things and
also among other denominations."

22. The *kos* was equivalent to a little over a mile (some sources say two
miles).
23. The censors were officials appointed especially to teach and enforce the
law of piety.
24. The Buddhist Order of monks, here probably including the lay disciples
also.
25. The Jains were an influential sect which engaged in severe ascetic practices and revered all forms of life.

7   Thus saith His Sacred and Gracious Majesty the King:—

"Both these and many other officers, heads of departments, are employed in the distribution of alms, both my own and those of the Queens[26]; and in all my female establishments both here [i.e., 'at the capital'] and in the provinces they indicate in diverse ways sundry places where satisfaction may be given.

"Those same officers are also employed in the distribution of the alms of my sons, and likewise of the other Princes, sons of the Queens, in order to promote the practice of the Law of Piety and conformity to that Law.

"The practice of the Law of Piety and the conformity referred to are those whereby compassion, liberality, truth, purity, gentleness, and saintliness will thus grow among mankind."

8   Thus saith His Sacred and Gracious Majesty the King:—

"Whatsoever meritorious deeds have been done by me, those deeds mankind will conform to and imitate, whence follows that they have grown and will grow in the virtues of hearkening to father and mother, hearkening to teachers (or 'elders'), reverence to the aged, and seemly treatment of Brahmans and ascetics, of the poor and wretched; yea, even of slaves and servants."

9   Thus saith His Sacred and Gracious Majesty the King:—

"Among men, however, when the aforesaid growth of piety has grown, it has been effected by twofold means, to wit, by regulations of the Law of Piety and by reflection. Of these two, however, regulations of the Law are of small account, whereas reflection is superior.

"Nevertheless, regulations of the Law of Piety have been made by me to the effect that such and such species are exempt from slaughter, not to speak of numerous other regulations of the Law of Piety which have been made by me.

"Yet the superiority of reflection is shown by the growth of piety among men and the more complete abstention from kill-

26. The queens were the principal royal consorts, possibly four in number, as distinguished from the ordinary women of the harem. Their sons ranked as princes.

ing animate beings and from the sacrificial slaughter of living creatures.

"So for this purpose has this been recorded, in order that my sons and descendants (lit. 'great grandsons') may conform thereto, and by thus conforming may win both this world and the next.

"When I had been consecrated twenty-seven years I had this scripture of the Law written."

10   Concerning this His Sacred Majesty saith:—

"This scripture of the Law of Piety, wheresoever pillars of stone or tables of stone exist, must there be recorded so that it may long endure."

Introduction to the Ramayana

The *Ramayana* is one of the two great epics of Indian literature. Its core consists of a heroic narrative—the adventures of prince Rama and his wife Sita—but as in the case of the *Mahabharata*, the original story has been substantially reworked, overlaid with supernatural elements, and modified by the addition of many pious speeches. When the epic was first written down is not certain. Valmiki, its traditional author, may indeed have collected a group of Rama-legends and transformed them into poetry, perhaps in the third century B.C. But all extant versions of the poem are much later, dating probably from about A.D. 200.

An abbreviated account of the story of Rama is actually contained in the *Mahabharata*, in a form suggesting that the *Ramayana* is its source. The two epics are in fact closely connected, having a number of verses in common. On the whole, the *Ramayana* is the later of the two and has fewer archaic elements. It is more compact in plot and much shorter, containing in its various recensions between 50,000 and 90,000 lines as against the *Mahabharata's* more than 200,000. The supernatural element is more prominent in the *Ramayana*: gods take a personal part in the action, human heroes commit superhuman feats, and magic plays a decisive role in the outcome of battles. But in contrast to the predominantly warlike character of the older epic, the entire first half of the *Ra-*

mayana is devoted to peaceful episodes; war breaks out only in response to the kidnapping of the hero's wife.

Elements of the *Ramayana* story undoubtedly go back to the period when the Aryan invaders had spread out from their base in the northwest, colonized the Ganges Valley, and pushed southward into the Deccan. Rama's journey across India may be taken as symbolic of this process of penetration. Indeed, the poem's description of his faithful allies—the native southern tribes—as monkeys, and of the inhabitants of Ceylon as monsters, reflects the typical prejudice of conquerors in all ages *vis-à-vis* subjugated and alien races. Kosala, Rama's home on the upper Ganges, became an Aryan kingdom in the ninth century B.C. Possibly Rama and his father Dasaratha were actual minor chieftains; Sita's father Janaka was certainly a historical personage, who is mentioned more than once in the Upanishads as the patron of hermits and mystics. His kingdom of Videha was an important state in the northeast, which disappeared in about the sixth century B.C. The *Ramayana* clearly describes a period when the tribal organization of the Aryans had given way to small kingdoms with a rudimentary administrative apparatus. But the social customs and the style of warfare it portrays often belong to a later period; and the various strata are not always easy to distinguish.

The historical portions of the *Ramayana* have been so altered that the poem as it now stands is as much a textbook of *dharma* as an epic narrative. Rama, the hero-prince, has become a god, the incarnation of Vishnu. His father Dasaratha is a perfectly wise and just ruler; his brother Lakshmana, a paragon of loyalty; his consort Sita, the embodiment of wifely virtue. The heroes examine every proposed action in the light of ethical imperatives. The plot develops in rigid conformance with the law of *karma,* according to which every evil deed must bring its appropriate punishment. When Dasaratha falls victim to a queen's wiles, sends his favorite son into exile, and dies in sorrow, it is revealed that this otherwise exemplary ruler had once accidentally slain a young man and thereby earned the curse of the youth's father. Sita's capture by the Titan Ravana and the consequent stain on her honor are attributed to the fact that, through excess of devotion to her husband, she once doubted the courage of his loyal brother Lakshmana. Even Rama must bear the consequences of having slain a member of the inviolate Brahmin class—even though the Brahmin was Ravana, the monster who had stolen his wife.

The *Ramayana* belongs to the class of literature called *smriti*, or sacred tradition, the recital of which confers innumerable religious benefits. Hearing it is sometimes described as equal in merit to reading the Vedas, or giving a hundred cows to a Brahmin, or performing a horse-sacrifice. The poem is popularly regarded as a kind of charm which can bring riches, offspring, a good husband, fame, and various other advantages. Even today in India the supposed route of Rama's journey is still pointed out; and the island chain connecting the mainland with Ceylon is believed to be the remains of the bridge by which Rama crossed over to recover his wife. Sita, whose faithfulness and devotion to her husband never wavered, remains the all-time favorite Indian heroine. For over two thousand years, the *Ramayana* has furnished materials for popular legend and fantasy in India and provided the illiterate masses with instruction in *dharma*.

The plot of the Ramayana begins when Dasaratha, the king of Kosala, resolves to appoint his son Rama as heir to the throne. The virtues of Rama clearly entitle him to this position; and the people rejoice. But one of Dasaratha's queens, ambitious for her own son, tricks the king into promising her a boon. The king promises; the queen requests that her son be made heir and Rama sent into exile. Dasaratha is unable to break his word; and Rama is informed of his coming banishment. Duty-bound to respect his father's will, Rama accepts this decision without murmur, but directs his wife Sita to remain behind in Ayodhya, the capital.

FROM THE RAMAYANA OF VALMIKI

Sita Entreats Rama To Allow Her To Accompany Him

The sweet-speaking Sita, worthy of Rama's love, thus being instructed to remain in Ayodhya, though filled with affection, indignantly replied: "O Offspring of a great king, O Rama, how canst thou speak in such wise? O Prince, thy words evoke laughter. O Chief of Men, father, mother, son and daughter-in-law live according to their merit and dependent on it, but a

From Valmiki, *The Ramayana*, trans. by Hari Prasad Shastri, 3 vols. (London: Shanti Sadan, 1957), I, 221, 227; II, 95-7, 99-103; III, 102-4, 287-9, 310-16, 334-8, 341-2.

wife enjoys the fortune of her husband since she is a part of himself. I am therefore entitled to share thy father's command and also go into exile.

"The happiness of a woman depends on her husband, neither father, mother, son, relative or companion avail her at death; in this world and in the other world, the husband alone is her all-in-all. If thou to-day depart for the forest, I will precede thee on foot, clearing the thorns and kusha grass from thy path. O Hero, relinquishing anger and pride, take me with thee without hesitation. There is no fault in me that merits my remaining here, without thee. The joy experienced by lords of men whether dwelling in a palace or transported in an aerial chariot through the heavens or possessing the eightfold psychic powers, is far inferior to the joy of the wife in the service of her lord. My royal father has instructed me fully in the duties of a wife and, therefore, I have no need of further instruction in the matter. Assuredly I shall accompany thee to the forest, uninhabited by men, filled with savage beasts, such as bears and bulls. O My Hero, I will dwell in the forest as happily as in the palace of my father, having no anxiety in the three worlds save the service of my spouse. O Hero, I will wander with thee in the forest according to the ancient spiritual ordinance, free from desire for pleasure, traversing the honey-scented woodland. O Lord of my Life, since thou canst protect and support innumerable people, canst thou not more easily protect me? Without doubt to-day I shall enter the forest with thee, O Fortunate Prince, none can break my resolve. . . .

Thus Sita, lamenting and embracing Shri[1] Rama, wept aloud. From her eyes, like a she elephant wounded by poisoned arrows, long-restrained tears issued, as fire is kindled by the friction of wood. Crystal drops fell from her eyes as water slips from the petals of the lotus flowers. The face of the princess resembling the full moon, withered by the fire of intense grief, looked like a lotus withdrawn from water.

Shri Ramachandra, taking Sita, afflicted and fainting, in his arms, spoke to her in the following wise: "O Devi,[2] I do not

1. A title of respect.
2. Goddess.

desire even to enter heaven if it causes thee pain! Nought do
I fear! Like Brahma,[3] I am wholly fearless! Though able to
protect thee in every way, yet not fully knowing thy mind, I
declined to let thee share my exile. Seeing thou art destined to
share my exile, I do not desire to abandon thee, as a man of
virtuous conduct determines not to sacrifice his good name. O
Beautiful One, following the example of the good of yore, I
shall act in the same manner; do thou follow me as Suvar-
chala[4] follows the sun. O Daughter of King Janaka, I am not
entering the forest by my own desire, but to obey the injunc-
tions of my father. O Devi, it is the duty of a son to obey his
parents, I could not endure life if I failed to observe my father's
command. Fate is invisible, who can control it, but the parents
and the spiritual preceptor are visible deities and their orders
must be obeyed. What in the world is so sacred as the worship
of that which grants dharma, prosperity and pleasure? By this
worship, homage is paid to the three worlds. O Sita, observance
of truth, charity and sacrifice accompanied by suitable offerings is of less avail in obtaining the spiritual realm than the
service of parents and the Guru.[5] Those who serve their parents
and the spiritual preceptor obtain heaven, wealth, learning and
progeny and nothing is impossible for them. Those who are devoted to their parents and their Guru obtain entrance to heaven
and the regions of the devas,[6] the gandharvas[7] and Brahma.
This is eternal righteousness—to obey the command of thy parents, fixed in the practice of truth. O Sita, not knowing thy
mind, I advised thee not to accompany me, but now seeing thy
fixed resolve I desire to take thee with me. . . .

.   .   .   .

[Rama is now living in the depths of the Dandaka forest with Sita
and his loyal brother, Lakshmana. After wandering across most of
India, they have built a hermitage near the sources of the Godavari
River. But their tranquil existence is rudely interrupted by the

3. The creator-god.
4. The consort of the sun-god.
5. The religious teacher.
6. Gods.
7. Celestial musicians.

visit of a hideous Titan princess. Observing the beauty of Rama, she falls in love with him; but he carelessly rejects her advances. Her brother Ravana, the king of Ceylon (Lanka), resolves to avenge this insult. Ravana sends a demon in the form of a deer to the vicinity of the hermitage in order to tempt Rama and Lakshmana into the forest. In their absence, he himself appears to Sita in the guise of a Brahmin.]

Ravana Approaches Sita

Thereupon Ravana, in the guise of a mendicant, availing himself of the opportunity, rapidly approached the hermitage with the purpose of seeking out Vaidehi.[8] With matted locks, clad in a saffron robe and carrying a triple staff and loshta,[9] that highly powerful one, knowing Sita to be alone, accosted her in the wood, in the form of an ascetic, at dusk when darkness shrouds the earth in the absence of the sun and moon. Gazing on Sita, the consort of Rama, Ravana resembled Rahu regarding Rohini in the absence of Shasi.[10]

Beholding that monstrous apparition, the leaves of the trees ceased to move, the wind grew still, the turbulent course of the river Godaveri subsided and began to flow quietly. The ten-headed Ravana, however, profiting by Rama's absence, drew near to Sita in the guise of a monk of venerable appearance while she was overcome with grief on account of her lord.

Approaching Vaidehi in an honourable guise, as Saturn draws near to the Chitra star, Ravana resembled a deep well overgrown with grass. He stood there gazing on the glorious consort of Rama of incomparable beauty, Sita, with her brilliant lips and teeth, her countenance as radiant as the full moon, seated on a carpet of leaves, overwhelmed with grief, weeping bitterly.

On seeing the Princess of Videha alone, clad in a yellow silken sari, whose eyes resembled lotus petals, the titan, struck by Kama's[11] arrow, joyfully accosted her, feigning the gentle

8. Sita, daughter of the king of Videha.
9. A vessel for receiving alms.
10. I.e., resembling the power of darkness (Rahu) casting its shadow on the beautiful star Rohini when the light of the moon (Shasi) fades.
11. The god of love.

accents of a brahmin. Praising her beauty, unequalled in the Three Worlds, which caused her to resemble Shri,[12] he said:—

"O Thou, possessed of the brilliance of gold and silver, who art clad in a yellow silken sari and who, like a pool of lilies, art wreathed in garlands of fresh flowers, art thou Lakshmi bereft of her lotus or Kirti or a nymph of graceful aspect? Art thou Bhuti of slender hips, or Rati[13] disporting herself in the forest?

"How even, sharp and white are thy teeth, how large thy slightly reddened eyes with their dark pupils, how well proportioned and rounded are thy thighs and how charming thy legs, resembling the tapering trunk of an elephant! How round and plump are thy cheeks, like unto the polished fruit of the Tala trees[14]; how enchanting is thy bosom, decorated with pearls! . . .

"Dost thou not fear to live amidst monkeys, lions, tigers, deer, wolves, bears, hyenas and leopards? O Fair One, dost thou not tremble before those terrible elephants, maddened with the exudation of temporal juices, in this great forest? Who art thou? To whom dost thou belong? For what reason dost thou range the Dandaka Forest alone, which is frequented by terrible titans?"

With these flattering words did the evil-minded Ravana address Sita, and seeing him in the guise of a brahmin, she entertained him with the traditional hospitality due to an uninvited guest. Leading him to a seat, she brought water to wash his feet and offered him food, saying:—"Be pleased to accept this repast!" Seeing him in the form of a Twice-born[15] with his loshta and saffron robe, unrecognizable in his disguise, Sita welcomed him as a true brahmin, saying:—

"Be seated, O Brahmin, and accept this water for washing thy feet, also this meal, composed of ripe fruits and roasted grain, prepared for thee, which please enjoy."

Thus did she receive him with hospitable words, but Ravana,

12. The goddess of beauty and wealth, wife of Vishnu.
13. Lakshmi, Kirti, Bhuti, and Rati are various goddesses and nymphs.
14. A species of palm.
15. A member of one of the upper classes who has undergone the ceremony of initiation.

his gaze fixed on the Princess of Mithila,[16] determined to bear her away, thus preparing his own destruction.

Sita, anxiously expecting the return from hunting of her illustrious lord, with Prince Lakshmana, searched the vast and darkening forest with her eyes but was unable to see either Rama or his brother there.

The Conversation of Ravana and Sita

[Sita has recounted the story of how she came to reside in the forest, and praised the virtue and nobility of her husband.]

.   .   .   .

Hearing the words of Sita, the consort of Rama, the mighty titan replied in these harsh words:—

"O Sita, I am that Ravana, King of the Titans,[17] in fear of whom the world, the Gods, titans and men tremble. O Source of Delight, since I beheld thee shining like gold, clad in silk, my consorts have ceased to find favour with me. Do thou become the chief queen of those countless women, stolen away from many quarters by me.

"Lanka, my capital, set in the midst of the sea, is built on the summit of a hill. There, O Sita, wander with me in the groves and thus forget the forest. O Lovely One, if thou dost become my wife, five thousand servants adorned with diverse ornaments shall attend on thee."

The blameless daughter of Janaka, being thus addressed by Ravana, was filled with indignation and answered that titan with contempt, saying:—

"I am dependent on my lord, Rama, who is as steadfast as a rock, calm as the ocean and equal to Mahendra[18] himself, Rama, endowed with every good quality, who resembles the Nyagrodha tree[19] in stature. I am dependent on that illustrious and noble warrior, whose arms are long, whose chest is broad, whose gait is like a lion's, nay, who resembles that king of beasts; to him, the greatest of men, I give my whole allegiance.

16. Mithila was the capital of Videha, where Sita's father was King.
17. *Rakshasas*—monsters of enormous size.
18. A name for the god Indra.
19. The Indian fig-tree, or banyan.

To Rama, whose countenance resembles the full moon, the son of a king, master of his passions, of immeasurable renown and power, I shall ever remain faithful.

"O Jackal, thou desirest a she-lion but art no more able to possess me than grasp the light of the sun! Thou Wretch, who seekest to carry off the beloved spouse of Raghava![20] Verily thou dost imagine the trees that thou seest before thee to be made of gold,[21] that thou art seeking to draw the teeth of a famished and courageous lion, that enemy of the deer, or extract the fangs of a poisonous snake. Dost thou desire to lift up the Mandara mountain with thy bare hands or live at ease after drinking poison? Thou dost seek to rub thine eyes with a needle and lick a razor with thy tongue! Thou desirest to cross the ocean with a stone round thy neck or grasp the sun and moon. O Thou who seekest to bear away the beloved wife of Rama, thou art endeavouring to carry a blazing fire in thy robe or walk on iron spikes.

"The disparity between thee and Rama is as that between a jackal and a lion, a brook and an ocean, the nectar of the Gods and sour barley gruel; between gold and iron, sandal and mud, an elephant and a cat, an eagle and a crow, a peacock and a duck, a swan and a vulture. Even shouldst thou steal me, if that mighty archer, Rama, whose prowess is equal to the Lord of a Thousand Eyes,[22] still lives, thou wilt no more be able to devour me than a fly can eat the clarified butter into which it has fallen."

Addressing that cruel Ranger of the Night thus, the guileless Sita shook like a leaf in the wind.

Perceiving her distress, Ravana, terrible as death, began to boast of his race, his power, his name and his exploits, in order to increase her fear.

Sita's Abduction by Ravana

Hearing those words of Sita, the mighty Ravana, striking one

20. Name for one belonging to the house of Raghu (here: Rama).
21. The trees of hell are said to be made of gold.
22. The god Indra. Since he is the chief god of the sky, his eyes are presumably the stars.

hand on the other, revealed his gigantic form and, skilled in speech, addressed her, saying:—

"Methinks thou hast taken leave of thy senses, hast thou not heard of my great prowess and valour? Standing in space, I am able to lift up the earth; I can drink the waters of the ocean and destroy death himself in combat. With my shafts I can pierce the sun and cleave the terrestial globe. Thou, who dost allow thyself to be deceived by any trick and dost follow any whim, behold how I can change my shape at will."

Speaking thus, Ravana, full of wrath, his eyes glowing like burning coals, resembled a flame, and discarding his benign aspect, he, the younger brother of Kuvera,[23] assumed a terrible shape, resembling death itself.

With smouldering eyes, a prey to anger, resplendent in ornaments of fine gold, like a dark cloud, that Ranger of the Night appeared before her with his ten heads and twenty arms. Abandoning his ascetic disguise, the King of the Titans took on his native form; wearing a blood-red robe, he fixed that pearl among women, Maithili,[24] with his gaze, thereafter addressing her, who resembled the sun, whose hair was dark and who was clothed in a robe and jewels, saying:—

"O Fair Lady, if thou desirest a master famed throughout the Three Worlds, then surrender thyself to me. I am a husband worthy of thee; do thou serve me forever! I shall do thee great honour nor will I ever displease thee. Renouncing thine attachment to a man, place thine affection on me. What binds thee to Rama, O Thou Foolish One who deemest thyself wise; he who has been banished from his domain, who has failed to fulfill his destiny and whose days are numbered, Rama, who on the injunction of a woman abandoned kingdom, friends and people to inhabit a forest frequented by wild beasts?"

Speaking thus to Maithili, who was worthy of tenderness and gentle of speech, that wicked titan, inflamed by passion, seized hold of her as Budha[25] seizes Rohini. With his left hand he grasped the hair of the lotus-eyed Sita, and with his right, her

23. The god of wealth.
24. Sita as daughter of the king of Mithila.
25. The planet Mercury.

thighs. Seeing Ravana with his sharp teeth like the peak of a mountain, resembling death itself, the Celestial Beings fled away in terror. Then instantly the great chariot belonging to Ravana, made of gold, to which braying mules were harnessed, appeared and, addressing Sita in harsh tones, he lifted her up and, clasping her, ascended the car.

.   .   .   .

[In search of Sita, Rama wanders through the southern mountains and concludes an alliance with the monkeys who inhabit that region. One of the monkeys jumps across the strait separating Ceylon from the mainland and discovers Sita in Ravana's palace. She has remained faithful to Rama despite all the Titan's blandishments, and she entrusts the monkey with a token of affection for her husband. Rama builds a bridge across the strait and crosses over with the monkeys into Ceylon.]

The Titans Make a Sortie

Then those titans approached the abode of Ravana and informed him that Rama and the monkeys had laid siege to the city.

This news enraged that Ranger of the Night, who, repeating his former commands went up into the palace. From there he surveyed Lanka with its hills, woods and groves, which was besieged on all sides by countless divisions of monkeys, eager to fight. Beholding the earth all brown with innumerable Plavagas,[26] in great perplexity he reflected: "How can they be exterminated?"

Having pondered long, Ravana regained his confidence and, opening his great eyes wide, he gazed on Raghava and the simian battalions.

Meanwhile Rama, at the head of his army was rapidly advancing on Lanka which was guarded on all sides and thronged with titans. Thereafter the son of Dasaratha, seeing that city furnished with flags and banners, remembered Sita and was filled with anguish. He reflected "That daughter of Janaka

26. Those who move by leaps and bounds; the monkeys.

whose eyes resemble a young doe's, will be a prey to anxiety on my account! Consumed with grief and emaciated, she is pining away, the bare ground her bed!"

Reflecting on the sufferings of Vaidehi, the virtuous Raghava speedily issued a command to the monkeys to prepare for the enemy's destruction.

Hearing the order of Raghava of imperishable exploits, the Plavagas, urging each other on, filled the air with their roaring.

"Let us demolish Lanka with rocks and stones or with our fists alone" was the resolve of the monkey leaders and, under the eyes of the King of the Titans, in order to accomplish Rama's cherished desire, those troops divided themselves into columns and began to scale the heights of Lanka. Hurling themselves on that city with rocks and trees, those golden-hued Plavamgamas[26] of coppery countenance, willing to lay down their lives in Rama's service, destroyed innumerable battlements, ramparts and arches with blows from trees, rocks and fists and filled the moats and trenches of clear water with sand, stones, grass and logs. . . .

Meanwhile, his heart filled with rage, the King of the Titans ordered his troops to make a rapid sortie. At this command falling from Ravana's lips, a tremendous clamour arose among the rangers of the night and the sound of kettledrums, their discs white as the moon, on which the titans beat with sticks of gold, broke out on every side, while hundreds and thousands of trumpets blared forth, blown by the titans with their cheeks extended to the full. With their dark limbs adorned with ornaments and their conches, those rangers of the night resembled clouds bordered with lightning or rows of cranes; and their battalions advanced gaily under Ravana's imperious commands as, at the time of Pralaya,[27] the tumultuous sea overflows.

At that moment from every side, a clamour arose from the army of the monkeys which filled Malaya[28] with its plains, valleys and chasms, and the sound of the trumpets and drums and the leonine roars of those warriors re-echoed over the earth, sky and sea, as also the trumpeting of elephants, the neighing

27. The time of the dissolution of the world at the end of a world cycle.
28. The mountain on the top of which lived the sage Agastya (see note 38).

of horses, the clatter of chariot wheels and the thunder of the titans marching.

Thereafter a terrible struggle ensued between the monkeys and the titans as, in former times between Gods and Asuras.[29] With their flaming maces, their spears, harpoons and axes, the titans, demonstrating their native prowess, struck the army of the monkeys and from their side, those gigantic apes attacked their adversaries ferociously with blows from trees, rocks, teeth and nails.

"Victory to King Sugriva!"[30] yelled the monkeys, "May our Sovereign prevail!" shouted the titans and each proclaimed his name, while other demons, standing on the walls, hacked at the monkeys below with hooks and harpoons and they, infuriated, leapt into the air and dragged down those soldiers stationed on the walls by seizing them with their arms, and that conflict between demons and monkeys was appalling and the earth was covered with mud and flesh in that astonishing fight.

[The struggle continues until many of the chief combatants on both sides are slain.]

Rama and Ravana Fight with Magic Weapons

. . . A great rage seized Ravana, who urged on his charioteer with these words:—

"By slaying Rama and Lakshmana I shall remove that double scourge, the cause of the slaughter of my faithful adherents and the siege of the city. In the fight I shall cut down Rama, that tree of which Sita is the flower and the fruit, whose branches are Sugriva . . . and all the leading monkeys."

Thereupon that mighty car-warrior, who caused the ten regions to resound, drove rapidly on Raghava with his chariot, and the earth, with its rivers, mountains and woods, trembled with the uproar, and the lions, gazelles and birds that inhabited it were seized with terror.

Then Ravana employed a dark and magic weapon that was

29. Demons.
30. King of the monkeys and ally of Rama.

formidable and terrifying and with it he consumed the monkeys, who fled hither and thither. Amidst the dust raised by their battalions, for they were unable to endure that weapon created by Brahma himself, Raghava, seeing those countless divisions taking refuge in innumerable places, pursued by Ravana's powerful shafts, stood ready waiting.

Meanwhile that Tiger among the Titans, having routed the army of monkeys, beheld Rama standing there unconquered with his brother Lakshmana, like unto Vasava[31] with Vishnu, and Rama seemed to touch the sky as it were as he stretched his great bow and those heroes with eyes as large as lotus petals were long-armed and the conquerors of their foes.

From his side the extremely illustrious and valiant Rama, who was accompanied by Saumitri,[32] seeing Ravana overwhelming the monkeys in the fight, joyfully took hold of the centre of his bow and immediately began to bend that excellent weapon that was stout and sonorous, riving the earth as it were. . . .

Thereafter, between those two warriors, each seeking to slay the other, an incomparable and unimaginable struggle ensued like unto the duel between Vritra[33] and Vasava. Both were furnished with excellent bows, both were skilled warriors, both brought exceptional knowledge in the science of arms to the fight. In all their manoeuvrings they were followed by a stream of shafts as the waves in two oceans that are whipped up by a tempest.

Then, with a skilful hand, Ravana, the Destroyer of the Worlds, aiming at Rama's forehead, loosed a formidable succession of iron shafts from his bow, which Rama received unmoved on his head like a garland of lotus leaves. Thereupon, reciting a sacred formula, arming himself with Rudra's[34] weapon and choosing a large number of spears, full of wrath, the illustrious Raghava bent his bow and with force let fly those weapons in rapid succession against that Indra of Titans but

31. A name for the god Indra.
32. A name for Rama's brother Lakshmana as son of Queen Sumitra.
33. The demon slain by Indra (Vasava). See Rig Veda I. 80, below, pp. 181-82.
34. The god of destruction.

those darts fell without breaking through the armour of Ravana, who, like an immense cloud, remained unmoved.

Then Rama, skilled in the use of arms, struck Ravana afresh on the forehead, as he stood in his chariot, with arrows to which he had joined a miraculous weapon, and it appeared as if five-headed serpents in the form of darts were penetrating hissing into the earth repelled by Ravana whom they sought to devour. Thereupon, having rendered Raghava's weapon void, Ravana, in a transport of rage, armed himself in his turn with the dreadful Asura weapon which he loosed joined to sharp and terrible arrows with huge points, having the heads of lions, tigers, herons, geese, vultures, falcons, jackals and wolves or resembling serpents with five heads. Others had the heads of donkeys, boars, dogs, cocks, aquatic monsters and venomous reptiles and those sharp arrows were the creation of his magic power. Struck by the Asuric shafts, that lion among the Raghus,[35] he who resembled the God of Fire himself, responded with the Agneya Dart that was full of power and to it he joined arrows of every kind with points that burnt like fire and which resembled suns, planets and stars in hue or great meteors like unto flaming tongues. Those formidable missiles belonging to Ravana striking against those loosed by Rama, disintegrated in space and were annihilated in their thousands.

Thereupon all the valiant monkeys with Sugriva at their head, able to change their form at will, beholding the titan's weapon destroyed by Rama of imperishable karma, let forth joyous acclamations and made a circle round him.

Then the magnanimous son of Dasaratha, the descendant of Raghu, having destroyed that weapon discharged by Ravana's own arm, was filled with felicity, whilst the leaders of the monkeys joyfully paid homage to him.

The Fluctuations of Combat

Then the desperate duel of chariots between Rama and Ravana broke out with increased fury so that all the worlds were seized with terror.

The battalions of titans and innumerable companies of mon-

35. The house to which Rama belonged.

keys stood motionless with weapons in their hands and, beholding those two warriors, man and titan, all were amazed, their hearts beating rapidly. Ready for combat, their arms filled with every kind of missile, they stood absorbed in the spectacle, forgetting to loose their shafts at one another, and the titans had their eyes riveted on Ravana and the monkeys on Rama so that both armies took on a strange aspect.

Meanwhile, witnessing those portents, both Raghava and Ravana, steady, resolute and full of anger, fought with determined courage. "I shall triumph" reflected Kakutstha,[36] "I must die" thought Ravana and both displayed their full strength with assurance in the encounter. . . .

Thus Rama and Ravana fought with an increasing supply of weapons and, in the struggle, they showered down their spears without pause to right and left, so that these formidable weapons covered the firmament; Rama striking Ravana's steeds and Ravana striking those belonging to Rama; thus, both exchanged blow for blow and both, in the height of anger, entered upon a tremendous duel causing the hair to stand on end. Then with sharpened arrows Rama and Ravana continued their combat and, contemplating his broken standard, Ravana was consumed with rage.

The Duel Continues

Witnessing the combat between Rama and Ravana, all beings were struck with amazement and those two warriors, assuming a dreadful aspect in the struggle, highly enraged, determined on mutual slaughter and, in their excellent cars, bore down on each other. Thereupon their drivers, parading their skill as charioteers, advanced, circled and manoeuvred in various ways. In their rapid course and swift evolutions, those two marvellous chariots ranged the battlefield, whilst the two warriors discharged countless shafts on each other, like unto clouds letting loose their showers.

Having displayed their immeasurable resource in the use of weapons, those two champions halted face to face, chariot shaft to chariot shaft, their horses' heads touching, their standards in-

---

36. A title for the descendants of Kakutstha; here applied to Rama.

tertwined. Then Rama loosed four sharp arrows, driving back
Ravana's four spirited steeds and he, furious on beholding them
retreat, let fly his penetrating shafts on Raghava. . . .

The Long-armed Warrior, the increaser of the glory of the
Raghus, Rama, placed an arrow, like unto a venomous reptile,
on his bow and cut off one of Ravana's heads, whereupon
that glorious head, adorned with sparkling earrings, rolled on
the earth in the presence of the Three Worlds. Nevertheless
another, equal to the former, grew immediately and Rama,
with a steady hand, dexterously sundered the second head with
his shafts. Hardly was it eliminated when another head appeared which was severed once more by Rama's darts like unto
thunderbolts. Thereafter he struck off a hundred more, being
unable to bring Ravana low. . . .

The Death of Ravana

At that moment, Matali[37] sought to recall Raghava's thoughts,
saying:—"How is it that thou dost act in regard to Ravana as
if thou wert unaware of thine own powers? In order to bring
about his end, discharge Brahma's Weapon upon him, O Lord!
Foretold by the Gods, the hour of his doom is at hand!"

Prompted by Matali, Rama took up a flaming shaft that was
hissing like a viper, formerly bestowed on him by the magnanimous and powerful Sage Agastya.[38] A gift of the Grand-
sire, that weapon never missed its target and it had been created
of yore by Brahma for Indra and bestowed on the King of the
Gods for the conquest of the Three Worlds. In its wings was
the wind, in its point the fire and the sun, in its haft space, and,
in size, it resembled the Mountains Meru and Mandara. With
its marvellous point, haft and gilding, it was composed of the
essence of all the elements and was as resplendent as the sun.
Resembling the Fire of Time enveloped in smoke, it was like
unto an enormous snake and was capable of riving men, elephants, horses, gateways, bars and even rocks. . . .

37. Charioteer of the god Indra.
38. A great rishi, supposed author of several Rig Vedic hymns, who had
entertained Rama, Sita, and Lakshmana in his hermitage.

That marvellous and powerful shaft that was to destroy the titan was the object of terror to the worlds, the remover of the fear of the supporters of the Ikshvakus,[39] the depriver of the glory of the foe, and it filled Rama with delight. Having charged it with the sacred formula, the valiant Rama of indescribable prowess placed that excellent weapon on his bow according to the method prescribed by the Veda and, when he made ready, all beings were seized with terror and the earth shook. Enraged, he stretched his bow with force and, deploying his whole strength, discharged that weapon, the destroyer of the vital parts, on Ravana, and that irresistible shaft like unto lightning, irrevocable as fate, loosed by the arm of one equal to the God who bears the Thunderbolt, struck Ravana's breast. Loosed with exceeding force, that missile, the supreme destroyer, pierced the breast of the wicked-hearted titan and, covered with blood, that fatal dart having extinguished his vital breaths, buried itself in the earth. Thereafter, having slain Ravana, that shaft, stained with blood which dripped therefrom, its purpose accomplished, returned submissively to the quiver. . . .

Seeing him stretched on the ground, the rangers of the night who had escaped the carnage, struck with terror, their sovereign being slain, fled in all directions and, from every side, the monkeys . . . hurled themselves upon them, armed with trees. Harassed by the monkey divisions, the titans, terror-stricken, took refuge in Lanka and, having lost their lord, in despair, gave way to tears. . . .

The blessed Raghava, by slaying that Bull among the Titans, fulfilled the ambitions of Sugriva, Angada and Bibishana;[40] peace reigned over all; the cardinal points were stilled; the air became pure, the earth ceased to tremble, the wind blew gently and the star of the day regained its full glory.

. . . .

39. Descendants of Ikshvaku, the son of Manu, the supposed forefather of the human race. Many subsequent Indian kings traced their descent back to Manu through Ikshvaku.
40. Sugriva and Angada were monkeys; Bibishana was the titan who fought for Rama.

[Following his victory over the Titans, Rama sends for Sita.]

Rama Repudiates Sita

Beholding Maithili standing humbly beside him, Rama gave expression to the feelings he had concealed in his heart, saying:—

"O Illustrious Princess, I have re-won thee and mine enemy has been defeated on the battlefield; I have accomplished all that fortitude could do; my wrath is appeased; the insult and the one who offered it have both been obliterated by me. To-day my prowess has been manifested, to-day mine exertions have been crowned with success, to-day I have fulfilled my vow and am free. As ordained by destiny the stain of thy separation and thine abduction by that fickle-minded titan has been expunged by me, a mortal. Of what use is great strength to the vacillating, who do not with resolution avenge the insult offered to them? . . .

When Sita heard Rama speak in this wise, her large doe-like eyes filled with tears and, beholding the beloved of his heart standing close to him, Rama, who was apprehensive of public rumour, was torn within himself. Then, in the presence of the monkeys and the titans, he said to Sita, whose eyes were as large as lotus petals, her dark hair plaited, and who was endowed with faultless limbs:—

"What a man should do in order to wipe out an insult, I have done by slaying Ravana for I guard mine honour jealously! Thou wert re-won as the southern region, inaccessible to man, was re-gained by the pure-souled Agastya through his austerities. Be happy and let it be known that this arduous campaign, so gloriously terminated through the support of my friends, was not undertaken wholly for thy sake. I was careful to wipe out the affront paid to me completely and to avenge the insult offered to mine illustrious House.

"A suspicion has arisen, however, with regard to thy conduct, and thy presence is as painful to me as a lamp to one whose eye is diseased! Henceforth go where it best pleaseth thee, I give thee leave, O Daughter of Janaka. O Lovely One, the ten regions are at thy disposal; I can have nothing more to do with

thee! What man of honour would give rein to his passion so far
as to permit himself to take back a woman who has dwelt in
the house of another? Thou hast been taken into Ravana's lap
and he has cast lustful glances on thee; how can I reclaim thee,
I who boast of belonging to an illustrious House? The end
which I sought in re-conquering thee has been gained; I no
longer have any attachment for thee; go where thou desirest!
This is the outcome of my reflections, O Lovely One! Turn to
Lakshmana or Bharata, Shatrughna,[41] Sugriva or the Titan
Bibishana, make thy choice, O Sita, as pleases thee best. Assuredly Ravana, beholding thy ravishing and celestial beauty,
will not have respected thy person during the time that thou
didst dwell in his abode."

On this, that noble lady, worthy of being addressed in sweet
words, hearing that harsh speech from her beloved lord, who
for long had surrounded her with every homage, wept bitterly,
and she resembled a creeper that has been torn away by the
trunk of a great elephant.

Sita's Lamentations; She Undergoes the Ordeal by Fire

Hearing these harsh words from the wrathful Raghava, causing
her to tremble, those fearful utterances, which till that time had
never been heard by her and were now addressed to her by her
lord in the presence of a great multitude, Maithili, the daughter
of Janaka, overwhelmed with shame, pierced to the heart by
that arrow-like speech, shed abundant tears. Thereafter, wiping
her face, she addressed her husband in gentle and faltering accents, saying:—

"Why dost thou address such words to me, O Hero, as a common man addresses an ordinary woman? I swear to thee, O
Long-armed Warrior, that my conduct is worthy of thy respect!
It is the behaviour of other women that has filled thee with
distrust! Relinquish thy doubts since I am known to thee! If
my limbs came in contact with another's, it was against my
will, O Lord, and not through any inclination on my part; it
was brought about by fate. That which is under my control, my

41. Bharata and Shatrughna were Rama's younger brothers.

heart, has ever remained faithful to thee; my body was at the
mercy of another; not being mistress of the situation, what
could I do? If despite the proofs of love that I gave thee whilst
I lived with thee, I am still a stranger to thee, O Proud Prince,
my loss is irrevocable!

"When, in Lanka, thou didst dispatch the great warrior
Hanuman to seek me out, why didst thou not repudiate me then?
As soon as I had received the tidings that I had been abandoned by thee, I should have yielded up my life in the presence
of that monkey, O Hero! Then thou wouldst have been spared
useless fatigue on mine account and others, lives would not have
been sacrificed, nor thine innumerable friends exhausted to no
purpose. But thou, O Lion among Men, by giving way to wrath
and by thus passing premature judgement on a woman, hast
acted like a worthless man.

"I have received my name from Janaka, but my birth was
from the earth and thou hast failed to appreciate fully the
nobility of my conduct, O Thou who are well acquainted with
the nature of others. Thou hast had no reverence for the joining of our hands in my girlhood and mine affectionate nature,
all these things hast thou cast behind thee!"

Having spoken thus to Rama, weeping the while, her voice
strangled with sobs, Sita addressed the unfortunate Lakshmana,
who was overwhelmed with grief, saying:—

"Raise a pyre for me, O Saumitri, this is the only remedy for
my misery! These unjust reproaches have destroyed me, I cannot go on living! Publicly renounced by mine husband, who is
insensible to my virtue, there is only one redress for me, to
undergo the ordeal by fire!"

Hearing Vaidehi's words, Lakshmana, the slayer of hostile
warriors, a prey to indignation, consulted Raghava with his
glance and by Rama's gestures he understood what was in his
heart, whereupon the valiant Saumitri, following his indications, prepared the pyre.

None amongst his friends dared to appeal to Rama, who resembled Death himself, the Destroyer of Time; none dared to
speak or even to look upon him.

Thereafter Vaidehi, having circumambulated Rama, who stood with his head bowed, approached the blazing fire and, paying obeisance to the Celestials and brahmins, Maithili, with joined palms, standing before the flames, spoke thus:—

"As my heart has never ceased to be true to Raghava, do thou, O Witness of all Beings, grant me thy protection! As I am pure in conduct, though Rama looks on me as sullied, do thou, O Witness of the Worlds, grant me full protection!"

With these words, Vaidehi circumambulated the pyre and with a fearless heart entered the flames.

And a great multitude were assembled there, amongst which were many children and aged people who witnessed Maithili entering the fire. And, resembling gold that has been melted in the crucible, she threw herself into the blazing flames in the presence of all. That large-eyed lady, entering the fire, who is the Bearer of Sacrificial Offerings, appeared to those who watched her to resemble a golden altar. That fortunate princess entering the fire, which is nourished by oblations, seemed, in the eyes of the Rishis, Devas and Gandharvas, to resemble a sacrificial offering.

.   .   .   .

Sita Is Restored to Rama

.   .   .   .

Thereafter the Witness of the whole world, Pavaka,[42] addressed Rama, saying:—

"Here is Vaidehi, O Rama, there is no sin in her! Neither by word, feeling or glance has thy lovely consort shown herself to be unworthy of thy noble qualities. Separated from thee, that unfortunate one was borne away against her will in the lonely forest by Ravana, who had grown proud on account of his power. Though imprisoned and closely guarded by titan women in the inner apartments, thou wast ever the focus of her

42. Name for Agni, god of fire.

thoughts and her supreme hope. Surrounded by hideous and sinister women, though tempted and threatened, Maithili never gave place in her heart to a single thought for that titan and was solely absorbed in thee. She is pure and without taint, do thou receive Maithili; it is my command that she should not suffer reproach in any way."

These words filled Rama's heart with delight and he, the most eloquent of men, that loyal soul, reflected an instant within himself, his glance full of joy. Then the illustrious, steadfast and exceedingly valiant Rama, the first of virtuous men, hearing those words addressed to him, said to the Chief of the Gods:—

"On account of the people, it was imperative that Sita should pass through this trial by fire; this lovely woman had dwelt in Ravana's inner apartments for a long time. Had I not put the innocence of Janaki[43] to the test, the people would have said:— 'Rama, the son of Dasaratha is governed by lust!' It was well known to me that Sita had never given her heart to another and that the daughter of Janaka, Maithili, was ever devoted to me. Ravana was no more able to influence that large-eyed lady, whose chastity was her own protection, than the ocean may pass beyond its bournes. Despite his great perversity, he was unable to approach Maithili even in thought, who was inaccessible to him as a flame. That virtuous woman could never belong to any other than myself for she is to me what the light is to the sun. Her purity is manifest in the Three Worlds; I could no more renounce Maithili, born of Janaka than a hero his honour. It behoveth me to follow your wise and friendly counsel, O Gracious Lords of the World."

Having spoken thus, the victorious and extremely powerful Rama, full of glory, adored for his noble exploits, was re-united with his beloved and experienced the felicity he had merited.

[So ends the original story of Rama and Sita as it appears in the first six books of the *Ramayana*. But subsequently a "supplemental" Book VII was added, in which the question of Sita's fate was re-

43. Daughter of Janaka.

opened. This final book—which fits awkwardly into the structure of
the epic—evidently arose in response to a popular feeling that the
honor of a wife who has dwelt, albeit innocently, in another man's
house is *ipso facto* irrevocably compromised. Rama remains convinced
of Sita's innocence, but agrees to banish her as a concession to public opinion. Sita goes to the forest hermitage of the poet Valmiki,
where she gives birth to twin sons who grow up as hermit-boys
and become the poet's pupils. Many years later Valmiki and the
two boys attend a great horse-sacrifice given by Rama; Rama recognizes his sons and determines to recall his wife. Sita comes, but
her heart has been broken. In response to her plea, the earth opens
up and she disappears forever into the abyss.]

Introduction to the Laws of Manu

Hindu legal science had its origins in the theological schools
formed to perpetuate the holy text of the Vedas and give instruction in the subsidiary disciplines connected with the sacrifice.* The
same schools produced textbooks for their students on the subject
of *dharma*, or moral law. These early law-books consist of quota-
tions from the Vedas as interpreted and applied in practice by
worthy Brahmins well versed in Aryan customs. They are composed in the form of *sutras* ("threads")—short, pithy sayings designed to express an idea in a few well-chosen words and thereby
render easier the task of memorization. Four of these ancient
Dharma Sutras† have come down to us, dating from between the
sixth and second centuries B.C. They are in no sense full and systematic expositions of the law, but didactic works dealing with
moral conduct, the sanctions for which were religious, not judicial. While in certain respects their stipulations are minute in the

---

* These subsidiary disciplines are known as the Vedangas, or "Limbs of the
Veda." They are six in number, namely: ritual (the correct performance of
the sacrifice); phonetics (correct pronunciation); prosody; etymology (inter-
pretation of obscure terms); grammar; and astronomy (calendar science).
† The Dharma Sutras attributed to Gautama, Baudhyana, Vasishtha, and
Apastamba respectively.

extreme, the Dharma Sutras omit many crucial areas of the law; and their treatment of civil and criminal law and legal procedure is quite rudimentary. The aim was not to provide for all possible contingencies, but rather to inculcate general principles.

As the accumulation of Vedic learning gradually became too great for any one person to master, more specialized schools were established for the various branches of Vedic study. Thereby the Sacred Law became a separate science, and a new form of literature came into being: the metrical Dharma Shastra.* Each of these later law-books seems to have been based upon a particular Dharma Sutra, which was expanded, remodeled, and rendered into verse. The Dharma Shastras treat legal topics in a more sophisticated and systematic fashion than did their predecessors; and regulations concerning the duties of kings and the administration of justice occupy a greater proportion of the whole.

The *Laws of Manu* (or *Manava Dharma Shastra*) is the earliest of these verse law-books now extant. Apparently it was based originally on a *Manava Dharma Sutra,* now lost, which belonged to a school in northwest India devoted to the Yajur Veda. Composed sometime between the first century B.C. and the second or third century A.D., the *Laws of Manu* represent an advance in precision and completeness over the Dharma Sutras, but are less technical than the later law-books of the Gupta period or the Middle Ages. They are still more concerned with moral duties than with exact legal distinctions and definitions; and they threaten offenders with divine as well as civil punishment.

In contrast to the Dharma Sutras, which admit that their authors were only human, the *Laws of Manu* profess to be of divine origin. The first chapter gives an account of the creation of the world, at which time the Supreme Being revealed his Sacred Law to Manu, the father of mankind. The name of Manu in India is surrounded by many legends. In the Vedas he is described as the founder of the human social order and the original teacher of *dharma*. Manu is a son of the Supreme Being, invoked in the sacrifice as Prajapati, the lord of creation; but also named as one of the (human) sages of antiquity. "Father Manu" is the Indian Noah. Tradition records that he was saved by the advice of a fish from a great flood which destroyed all other living creatures. After the flood he engaged in

---

* Though Dharma Sutras and Dharma Shastras are sometimes referred to collectively as Dharma Shastras, here the term is used to signify only the metrical law-books.

ascetic practices and produced a woman, through whom he created the ancestors of the human race.

The claim of the *Laws of Manu* to be the original Indian law-book is obviously fictitious, and is in fact a rather late addition to the work. A number of verses openly admit an acquaintance with the Dharma Sutras and refer to the opinions of predecessors on various points. The evident contradictions in some of the views expressed likewise suggest that the compiler was remodeling an earlier work. It is significant that a large number of verses from the *Laws of Manu* can also be found, partially or wholly, in the *Mahabharata*, the Puranas (popular compendia of mythology), and certain Buddhist writings. The correspondences are insufficiently exact to permit the assumption that one work borrowed directly from another; probably all of them drew upon a common store of traditional wisdom. An ancient compiler would have found no incongruity in attributing various well-known sayings to Manu: any valid maxim could be regarded as derived from the original teacher of *dharma*.

Though the precepts of each Dharma Sutra seem to have applied only to its particular sect, the *Laws of Manu* admit no such exclusiveness. Evidently the book was produced by one of the specialized schools of the Sacred Law, who regarded their rules as binding on all Aryans. The very fact that the *Laws* are ascribed to the father of the human race indicates that they were intended to be valid for all Hindu schools of thought. Later Indian jurists regarded the work with great reverence and frequently quoted from it; it was classed as *smriti*, or sacred tradition. In the eighteenth century the book gained a fresh lease on life. The British East India Company sought to rule its Indian territories by a system familiar to the people; and the code selected for this purpose was none other than the *Laws of Manu*.

The Four Stages of Life

In traditional Indian theory, the well-spent life for an upper-class male consisted of four stages—that of the student, the house-holder, the forest-dweller, and finally, the wandering ascetic. This scheme—already pre-supposed by the Dharma Sutras, but formulated more precisely by the *Laws of Manu*—represented a balance between world-affirmation and world-renunciation. Following a period of preparatory education, the Indian was supposed to lead the ordinary life of husband, father, and provider; and only in late middle life devote himself exclusively to the pursuit of spiritual redemption. But certainly this ideal program was never followed by more than a small proportion of men: many undoubtedly never went beyond the householding stage; a few might become ascetics without ever having been householders; and the third and fourth stages tended to merge into one.

All the law books devote considerable attention to the stage of studentship, when the boy received instruction in the Vedas. The Vedas were *shruti*—scriptures directly revealed by God—in which every syllable was holy and semi-magical in its efficacy. It was of utmost importance that only the proper persons—members of the three highest classes leading a pure life—should have access to them. Detailed regulations prescribed the places and seasons at which the Vedas might be studied. Typically, the student lived as a servant in his teacher's house, learning the sacred lore by rote. The teacher was expected to lead a holy life, in conformance with his teaching; the student owed him reverence and unquestioned trust.

Having completed his course of instruction, the student returned home, married, and entered upon the life of a householder. He engaged in all the usual worldly activities and was free to pursue *artha* and *kama*. His obligations (*dharma*) included the performance of certain religious rites and conformity with prescribed norms of personal behavior. The law books set down in minute detail such matters as what he might and might not eat, when he could approach his wife, how he ought to treat guests, and what occupations he was allowed to pursue.

When his sons were grown, he was free to enter the third stage, that of the hermit in the forest. Perhaps together with his wife, he then began another period of preparation, free from the concerns and distractions of his former householder's life. While in the forest, he was supposed to live simply, restricting his diet to certain items, performing ceremonies in honor of the gods, and meditating. Thereby he acquired sufficient spiritual merit to pass into the fourth stage. As a wandering ascetic, he would live out the remainder of his life, indifferent to the world and absorbed solely by the search for salvation.

FROM THE LAWS OF MANU

THE STUDENT (*brahmacharyin*)
Chapter II

109 According to the sacred law the (following) ten (persons, viz.) the teacher's son, one who desires to do service, one who imparts knowledge, one who is intent on fulfilling the law, one who is pure, a person connected by marriage or friendship, one who possesses (mental) ability, one who makes presents of money, one who is honest, and a relative, may be instructed (in the Veda).

110 Unless one be asked, one must not explain (anything) to anybody, nor (must one answer) a person who asks improperly; let a wise man, though he knows (the answer), behave among men as (if he were) an idiot.

111 Of the two persons, him who illegally explains (anything), and him who illegally asks (a question), one (or both) will die[1] or incur (the other's) enmity.

112 Where merit and wealth are not (obtained by teaching) nor (at least) due obedience, in such (soil) sacred knowledge must not be sown, just as good seed (must) not (be thrown) on barren land.

113 Even in times of dire distress a teacher of the Veda should rather die with his knowledge than sow it in barren soil.

114 Sacred Learning approached a Brahmin and said to him: "I am thy treasure, preserve me, deliver me not to a scorner; so (preserved) I shall become supremely strong.[2]

115 "But deliver me, as to the keeper of thy treasure, to a Brahmin whom thou shalt know to be pure, of subdued senses, chaste and attentive."

The following selections, from the Four Stages of Life through Personal Injury, are from *The Laws of Manu*, trans. by Georg Buehler in Vol. 25 of *The Sacred Books of the East* (Oxford: at the Clarendon Press, 1886).

1. The offender will die; if both offend, both will die.
2. This was a favorite verse of the Brahmins; it appears also in other ancient texts.

116 But he who acquires without permission the Veda from one who recites it, incurs the guilt of stealing the Veda, and shall sink into hell.

.   .   .   .

146 Of him who gives natural birth and him who gives (the knowledge of) the Veda, the giver of the Veda is the more venerable father; for the birth for the sake of the Veda (ensures) eternal (rewards) both in this (life) and after death.

147 Let him consider that (he received) a (mere animal) existence, when his parents begat him through mutual affection, and when he was born from the womb (of his mother).

148 But that birth which a teacher acquainted with the whole Veda, in accordance with the law, procures for him through the *Savitri*,[3] is real, exempt from age and death.

149 (The pupil) must know that that man also who benefits him by (instruction in) the Veda, be it little or much, is called in these (Institutes) his Guru, in consequence of that benefit (conferred by instruction in) the Veda.

150 That Brahmin who is the giver of the birth for the sake of the Veda and the teacher of the prescribed duties becomes by law the father of an aged man, even though he himself be a child.

151 Young Kavi, the son of Angiras,[4] taught his (relatives who were old enough to be) fathers, and, as he excelled them in (sacred) knowledge, he called them "Little sons."

152 They, moved with resentment, asked the gods concerning that matter, and the gods, having assembled, answered, "The child has addressed you properly.

153 "For (a man) destitute of (sacred) knowledge is indeed a child, and he who teaches him the Veda is his father; for (the sages) have always said 'child' to an ignorant man, and 'father' to a teacher of the Veda."

3. The *Savitri* is the holiest verse of the Vedas. It is repeated at all sacred ceremonies, especially at the rite of initiation in which the boy becomes a full member of his class.
4. The Angiras were an ancient priestly family mentioned prominently in the Rig Veda.

154 Neither through years, nor through white (hairs), nor through wealth, nor through (powerful) kinsmen (comes greatness). The sages have made this law, "He who has learnt the Veda together with the Angas[5] is (considered) great by us."

155 The seniority of Brahmins is from (sacred) knowledge, that of Kshatriyas from valour, that of Vaishyas from wealth in grain (and other goods), but that of Shudras alone from age.

156 A man is not therefore (considered) venerable because his head is gray; him who, though young, has learned the Veda, the gods consider to be venerable.

. . . .

175 A student who resides with his teacher must observe the following restrictive rules, duly controlling all his organs, in order to increase his spiritual merit.

176 Every day, having bathed, and being purified, he must offer libations of water to the gods, sages and spirits, worship (the images of) the gods, and place fuel on (the sacred fire).

177 Let him abstain from honey, meat, perfumes, garlands, substances (used for) flavouring (food), women, all substances turned acid, and from doing injury to living creatures.

178 From anointing (his body), applying collyrium to his eyes, from the use of shoes and of an umbrella (or parasol), from (sensual) desire, anger, covetousness, dancing, singing, and playing (musical instruments),

179 From gambling, idle disputes, backbiting, and lying, from looking at and touching women, and from hurting others.

180 Let him always sleep alone, let him never waste his manhood; for he who voluntarily wastes his manhood, breaks his vow.

181 A twice-born[6] student, who has involuntarily wasted his

5. Or Vedangas, "limbs of the Veda"—the six auxiliary disciplines necessary for the performance of the sacrifice, namely phonetics, ritual, grammar, etymology, prosody, and astronomy.

6. The twice-born were those members of the three upper *varnas* who had undergone the sacred initiation, which constituted a "second birth."

manly strength during sleep, must bathe, worship the sun, and afterwards thrice mutter the Rig-verse (which begins), "Again let my strength return to me."

182 Let him fetch a pot full of water, flowers, cowdung, earth, and *kusha* grass, as much as may be required (by his teacher), and daily go to beg food.

183 A student, being pure, shall daily bring food from the houses of men who are not deficient in (the knowledge of) the Veda and in (performing) sacrifices, and who are famous for (following their lawful) occupations.

184 Let him not beg from the relatives of his teacher, nor from his own or his mother's blood-relations; but if there are no houses belonging to strangers, let him go to one of those named above, taking the last-named first;

185 Or, if there are no (virtuous men of the kind) mentioned above, he may go to each (house in the) village, being pure and remaining silent; but let him avoid those accused of mortal sin.

186 Having brought sacred fuel from a distance, let him place it anywhere but on the ground, and let him, unwearied, make with it burnt oblations to the sacred fire, both evening and morning.

187 He who, without being sick, neglects during seven (successive) days to go out begging, and to offer fuel in the sacred fire, shall perform the penance of one who has broken his vow.

188 He who performs the vow (of studentship) shall constantly subsist on alms, (but) not eat the food of one (person only); the subsistence of a student on begged food is declared to be equal (in merit) to fasting.

189 At his pleasure he may eat, when invited, the food of one man at (a rite) in honour of the gods, observing (however the conditions of) his vow, or at a (funeral meal) in honour of the spirits, behaving (however) like a hermit.

190 This duty is prescribed by the wise for a Brahmin only; but no such duty is ordained for a Kshatriya and a Vaishya.

191 Both when ordered by his teacher, and without a (special) command, (a student) shall always exert himself in study-

ing (the Veda), and in doing what is serviceable to his
teacher.

THE HOUSEHOLDER *(grhastha)*
Chapter III

1   The vow (of studying) the three Vedas under a teacher
    must be kept for thirty-six years, or for half that time, or
    for a quarter, or until the (student) has perfectly learnt
    them.

2   (A student) who has studied in due order the three Vedas,
    or two, or even one only, without breaking the (rules of)
    studentship, shall enter the order of householders.

3   He who is famous for (the strict performance of) his duties
    and has received his heritage, the Veda, from his father,[7]
    shall be honoured, sitting on a couch and adorned with a
    garland, with (the present of) a cow (and the honey-
    mixture).

4   Having bathed, with the permission of his teacher, and
    performed according to the rule the rite on returning home,
    a twice-born man shall marry a wife of equal caste who is
    endowed with auspicious (bodily) marks.

5   A (damsel) who is neither a *Sapinda*[8] on the mother's side,
    nor belongs to the same family on the father's side, is rec-
    ommended to twice-born men for wedlock and conjugal
    union.

6   In connecting himself with a wife, let him carefully avoid
    the ten following families, be they ever so great, or rich in
    kine, horses, sheep, grain, or (other) property,

7   (Viz.) one which neglects the sacred rites, one in which no
    male children (are born), one in which the Veda is not
    studied, one (the members of) which have thick hair on
    the body, those which are subject to hemorrhoids, phthisis,
    weakness of digestion, epilepsy, or white and black leprosy.

10 Let him wed a female free from bodily defects, who has

---

7. The term includes "spiritual father."
8. A *Sapinda* is someone descended from one's maternal ancestors within
the sixth degree.

an agreeable name, the (graceful) gait of a *Hamsa*[9] or of an elephant, a moderate (quantity of) hair on the body and on the head, small teeth, and soft limbs.

11 But a prudent man should not marry (a maiden) who has no brother, nor one whose father is not known, through fear lest (in the former case she be made) an appointed daughter[10] (and in the latter) lest (he should commit) sin.[11]

12 For the first marriage of twice-born men (wives) of equal caste are recommended; but for those who through desire proceed (to marry again) the following females, (chosen) according to the (direct) order (of the castes), are most approved.[12]

13 It is declared that a Shudra woman alone (can be) the wife of a Shudra, she and one of his own caste (the wives) of a Vaishya, those two and one of his own caste (the wives) of a Kshatriya, those three and one of his own caste (the wives) of a Brahmin.

14 A Shudra woman is not mentioned even in any (ancient) story as the (first) wife of a Brahmin or of a Kshatriya, though they lived in the (greatest) distress.

15 Twice-born men who, in their folly, wed wives of the low (Shudra) caste, soon degrade their families and their children to the state of Shudras.

THE FOREST DWELLER *(vanaprastha)*
Chapter VI

2 When a householder sees his (skin) wrinkled, and (his hair) white, and the sons of his sons, then he may resort to the forest.

3 Abandoning all food raised by cultivation, and all his be-

9. A kind of large bird.
10. Lest the father should take her first son as his own to perform his funeral rites.
11. That is, contract marriage with someone of a forbidden class.
12. This stipulation is now obsolete in India; among those who respect caste regulations, marriages are contracted only within much smaller groupings.

longings, he may depart into the forest, either committing his wife to his sons, or accompanied by her.

4 Taking with him the sacred fire and the implements required for domestic (sacrifices), he may go forth from the village into the forest and reside there, duly controlling his senses.

5 Let him offer those five great sacrifices according to the rule, with various kinds of pure food fit for ascetics, or with herbs, roots, and fruit.

6 Let him wear a skin or a tattered garment; let him bathe in the evening or in the morning; and let him always wear (his hair in) braids, the hair on his body, his beard, and his nails (being unclipped).

7 Let him perform the Bali-offering[13] with such food as he eats, and give alms according to his ability; let him honour those who come to his hermitage with alms consisting of water, roots, and fruit.

8 Let him be always industrious in privately reciting the Veda; let him be patient of hardships, friendly (towards all), of collected mind, ever liberal and never a receiver of gifts, and compassionate towards all living creatures.

23 In summer let him expose himself to the heat of five fires, during the rainy season live under the open sky, and in winter be dressed in wet clothes, (thus) gradually increasing (the rigour of) his austerities.

24 When he bathes at sunrise, midday, and sunset, let him offer libations of water to the spirits and the gods, and practising harsher and harsher austerities, let him dry up his bodily frame.

25 Having reposited the three sacred fires in himself, according to the prescribed rule, let him live without a fire, without a house, wholly silent, subsisting on roots and fruit,

26 Making no effort (to procure) things that give pleasure, chaste, sleeping on the bare ground, not caring for any shelter, dwelling at the roots of trees.

27 From Brahmins (who live as) ascetics, let him receive

13. The offering of edible fruits to the divinities.

alms, (barely sufficient) to support life, or from other householders of the twice-born (castes) who reside in the forest.

28 Or (the hermit) who dwells in the forest may bring (food) from a village, receiving it either in a hollow dish (of leaves), in (his naked) hand, or in a broken earthen dish, and may eat eight mouthfuls.

29 These and other observances must a Brahmin who dwells in the forest diligently practise, and in order to attain complete (union with) the (supreme) Soul, (he must study) the various sacred texts contained in the Upanishads,[14]

30 (As well as those rites and texts) which have been practised and studied by the sages (Rishis), and by Brahmin householders, in order to increase their knowledge (of Brahman[15]), and their austerity, and in order to sanctify their bodies;

31 Or let him walk, fully determined and going straight on, in a north-easterly direction, subsisting on water and air, until his body sinks to rest.

32 A Brahmin, having got rid of his body by one of those modes practised by the great sages,[16] is exalted in the world of Brahman, free from sorrow and fear.

THE WANDERING ASCETIC (*sannyasin*)
Chapter VI

33 But having thus passed the third part of (a man's natural term of) life in the forest, he may live as an ascetic during the fourth part of his existence, after abandoning all attachment to worldly objects.

34 He who after passing from order to order, after offering sacrifices and subduing his senses, becomes, tired with (giving) alms and offerings of food, an ascetic, gains bliss after death.

35 When he has paid the three debts, let him apply his mind

14. For a sample of Upanishadic texts, see below, pp. 186-96.
15. The world-spirit, or Supreme Soul.
16. I.e., by drowning oneself, throwing oneself from a high place, burning oneself, or starving oneself to death.

to (the attainment of) final liberation; he who seeks it
without having paid (his debts) sinks downwards.

36 Having studied the Vedas in accordance with the rule,
having begat sons according to the sacred law, and having
offered sacrifices according to his ability, he may direct
his mind to (the attainment of) final liberation.

37 A twice-born man who seeks final liberation, without having studied the Vedas, without having begotten sons, and
without having offered sacrifices, sinks downwards.

. . . .

41 Departing from his house fully provided with the means
of purification,[17] let him wander about absolutely silent,
and caring nothing for enjoyments that may be offered
(to him).

42 Let him always wander alone, without any companion, in
order to attain (final liberation), fully understanding that
the solitary (man, who) neither forsakes nor is forsaken,
gains his end.

43 He shall possess neither a fire, nor a dwelling, he may go
to a village for his food, (he shall be) indifferent to everything, firm of purpose, meditating (and) concentrating his
mind on Brahman.

44 A potsherd (instead of an alms-bowl), the roots of trees
(for a dwelling), coarse worn-out garments, life in solitude
and indifference towards everything, are the marks of one
who has attained liberation.

45 Let him not desire to die, let him not desire to live; let him
wait for (his appointed) time, as a servant (waits) for the
payment of his wages.

46 Let him put down his foot purified by his sight, let him
drink water purified by (straining with) a cloth, let him
utter speech purified by truth, let him keep his heart pure.

47 Let him patiently bear hard words, let him not insult anybody, and let him not become anybody's enemy for the
sake of this (perishable) body.

17. His staff, water-pot, perhaps also the sacred *kusha* grass and the skin of
a black antelope.

48 Against an angry man let him not in return show anger,
    let him bless when he is cursed, and let him not utter
    speech, devoid of truth, scattered at the seven gates.

49 Delighting in what refers to the Soul, sitting (in the pos-
    tures prescribed by the Yoga),[18] independent (of external
    help), entirely abstaining from sensual enjoyments, with
    himself for his only companion, he shall live in this world,
    desiring the bliss (of final liberation).

18. On Yoga, see below, pp. 197-202.

The Four Varnas

The word *varna* means "color" and refers to the organization of
Indian society into four occupational classes: Brahmins (priests
and teachers), Kshatriyas (warriors), Vaishyas (artisans and busi-
nessmen), and Shudras (servants). This division of labor, together
with the tendency of sons to continue in the professions of their
fathers, is characteristic of many developing societies. But in India,
occupational distinctions became hereditary. The barriers became
progressively more rigid between the classes—and between those
belonging to the class-order and those excluded from it.

The earliest portions of the Vedas, which go back to the period
of the Aryan invasions of India, give evidence of a much more fluid
social structure than that described in subsequent literature. Presumably the Aryans' sense of exclusiveness developed gradually in
the course of their wars against the indigenous inhabitants of the
country—the so-called *Dasyus*, who probably represent the sur-
vivors of the ancient Indus culture. In any event, the distinctions
of *varna* gradually acquired a sacred character. The Dharma Sutras and the *Laws of Manu* accept them as part of the immemorial
order of the universe.

The notion of *varna* thus became inseparably intertwined with
that of *dharma*. The class into which a person was born determined
the nature of his moral and religious obligations. Nothing in this
present life could alter his class affiliation; according to the law of

karma, one's current status was the direct result of actions in previous lives. Those fortunate persons who belonged to one of the
higher classes felt they had earned their places through past merit;
those of the lower classes could hope to be reborn into a higher
one through faithfully fulfilling the duties of their present station in
life. Thus the duties of each class as taught in the law books had a
supernatural sanction, affecting a person's status in many lives to
come.

But the regulations set down in the Dharma Sutras and the *Laws
of Manu* did not yet approach the rigidity and complexity of the
later Hindu caste system. In the twelfth and thirteenth centuries A.D.,
large numbers of Muslims settled down in north India, thereby
introducing a permanently alien element into the social fabric. Islam
recognizes no inborn, hereditary class distinctions; Hindu society
responded by making its own class divisions stricter and more complicated. Close association among persons of different castes became
almost unthinkable; and non-Hindus (even the later British over-
lords) were regarded as totally beyond the pale.

The word *varna* is often translated as "caste," though this is not
quite accurate. Caste is a more minute designation, with no necessary relation to *varna;* the Indian term for it is *jati,* "species."
Nowadays there are probably several thousand castes in India, each
separated from the others by elaborate rules prescribing with whom
a member may eat and whom he or she may marry. Although the
ancient division into *varnas* is still maintained, the modern Indian's social status is determined rather by caste than by *varna.* In
recent decades the Government of India—following the example of
Gandhi—has made extensive efforts to mitigate the worst effects of
caste prejudice. But even for those who intellectually reject the idea
of caste, the weight of tradition often proves overwhelming. For the
vast majority of Hindus, the regulations of caste still govern the
major forms of personal intercourse.

FROM THE LAWS OF MANU
Chapter IX

317 A Brahmin, be he ignorant or learned, is a great divinity,
just as the fire, whether carried forth (for the performance
of a burnt-oblation) or not carried forth, is a great divinity.
318 The brilliant fire is not contaminated even in burial-

places,[1] and, when presented with oblations (of butter) at sacrifices, it again increases mightily.

319 Thus, though Brahmins employ themselves in all (sorts of) mean occupations, they must be honoured in every way; for (each of) them is a very great deity.

320 When the Kshatriyas become in any way overbearing towards the Brahmins, the Brahmins themselves shall duly restrain them; for the Kshatriyas sprang from the Brahmins.

321 Fire sprang from water,[2] Kshatriyas from Brahmins,[3] iron from stone; the all-penetrating force of those (three) has no effect on that whence they were produced.

322 Kshatriyas prosper not without Brahmins, Brahmins prosper not without Kshatriyas; Brahmins and Kshatriyas, being closely united, prosper in this (world) and in the next.

.   .   .   .

326 After a Vaishya has received the sacraments and has taken a wife, he shall be always attentive to the business whereby he may subsist and to (that of) tending cattle.

327 For when the Lord of creatures (Prajapati) created cattle, he made them over to the Vaishya; to the Brahmin, and to the king he entrusted all created beings.

328 A Vaishya must never (conceive this) wish, "I will not keep cattle"; and if a Vaishya is willing (to keep them), they must never be kept by (men of) other (castes).

329 (A Vaishya) must know the respective value of gems, of pearls, of coral, of metals, of (cloth) made of thread, of perfumes, and of condiments.

330 He must be acquainted with the (manner of) sowing of seeds, and of the good and bad qualities of fields, and he must perfectly know all measures and weights.

331 Moreover, the excellence and defects of commodities, the

1. Burial places, like corpses, were regarded as contaminating.
2. As in the case of lightning from rain.
3. Possibly this refers to a story in the Puranas according to which, after all Kshatriya men had been destroyed, the Brahmins produced a new Kshatriya race through intercourse with Kshatriya women.

advantages and disadvantages of (different) countries, the (probable) profit and loss on merchandise, and the means of properly rearing cattle.

332 He must be acquainted with the (proper) wages of servants, with the various languages of men, with the manner of keeping goods, and (the rules of) purchase and sale.

333 Let him exert himself to the utmost in order to increase his property in a righteous manner, and let him zealously give food to all created beings.

334 But to serve Brahmins (who are) learned in the Vedas, householders, and famous (for virtue) is the highest duty of a Shudra, which leads to beatitude.

335 (A Shudra who is) pure, the servant of his betters, gentle in his speech, and free from pride, and always seeks a refuge with Brahmins, attains (in his next life) a higher caste.

336 The excellent law for the conduct of the (four) castes (*varna*), (when they are) not in distress, has been thus promulgated; now hear in order their (several duties) in times of distress.

Chapter X

51 The dwellings of *Chandalas*[4] and *Svapakas*[5] shall be outside the village, they must be made *Apapatras*,[6] and their wealth (shall be) dogs and donkeys.

52 Their dress (shall be) the garments of the dead, (they shall eat) their food from broken dishes, black iron (shall be) their ornaments, and they must always wander from place to place.

53 A man who fulfils a religious duty,[7] shall not seek intercourse with them; their transactions (shall be) among

4. Outcastes; persons not belonging to any of the four *varnas*. According to Manu, a Chandala is the offspring of a Shudra man and a Brahmin woman.
5. Another type of outcaste, the offspring of a Kshatriya man and a woman of mixed Kshatriya-Shudra parentage.
6. According to one ancient Indian commentator, Apapatras are persons to whom the following stipulations apply: vessels used by them must be thrown away; if food is given to them, it must be placed in vessels standing on the ground or held by others; they must use only broken vessels.
7. Or: a righteous man.

themselves, and their marriages with their equals.

54 Their food shall be given to them by others (than an Aryan giver) in a broken dish; at night they shall not walk about in villages and in towns.

55 By day they may go about for the purpose of their work, distinguished by marks[8] at the king's command, and they shall carry out the corpses (of persons) who have no relatives; that is a settled rule.

56 By the king's order they shall always execute the criminals, in accordance with the law, and they shall take for themselves the clothes, the beds, and the ornaments of (such) criminals.

57 A man of impure origin, who belongs not to any *varna*, (whose character is) not known, who, (though) not an Aryan, has the appearance of an Aryan, one may discover by his acts.

58 Behaviour unworthy of an Aryan, harshness, cruelty, and habitual neglect of the prescribed duties betray in this world a man of impure origin.

59 A base-born man either resembles in character his father, or his mother, or both; he can never conceal his real nature.

60 Even if a man, born in a great family, sprang from criminal intercourse, he will certainly possess the faults of his (father), be they small or great.

61 But that kingdom in which such bastards, sullying (the purity of) the castes, are born, perishes quickly together with its inhabitants.

62 Dying, without the expectation of a reward, for the sake of Brahmins and of cows, or in the defence of women and children, secures beatitude to those excluded (from the Aryan community).

. . . .

74 Brahmins who are intent on the means (of gaining union with) Brahman and firm in (discharging) their duties, shall live by duly performing the following six acts, (which are enumerated) in their (proper) order.

8. I.e., carrying axes or other implements used for executing criminals; or possibly branded on the forehead.

75 Teaching, studying, sacrificing for himself, sacrificing for others, making gifts and receiving them are the six acts (prescribed) for a Brahmin.

76 But among the six acts (ordained) for him three are his means of subsistence, (viz.) sacrificing for others, teaching, and accepting gifts from pure men.

77 (Passing) from the Brahmin to the Kshatriya, three acts (incumbent on the former) are forbidden, (viz.) teaching, sacrificing for others, and, thirdly, the acceptance of gifts.

78 The same are likewise forbidden to a Vaishya, that is a settled rule; for Manu, the lord of creatures (Prajapati), has not prescribed them for (men of) those two (castes).

79 To carry arms for striking and for throwing (is prescribed) for Kshatriyas as a means of subsistence; to trade, (to rear) cattle, and agriculture for Vaishyas; but their duties are liberality, the study of the Veda, and the performance of sacrifices.

80 Among the several occupations the most commendable are, teaching the Veda for a Brahmin, protecting (the people) for a Kshatriya, and trade for a Vaishya.

81 But a Brahmin, unable to subsist by his peculiar occupations just mentioned, may live according to the law applicable to Kshatriyas; for the latter is next to him in rank.

82 If it be asked, "How shall it be, if he cannot maintain himself by either (of these occupations?" the answer is), he may adopt a Vaishya's mode of life, employing himself in agriculture and rearing cattle.

83 But a Brahmin, or a Kshatriya, living by a Vaishya's mode of subsistence, shall carefully avoid (the pursuit of) agriculture, (which causes) injury to many beings and depends on others.[9]

84 (Some) declare that agriculture is something excellent, (but) that means of subsistence is blamed by the virtuous; (for) the wooden (implement) with iron point injures the earth and (the beings) living in the earth.

9. E.g., on draft animals. According to the *Laws of Manu* IV, 159-60, the virtuous man should avoid all undertakings the success of which depends upon others.

85 But he who, through a want of means of subsistence, gives up the strictness with respect to his duties, may sell, in order to increase his wealth, the commodities sold by Vaishyas, making (however) the (following) exceptions.

86 He must avoid (selling) condiments of all sorts, cooked food and sesamum, stones, salt, cattle, and human (beings),

87 All dyed cloth, as well as cloth made of hemp, or flax, or wool, even though they be not dyed, fruit, roots, and (medical) herbs;

88 Water, weapons, poison, meat, *soma*,[10] and perfumes of all kinds, fresh milk, honey, sour milk, clarified butter, oil, wax, sugar, *kusha* grass;

89 All beasts of the forest, animals with fangs or tusks, birds, spirituous liquor, indigo, lac, and all one-hoofed beasts.

90 But he who subsists by agriculture, may at pleasure sell unmixed sesamum grains for sacred purposes provided he himself has grown them and has not kept them long.

91 If he applies sesamum to any other purpose but food, anointing, and charitable gifts, he will be born (again) as a worm and, together with his ancestors, be plunged into the ordure of dogs.

92 By (selling) flesh, salt, and lac a Brahmin at once becomes an outcast; by selling milk he becomes (equal to) a Shudra in three days.

93 But by willingly selling in this world other (forbidden) commodities, a Brahmin assumes after seven nights the character of a Vaishya.

94 Condiments may be bartered for condiments, but by no means salt for (other) condiments; cooked food (may be exchanged) for (other kinds of) cooked food, and sesamum seeds for grain in equal quantities.

95 A Kshatriya who has fallen into distress, may subsist by all these (means); but he must never arrogantly adopt the mode of life (prescribed for his) betters.

96 A man of low caste who through covetousness lives by the

10. Soma was an intoxicating juice used in the sacrifice.

occupations of a higher one, the king shall deprive of his property and banish.

97 It is better (to discharge) one's own (appointed) duty incompletely than to perform completely that of another; for he who lives according to the law of another (caste) is instantly excluded from his own.[11]

98 A Vaishya who is unable to subsist by his own duties, may even maintain himself by a Shudra's mode of life, avoiding (however) acts forbidden (to him), and he should give it up, when he is able (to do so).

99 But a Shudra, being unable to find service with the twice-born[12] and threatened with the loss of his sons and wife (through hunger), may maintain himself by handicrafts.

100 (Let him follow) those mechanical occupations and those various practical arts by following which the twice-born are (best) served.

101 A Brahmin who is distressed through a want of means of subsistence and pines (with hunger), (but) unwilling to adopt a Vaishya's mode of life and resolved to follow his own (prescribed) path, may act in the following manner.

102 A Brahmin who has fallen into distress may accept (gifts) from anybody; for according to the law it is not possible (to assert) that anything pure can be sullied.

103 By teaching, by sacrificing for, and by accepting gifts from despicable (men) Brahmins (in distress) commit not sin; for they (are as pure) as fire and water.

104 He who, when in danger of losing his life, accepts food from any person whatsoever, is no more tainted by sin than the sky by mud.

116 Learning,[13] mechanical arts, work for wages, service, rearing cattle, traffic, agriculture, contentment (with little), alms, and receiving interest on money, are the ten modes of subsistence (permitted to all men in times of distress).

117 Neither a Brahmin, nor a Kshatriya must lend (money at)

11. A similar verse may be found in the *Bhagavad Gita*, III. 35.
12. Members of the Brahmin, Kshatriya, or Vaishya classes.
13. I.e., teaching other than Vedic sciences, e.g., logic, charms, exorcism.

interest; but at his pleasure (either of them) may, in times of distress (when he requires money) for sacred purposes, lend to a very sinful man at a small interest.

118 A Kshatriya (king) who, in times of distress, takes even the fourth part (of the crops), is free from guilt, if he protects his subjects to the best of his ability.

119 His peculiar duty is conquest, and he must not turn back in danger; having protected the Vaishyas by his weapons, he may cause the legal tax to be collected;

120 (Viz.) from Vaishyas one-eighth as the tax on grain, one-twentieth (on the profits on gold and cattle), which amount at least to one *karshapana*;[14] Shudras, artisans, and mechanics (shall) benefit (the king) by (doing) work (for him).

121 If a Shudra, (unable to subsist by serving Brahmins,) seeks a livelihood, he may serve Kshatriyas, or he may also seek to maintain himself by attending on a wealthy Vaishya.

122 But let a (Shudra) serve Brahmins, either for the sake of heaven, or with a view to both (this life and the next); for he who is called the servant of a Brahmin thereby gains all his ends.

123 The service of Brahmins alone is declared (to be) an excellent occupation for a Shudra; for whatever else besides this he may perform will bear him no fruit.

124 They must allot to him out of their own family (-property) a suitable maintenance, after considering his ability, his industry, and the number of those whom he is bound to support.

125 The remnants of their food must be given to him, as well as their old clothes, the refuse of their grain, and their old household furniture.

126 A Shudra cannot commit an offence, causing loss of caste, and he is not worthy to receive the sacraments; he has no right to (fulfil) the sacred law (of the Aryans, yet) there is no prohibition against (his fulfilling certain portions of) the law.

14. The *karshapana* (or *pana*) was a silver coin valued at 57.8 grains.

127 (Shudras) who are desirous to gain merit, and know (their) duty, commit no sin, but gain praise, if they imitate the practice of virtuous men without reciting sacred texts.

128 The more a (Shudra), keeping himself free from envy, imitates the behaviour of the virtuous, the more he gains, without being censured, (exaltation in) this world and the next.

129 No collection of wealth must be made by a Shudra, even though he be able (to do it); for a Shudra who has acquired wealth, gives pain to Brahmins.

130 The duties of the four castes (*varna*) in times of distress have thus been declared, and if they perform them well, they will reach the most blessed state.

Origin of the Laws

The following account of the creation of the world and the derivation of the laws from the Supreme Being lacks a counterpart in any of the earlier law-books. It is unquestionably a late addition, put in to establish the validity of the *Laws of Manu* for all Hindus.

FROM THE LAWS OF MANU

Chapter I

23 But from fire, wind, and the sun he [the Lord] drew forth the threefold eternal Veda, called Rig, Yajur, and Sama,[1] for the due performance of the sacrifice.

58 But he [the Lord] having composed these Institutes (of the sacred law), himself taught them, according to the rule, to me [Manu] alone in the beginning; next I (taught them) to Mariki[2] and the other sages.

1. The fourth Veda, the Atharva, is the youngest and in some texts is not numbered among the Vedas.
2. Mariki was the first of the ten sages who, according to legend, was created directly by God.

Chapter II

6 The whole Veda is the (first) source of the sacred law, next the tradition and the virtuous conduct of those who know the (Veda further), also the customs of holy men, and (finally) self-satisfaction.

7 Whatever law[3] has been ordained for any (person) by Manu, that has been fully declared in the Veda: for that (sage was) omniscient.

8 But a learned man after fully scrutinising all this with the eye of knowledge, should, in accordance with the authority of the revealed texts, be intent on (the performance of) his duties.[4]

9 For that man who obeys the law prescribed in the revealed texts and in the sacred tradition, gains fame in this (world) and after death unsurpassable bliss.

10 But by *shruti* (revelation) is meant the Veda, and by *smriti* (tradition) the Institutes of the sacred law: those two must not be called into question in any matter, since from those two the sacred law shone forth.

11 Every twice-born man, who, relying on the Institutes of dialectics,[5] treats with contempt those two sources (of the law), must be cast out by the virtuous, as an atheist and a scorner of the Veda.

12 The Veda, the sacred tradition, the customs of virtuous men, and one's own pleasure,[6] they declare to be visibly the fourfold means of defining the sacred law.

13 The knowledge of the sacred law is prescribed for those who are not given to the acquisition of wealth and to the gratification of their desires; to those who seek the knowledge of the sacred law the supreme authority is the revelation (*shruti*).

---

3. In the original: *dharma*.
4. *Dharma*.
5. Methods of reasoning, probably meaning the speculations of the Buddhists and materialists.
6. I.e., satisfaction with one's own conduct.

14 But when two sacred texts (*shruti*) are conflicting, both
are held to be law[7]; for both are pronounced by the wise
(to be) valid law.

7. I.e., either may be followed.

The King's Justice

The specific legal provisions of the *Laws of Manu* belong to its later
portions and have few parallels in the Dharma Sutras. Though many
important areas of jurisprudence are still left unmentioned, civil
and criminal law receive far more extensive and detailed treatment
than in the earlier law books. The *Laws of Manu* thus represents a
decided step forward in the direction of a comprehensive, secular
system of law in which penalties are administered by government
officials rather than left to private vengeance, divine retribution, or
the moral law of *karma*.

FROM THE LAWS OF MANU
Chapter VIII

41 (A king) who knows the sacred law, must inquire into the
laws of castes (*jati*), of districts, of guilds, and of families,
and (thus) settle the peculiar law of each.

42 For men who follow their particular occupations and
abide by their particular duty, become dear to people,
though they may live at a distance.

43 Neither the king nor any servant of his shall themselves
cause a lawsuit to be begun,[1] or hush up one that has been
brought (before them) by (some) other (man).

1. According to the old Indian commentators, because this would indicate
greed.

44 As a hunter traces the lair of a (wounded) deer by the drops of blood, even so the king shall discover on which side the right lies, by inferences[2] (from the facts).

45 When engaged in judicial proceedings he must pay full attention to the truth, to the object (of the dispute), (and) to himself, next to the witnesses, to the place, to the time, and to the aspect.

46 What may have been practised by the virtuous, by such twice-born men as are devoted to the law, that he shall establish as law, if it be not opposed to the (customs of) countries, families, and castes (jati).

.   .   .   .

170 No king, however indigent, shall take anything that ought not to be taken, nor shall he, however wealthy, decline taking that which he ought to take, be it ever so small.

171 In consequence of his taking what ought not to be taken, or of his refusing what ought to be received, a king will be accused of weakness and perish in this (world) and after death.

172 By taking his due, by preventing the confusion of the castes (varna), and by protecting the weak, the power of the king grows, and he prospers in this (world) and after death.

173 Let the prince, therefore, like Yama,[3] not heeding his own likings and dislikings, behave exactly like Yama, suppressing his anger and controlling himself.

174 But that evil-minded king who in his folly decides causes unjustly, his enemies soon subjugate.[4]

175 If, subduing love and hatred, he decides the causes according to the law, (the hearts of) his subjects turn towards him as the rivers (run) towards the ocean.

---

2. In Indian logic, inference is one of the three means of arriving at a conclusion.

3. Yama was the god of death and judge of the dead, supposed to be absolutely fair in his decisions.

4. I.e., the king's estranged people support the enemy.

Judicial Procedure

FROM THE LAWS OF MANU

WITNESSES

Chapter VIII

61 I will fully declare what kind of men may be made witnesses in suits by creditors, and in what manner those (witnesses) must give true (evidence).

62 Householders, men with male issue, and indigenous (inhabitants of the country, be they) Kshatriyas, Vaishyas, or Shudras, are competent, when called by a suitor, to give evidence, not any persons whatever (their condition may be) except in cases of urgency.[1]

63 Trustworthy men of all the (four) castes (*varna*) may be made witnesses in lawsuits, (men) who know (their) whole duty, and are free from covetousness; but let him reject those (of an) opposite (character).

64 Those must not be made (witnesses) who have an interest in the suit, nor familiar (friends), companions, and enemies (of the parties), nor (men) formerly convicted (of perjury), nor (persons) suffering under (severe) illness, nor (those) tainted (by mortal sin).[2]

68 Women should give evidence for women,[3] and for twice-born men twice-born men (of the) same (kind), virtuous Shudras for Shudras, and men of the lowest castes for the lowest.

---

1. The cases of urgency are those specified in verse 69 below, probably also the cases where no other witnesses are obtainable.
2. Possibly meaning "capital offenders."
3. In matters concerning women, only other women may be supposed to be well informed.

69 .But any person whatsoever, who has personal knowledge (of an act committed) in the interior apartments (of a house), or in a forest, or of (a crime causing) loss of life, may give evidence between the parties.

70 On failure (of qualified witnesses, evidence) may be given (in such cases) by a woman, by an infant, by an aged man, by a pupil, by a relative, by a slave, or by a hired servant.

71 But the (judge) should consider the evidence of infants, aged and diseased men, who (are apt to) speak untruly, as untrustworthy, likewise that of men with disordered minds.

72 In all cases of violence, of theft and adultery, of defamation and assault, he must not examine the (competence of) witnesses (too strictly).

73 On a conflict of the witnesses the king shall accept (as true) the (evidence of the) majority; if (the conflicting parties are) equal in number, (that of) those distinguished by good qualities; on a difference between (equally) distinguished (witnesses, that of) the best among the twice-born.

OATHS AND ORDEALS

Chapter VIII

109 If two (parties) dispute about matters for which no witnesses are available, and the (judge) is unable to really ascertain the truth, he may cause it to be discovered even by an oath.

110 Both by the great sages and the gods oaths have been taken for the purpose of (deciding doubtful) matters . . .[4]

111 Let no wise man swear an oath falsely, even in a trifling matter; for he who swears an oath falsely is lost in this (world) and after death.

112 No crime, causing loss of caste, is committed by swearing

4. Various instances of this occur, for example, in the *Mahabharata*.

(falsely) to women, the objects of one's desire, at marriages, for the sake of fodder for a cow, or of fuel, and in (order to show) favour to a Brahmin.

113 Let the (judge) cause a Brahmin to swear by his veracity, a Kshatriya by his chariot or the animal he rides on and by his weapons, a Vaishya by his kine, grain, and gold, and a Shudra by (imprecating on his own head the guilt) of all grievous offences.

114 Or the (judge) may cause the (party) to carry fire or to dive under water, or severally to touch the heads of his wives and children.[5]

115 He whom the blazing fire burns not, whom the water forces not to come (quickly) up,[6] who meets with no speedy misfortune,[7] must be held innocent on (the strength of) his oath.

5. The major Indian commentators on this text assert that ordeals may be used only in the most important cases.
6. Apparently the test is whether he can stay under water, i.e., whether the water will receive him.
7. Within a period of a few weeks.

Family Law

FROM THE LAWS OF MANU
Chapter VIII

352 Men who commit adultery with the wives of others, the king shall cause to be marked by punishments which cause terror, and afterwards banish.

353 For by (adultery) is caused a mixture of the castes (*varna*) among men; thence (follows) sin, which cuts up even the roots and causes the destruction of everything.[1]

1. Because qualified persons are not available to perform the sacrifices; without sacrifices, no rain will fall.

354 A man formerly accused of (such) offences, who secretly converses with another man's wife, shall pay the first (or lowest) amercement.

355 But a man, not before accused, who (thus) speaks with (a woman) for some (reasonable) cause, shall not incur any guilt, since in him there is no transgression.

359 A man who is not a Brahmin ought to suffer death for adultery[2]; for the wives of all the four castes even must always be carefully guarded.

360 Mendicants,[3] bards, men who have performed the initiatory ceremony of a Vedic sacrifice, and artisans[4] are not prohibited from speaking to married women.

361 Let no man converse with the wives of others after he has been forbidden (to do so)[5]; but he who converses (with them), in spite of a prohibition, shall be fined one *suvarna*.[6]

364 He who violates an unwilling maiden shall instantly suffer corporal punishment[7]; but a man who enjoys a willing maiden shall not suffer corporal punishment, if (his caste be) the same (as hers).

365 From a maiden[8] who makes advances to a (man of) high (caste), he [the king] shall not take any fine; but her, who courts a (man of) low (caste), let him force to live confined in her house.[9]

366 A (man of) low (caste) who makes love to a maiden (of) the highest (caste)[10] shall suffer corporal punishment[11];

2. That is, with a woman of a higher class than his own.
3. Religious mendicants.
4. Because they have reason to be in the house and may speak about their business.
5. By the husband.
6. The *suvarna* or *dinara* was a coin based on the Roman denarius, consisting of 124 grains of gold.
7. According to the class of the offender, the punishment is mutilation or death.
8. I.e., from her relatives or guardians.
9. I.e., until her feeling for the low-caste man is extinguished.
10. Probably: "a high*er* caste," meaning that the punishment applies to an man who makes love to a woman of a higher class than his own.
11. See note 7, above.

he who addresses a maiden (of) equal (caste) shall pay the nuptial fee,[12] if her father desires it.

Chapter IX

94 A man, aged thirty years, shall marry a maiden of twelve who pleases him, or a man of twenty-four a girl eight years of age[13]; if (the performance of) his duties would (otherwise) be impeded,[14] (he must marry) sooner.

95 The husband receives his wife from the gods, (he does not wed her) according to his own will; doing what is agreeable to the gods, he must always support her (while she is) faithful.

96 To be mothers were women created, and to be fathers men; religious rites, therefore, are ordained in the Veda to be performed (by the husband) together with the wife.

97 If, after the nuptial fee has been paid for a maiden, the giver of the fee dies, she shall be given in marriage to his brother, in case she consents.

98 Even a Shudra ought not to take a nuptial fee, when he gives away his daughter; for he who takes a fee sells his daughter, covering (the transaction by another name).[15]

99 Neither ancients nor moderns who were good men have done such (a deed) that, after promising (a daughter) to one man, they gave her to another;

100 Nor, indeed, have we heard, even in former creations, of such (a thing as) the covert sale of a daughter for a fixed price, called a nuptial fee.

101 "Let mutual fidelity continue until death," this may be considered as the summary of the highest law for husband and wife.

12. I.e., marry her.
13. The general rule is that the bride should be about a third as old as the bridegroom; these are illustrations only.
14. I.e., his duties as a householder, which must begin as soon as the period of studentship is completed, possibly before age twenty-four.
15. This verse stands in evident contradiction to the one which precedes. Obviously the nuptial fee was common practice, even if the law books disapproved of it. Probably verses 98-100 are a late addition to the Laws, inserted without modification of the original text.

Theft

FROM THE LAWS OF MANU

Chapter VIII

336 Where another common man would be fined one *kar-shapana*,[1] the king shall be fined one thousand[2], that is the settled rule.

337 In (a case of) theft the guilt[3] of a Shudra shall be eightfold, that of a Vaishya sixteenfold, that of a Kshatriya two-and-thirtyfold,

338 That of a Brahmin sixty-fourfold, or quite a hundredfold, or (even) twice four-and-sixtyfold; (each of them) knowing the nature of the offence.

Chapter IX

256 Let the king who sees (everything) through his spies, discover the two sorts of thieves who deprive others of their property, both those who (show themselves) openly and those who (lie) concealed.

257 Among them, the open rogues (are those) who subsist by (cheating in the sale of) various marketable commodities, but the concealed rogues are burglars, robbers in forests, and so forth.

258 Those who take bribes, cheats and rogues,[4] gamblers, those

---

1. This was the basic Indian silver coin, worth 57.8 grains.
2. According to Manu IX, 244, the king shall throw the fine into the water or give it to Brahmins.
3. I.e., the fine.
4. Examples of cheats and rogues as given by some ancient Indian commentators are: persons who extort money by threats or take money under false pretenses, use false weights and measures, or break promises of transacting certain business.

who live by teaching (the performance of) auspicious ceremonies, sanctimonious hypocrites, and fortune-tellers,

259 Officials of high rank and physicians who act improperly,
men living by showing their proficiency in arts,[5] and
clever harlots,

260 These and the like who show themselves openly, as well
as others who walk in disguise (such as) non-Aryans who
wear the marks of Aryans, he should know to be thorns (in
the side of his people).

261 Having detected them by means of trustworthy persons,
who, disguising themselves, (pretend) to follow the same
occupations and by means of spies, wearing various dis-
guises, he must cause them to be instigated (to commit
offences), and bring them into his power.

262 Then having caused the crimes, which they committed
by their several actions, to be proclaimed in accordance
with the facts, the king shall duly punish them according
to their strength[6] and their crimes.

263 For the wickedness of evil-minded thieves, who secretly
prowl over this earth, cannot be restrained except by
punishment.

264 Assembly-houses, houses where water is distributed or
cakes are sold, brothels, taverns and victuallers' shops,
cross-roads, well-known trees, festive assemblies, and play-
houses and concert-rooms,

265 Old gardens, forests, the shops of artisans, empty dwellings, natural and artificial groves,

266 These and the like places the king shall cause to be guarded
by companies of soldiers, both stationary and patrolling,
and by spies, in order to keep away thieves.

270 A just king shall not cause a thief to be put to death, (unless taken) with the stolen goods (in his possession); him
who (is taken) with the stolen goods and the implements
(of burglary), he may, without hesitation, cause to be
slain.

5. I.e., wood-carvers, painters, hairdressers, umbrella and fan makers.
6. Possibly: according to their wealth.

271 All those also who in villages give food to thieves or grant them room for (concealing their implements), he shall cause to be put to death.

272 Those who are appointed to guard provinces and his vassals who have been ordered (to help), he shall speedily punish like thieves, (if they remain) inactive in attacks (by robbers).

273 Moreover if (a man), who subsists by (the fulfilment of) the law,[7] departs from the established rule of the law, the (king) shall severely punish him by a fine, (because he) violated his duty.

274 Those who do not give assistance according to their ability when a village is being plundered, a dyke is being destroyed, or a highway robbery committed, shall be banished with their goods and chattels.

275 On those who rob the king's treasury . . . he shall inflict various kinds of capital punishment, . . .

276 But the king shall cut off the hands of those robbers who, breaking into houses, commit thefts at night, and cause them to be impaled on a pointed stake.[8]

277 On the first conviction, let him cause two fingers of a cutpurse to be amputated; on the second, one hand and one foot; on the third, he shall suffer death.

280 Those who break into a (royal) storehouse, an armoury, or a temple, and those who steal elephants, horses, or chariots, he shall slay without hesitation.

293 For the theft of agricultural implements, of arms and of medicines, let the king award punishment, taking into account the time (of the offence) and the use (of the object).[9]

---

7. I.e., priests who officiate at sacrifices and other Brahmins who obtain alms on account of their piety.

8. I.e., executed. This form of punishment seems to have been common; e.g., it is mentioned several times in the *Mahabharata*.

9. I.e., the theft of a plow during the plowing season, or of weapons just before or during a fight, should be punished more severely than the same act committed at another time.

Commerce and Debt

FROM THE LAWS OF MANU
Chapter VIII

47 When a creditor sues (before the king) for the recovery of money from a debtor, let him make the debtor pay the sum which the creditor proves (to be due).

48 By whatever means a creditor may be able to obtain possession of his property, even by those means may he force the debtor and make him pay.

49 By moral suasion, by suit of law, by artful management, or by the customary proceeding,[1] a creditor may recover property lent; and fifthly, by force.

50 A creditor who himself recovers his property from his debtor, must not be blamed by the king for retaking what is his own.

51 But him who denies a debt which is proved by good evidence, he shall order to pay that debt to the creditor and a small fine[2] according to his circumstances.

52 On the denial (of a debt) by a debtor who has been required in court to pay it, the complainant must call (a witness) who was present (when the loan was made), or adduce other evidence.

.   .   .   .

139 A debt being admitted as due, (the defendant) shall pay five in the hundred (as a fine), if it be denied (and proved) twice as much; that is the teaching of Manu.

---

1. I.e., by the creditor's sitting at the debtor's door, or by fasting, or by starving himself to death.
2. The amount is specified in verse 139, below.

140 A money-lender may stipulate as an increase of his capital the interest allowed by Vasishtha,[3] and take monthly the eightieth part of a hundred.[4]

141 Or, remembering the duty of good men, he may take two in the hundred (by the month), for he who takes two in the hundred becomes not a sinner for gain.

142 Just two in the hundred, three, four, and five (and not more), he may take as monthly interest according to the order of the castes (*varna*).[5]

143 But if a beneficial pledge (i.e. one from which profit accrues, has been given), he shall receive no interest on the loan; nor can he, after keeping (such) a pledge for a very long time, give or sell it.

144 A pledge (to be kept only) must not be used by force,[6] (the creditor), so using it, shall give up his (whole) interest, or, (if it has been spoilt by use)[7] he shall satisfy the (owner) by (paying its) original price; else he commits a theft of the pledge.

145 Neither a pledge nor a deposit can be lost by lapse of time; they are both recoverable, though they have remained long (with the bailee).

151 In money transactions interest paid at one time (not by instalments) shall never exceed the double (of the principal)[8]; on grain, fruit, wool or hair, (and) beasts of burden it must not be more than five times (the original amount).

152 Stipulated interest beyond the legal rate, being against (the law), cannot be recovered; they call that a usurious way (of lending); (the lender) is (in no case) entitled to (more than) five in the hundred.

. . . .

401 Let (the king) fix (the rates for) the purchase and sale of all marketable goods, having (duly) considered whence

3. Vasishtha was the reputed author of one of the Dharma Sutras.
4. Or 15 per cent yearly.
5. Beginning with the Brahmin caste.
6. I.e., without the owner's permission.
7. Evidently household goods, clothes, or ornaments are meant.
8. I.e., the interest plus the principal must not exceed twice the principal.

they come, whither they go,[9] how long they have been kept, the (probable) profit and the (probable) outlay.

402 Once in five nights, or at the close of each fortnight, let the king publicly settle the prices for the (merchants).[10]

403 All weights and measures must be duly marked, and once in six months let him re-examine them.

404 At a ferry an (empty) cart shall be made to pay one *pana*, a man's (load) half a *pana*, an animal and a woman one quarter of a (*pana*), an unloaded man one-half of a quarter.

405 Carts (laden) with vessels full (of merchandise) shall be made to pay toll at a ferry according to the value (of the goods), empty vessels[11] and men without luggage some trifle.

406 For a long passage the boat-hire must be proportioned to the places and times; know that this (rule refers) to (passages along) the banks of rivers; at sea there is no settled (freight).

9. I.e., the distance traveled.
10. Or: in the presence of the merchants.
11. Jars, leather bags, or baskets which serve to transport merchandise.

Property Rights

FROM THE LAWS OF MANU
Chapter VIII

229 I will fully declare in accordance with the true law (the rules concerning) the disputes, (arising) from the transgressions of owners of cattle and of herdsmen.

230 During the day the responsibility for the safety (of the cattle rests) on the herdsman, during the night on the owner, (provided they are) in his house; (if it be) otherwise,[1] the herdsman will be responsible (for them also during the night).

1. I.e., if they remain out-of-doors.

231 A hired herdsman who is paid with milk, may milk with the consent of the owner the best (cow) out of ten; such shall be his hire if no (other) wages (are paid).

232 The herdsman alone shall make good (the loss of a beast) strayed, destroyed by worms, killed by dogs[2] or (by falling) into a pit, if he did not duly exert himself (to prevent it).

233 But for (an animal) stolen by thieves, though he raised an alarm, the herdsman shall not pay, provided he gives notice to his master at the proper place and time.[3]

234 If cattle die, let him carry to his master their ears, skin, tails, bladders, tendons, and the yellow concrete bile, and let him point out their particular marks.

235 But if goats or sheep are surrounded by wolves and the herdsman does not hasten (to their assistance), he shall be responsible for any (animal) which a wolf may attack and kill.

236 But if they, kept in (proper) order, graze together in the forest, and a wolf, suddenly jumping on one of them, kills it, the herdsman shall bear in that case no responsibility.

237 On all sides of a village a space, one hundred *dhanus*[4] or three *samya*-throws[5] (in breadth), shall be reserved (for pasture), and thrice (that space) round a town.

238 If the cattle do damage to unfenced crops on that (common), the king shall in that case not punish the herdsmen.[6]

239 (The owner of the field) shall make there a hedge over which a camel cannot look, and stop every gap through which a dog or a boar can thrust his head.

240 (If cattle do mischief) in an enclosed field near a highway or near a village, the herdsman shall be fined one hundred (*panas*)[7]; (but cattle), unattended by a herdsman, (the watchman in the field) shall drive away.

2. Or doglike animals, such as jackals.
3. I.e., the same evening and at the place where it happened, or wherever the owner is.
4. The *dhanu* was equivalent to a bow's length, or about six feet.
5. The *samya* was a short, thick piece of wood used at sacrifices.
6. Because this is common land which is not supposed to be cultivated.
7. The *pana* or *karshapana* was a silver coin worth 57.8 grains.

241 (For damage) in other fields (each head of) cattle shall (pay[8] a fine of) one (*pana*) and a quarter, and in all (cases the value of) the crop (destroyed) shall be made good to the owner of the field; that is the settled rule.

242 But Manu has declared that no fine shall be paid for (damage done by) a cow within ten days after her calving,[9] by bulls[10] and by cattle sacred to the gods,[11] whether they are attended by a herdsman or not.

. . . .

245 If a dispute has arisen between two villages concerning a boundary, the king shall settle the limits in the month of *Gyaishtha*,[12] when the landmarks are most distinctly visible.

246 Let him mark the boundaries (by) trees, (e.g.) . . . cotton-trees, . . . palms, and trees with milky juice,[13]

247 By clustering shrubs, bamboos of different kinds, . . . creepers and raised mounds, reeds, thickets . . . ; thus the boundary will not be forgotten.

248 Tanks, wells, cisterns, and fountains should be built where boundaries meet, as well as temples,

249 And as he will see that through men's ignorance of the boundaries trespasses constantly occur in the world, let him cause to be made other hidden marks for boundaries,

250 Stones, bones, cow's hair, chaff, ashes, potsherds, dry cow-dung, bricks, cinders, pebbles, and sand,

251 And whatever other things of a similar kind the earth does not corrode even after a long time, those he should cause to be buried[14] where one boundary joins (the other).

252 By these signs, by long continued possession, and by constantly flowing streams of water the king shall ascertain the boundary (of the land) of two disputing parties.

8. I.e., the herdsman shall pay for the cattle.
9. At this time the cow is supposed to be utterly unmanageable.
10. Bulls set at liberty.
11. Cattle set apart for sacrifices, or dedicated to temples.
12. May-June, when the grass has been dried out by the heat.
13. All the trees named are either very tall or otherwise conspicuous, and especially enduring.
14. Evidently these objects were to be placed in jars.

253 If there be a doubt even on inspection of the marks, the settlement of a dispute regarding boundaries shall depend on witnesses.

Personal Injury

FROM THE LAWS OF MANU
Chapter VIII

279 With whatever limb a man of a low caste does hurt to (a man of the three) highest (castes), even that limb shall be cut off; that is the teaching of Manu.

280 He who raises his hand or a stick, shall have his hand cut off; he who in anger kicks with his foot, shall have his foot cut off.

281 A low-caste man who tries to place himself on the same seat with a man of a high caste, shall be branded on his hip and be banished, or (the king) shall cause his buttock to be gashed.

283 If he lays hold of the hair (of a superior), let the (king) unhesitatingly cut off his hands, likewise (if he takes him) by the feet, the beard, the neck, or the scrotum.

284 He who breaks the skin (of an equal) or fetches blood from him) shall be fined one hundred (*panas*), he who cuts a muscle six *nishkas*,[1] he who breaks a bone shall be banished.

286 If a blow is struck against men or animals in order to (give them) pain, (the judge) shall inflict a fine in proportion to the amount of pain (caused).

287 If a limb is injured, a wound (is caused), or blood (flows, the assailant) shall be made to pay (to the sufferer) the expenses of the cure, or the whole (both the usual amercement and the expenses of the cure as a) fine (to the king).[2]

1. According to Manu, the *nishka* was equal to a *pana*.
2. I.e., if the injured person refused the compensation.

IV

Moksha

Karma and Transmigration

Fundamental to all the major religious and philosophical systems of India is a belief in the laws of *karma* and transmigration (*samsara*). *Karma*, which literally means "act" or "deed," is understood as a moral force bearing the seeds of future good or bad fortune. The law of *karma* is a theory of cause and effect according to which the acts or thoughts of all living creatures inevitably produce conse-- quences, either in this life or in a subsequent one. Whether a soul will be re-born in human, animal, or plant form, and whether its future existences will be happy or wretched, depends upon the good or evil nature of its previously-accumulated *karma*. Thus transmigration is the unavoidable fate of every un-liberated soul. The body is merely its temporary residence; at the death of a particular body it enters into another which is just being born.

Extant Indian sources do not record that either *karma* or transmigration formed part of the earlier Vedic thought-world. According to the *Rig Veda*, dead souls passed either to the "World of the Fathers" —a kind of heaven where they remained indefinitely—or to a shadowy, subterranean hell. The earliest suggestion of transmigration in Indian literature occurs in a passage of the *Brhadaranyaka Upanishad* which declares that souls resident in the "World of the Fathers" subsequently return to earth. Scholars suppose that the ideas of *karma* and transmigration, in some form, were part of the religious lore of the indigenous non-Aryan population of India. Lack of information about the pre-Aryan period—e.g., the script of the Indus civilization has never been deciphered—makes any such theory impossible to prove. But by the time of the Buddha (*ca.* 500 B.C.), both *karma* and transmigration seem to have been widely accepted ideas.

For example, Jainism, a sect founded at about the same time as Buddhism, conceived the law of *karma* in a strictly materialistic way. Jains regarded the soul (*jiva*) in its pristine state as analogous to a perfectly transparent crystal, capable of being contaminated by karmic material. Every good or evil act produced karmic coloring on the soul—light colors for virtuous acts and minor offenses, darker shades for more serious sins. Since dark-colored stains weighted down the soul, while brighter ones allowed it to rise, the light-colored souls would be re-born as human beings or gods, the darker ones as animals or plants, or as inhabitants of hell.

Sankhya, one of the major Hindu systems of philosophy, taught that the soul (*purusha*) was spiritual, incapable of being affected by material qualities like color. But the Sankhya theory of transmigration was nonetheless materialistic. The visible human body was believed to contain a subtler inner body composed of the sense faculties, the vital breaths, and the mind. This subtle body was the receiver of karmic influences and the basis of the re-incarnated personality. According to the number and depth of karmic scars upon it, the subtle body would be reborn in human, plant, or animal form. Liberation from the succession of births and deaths was possible only through recognition that the true soul was pure and free, and that its association with matter was illusory.

The Upanishads treat *karma* and transmigration in an immaterial, psychological sense. The soul (Atman) is described in negative or contradictory terms which convey that it cannot be comprehended through reason and is certainly not material. *Karma* attaches to the Atman in some mysterious way which is left unexplained. As in the Sankhya system, liberation from future births comes only through knowledge—in this case, recognition that the Atman is fundamentally identical with the essence of the entire universe (Brahman).

Buddhism is even farther removed from materialism. Buddhists regard the entire universe as in a state of continual flux, and deny the existence of any permanent, concrete entity which may be termed a soul. At the same time, they accept the validity of the laws of *karma* and transmigration. The juxtaposition of these several ideas has often troubled critical scholars; since if no soul exists it is difficult to understand what it is that transmigrates. But at least in its original form—as far as we can tell from extant scriptures—Buddhism ignored this difficulty. Perhaps its earliest adherents considered the notions of *karma* and transmigration as too self-evident to be questioned. In any event, Buddha himself had regarded metaphysical speculation as an obstacle to the practical goal of salvation; and the early Buddhists apparently followed his lead. The Mahayana school, with its greater penchant for speculation, explained *karma* as a kind of psychic energy which, though not attached to an eternal soul, was carried over from present to future as part of the self-contained system of the universe.

The related concepts of *karma* and transmigration thus transformed ethics into a natural law, operating automatically without the intervention of divine personalities. Once an act had been committed, its effects were believed to be as certain and inevitable as the fact that day and night follow each other. The result of this was to invest each act of the individual with far-reaching significance and make each person feel responsible for his own fate. From the standpoint of society, it provided firm ethical justification for the existing order of things.

The universal applicability of the laws of *karma* and transmigration served also to bind all the creatures of the universe into a single, all-embracing cosmological and ethical system. Each living being was thought capable of producing *karma*, though the opportunities for gaining favorable *karma* increased as one progressed up the scale from plants and animals through the lower to the higher classes of humans. Birth into the Brahmin class—the most desirable earthly state—granted not merely external advantages, but also the best possible milieu for winning salvation without further re-births. But whether faith, works, or wisdom were emphasized, all the major Indian schools of thought agreed that liberation from the round of births and deaths was possible only through putting an end to the accumlation of *karma*.

Introduction to the Vedic Hymns

A large proportion of the hymns of the Vedas are marked by a simple animism, polytheism, and a quid-pro-quo philosophy whereby praise and sacrifice to the gods are exchanged for mundane benefits. The forces of nature are each personified as deities— gods of sun, rain, fertility, etc. Frequently a long list of gods is invoked in a single short composition; hymns which are dedicated to one particular deity in no way deny the existence of other divine beings. The gods deign to confer their blessings only upon those worshippers who have provided them with abundant flattery, food, and drink at the sacrifice. A few Vedic hymns, however, give evidence of a profounder cosmology, a tendency toward monotheism, and a less mechanical concept of ethics.

Rta, for instance, is no one specific natural force, but the universal order of the cosmos. *Rta* signifies the regularity and life-giving quality of the cosmic process: the succession of days and nights, months and years; the alternation of rainfall and sunshine. The gods are the guardians of *rta* against the demonic forces which seek to disturb it. This idea is expressed, for example, in the myth of Indra and the dragon. Indra was one of the chief Vedic gods, a deity both of war and weather, who rode at the head of his troops of storm-gods and destroyed his enemies with thunderbolts. As god of war, he was a natural defender of *rta* against the dragon Vritra (the name means "enemy of *rta*"), who held back the rains and thus prevented the growth of crops. Indra slew the dragon, brought relief to the parched earth, and thereby preserved the cosmic order.

Monotheistic tendencies appear in certain hymns to Agni. Agni was fire, or the fire-god (his name is etymologically related to the Latin *ignis*). He was the patron of the priests who officiated at sacrifices, and also the intermediary who consumed the sacrifice and carried it to the gods. As fire, he dwelt in many places: in the sky as lightning, in the domestic hearth, in the warmth of the sun, in the fire-sticks which produced sparks when rubbed, in the fire-sacrifice. Agni's ubiquitous presence gave rise to the question how it was possible that he was everywhere at once, but was nonetheless One. *Rig Veda* II. 1., by identifying all the other chief gods with Agni, treats him in effect as the sole existing deity.

Of all the Vedic gods, Varuna (the Persian Ahura, Greek Uranos) has the strongest ethical character. Unlike his colleagues, who were regarded as good-natured as long as they received their due at the sacrifice, Varuna was portrayed as a solemn judge who punished mankind for its sins. Though the concept of sin in Vedic times was bound up with the mores of sacrifice, and certainly included ritual errors and the breaking of taboos, it also encompassed intoxication, gambling, lying, and deeds done in anger. Varuna is the omnipresent observer of all actions; even in the most remote, hidden places no one can evade his gaze. He punishes sinners (and their descendants) with ill-fortune and disease on earth, and after death consigns them to a gloomy, subterranean hell.

FROM THE VEDIC HYMNS

Indra's Self-Dominion (Rig Veda I. 80)

1   Thus in the soma[1] and his raptures
      the priest has glorified thee. And
    thou, mightiest, thunder-armed, by valour
      hast expelled Ahi[2] from the earth,
        acclaiming self-dominion.

2   That enraptured thee—the strong,
      rousing soma, brought by the hawk[3] and pressed—
    with which thou, thunder-armed, didst drive,
      by thy valour, Vritra from the floods,[4]
        acclaiming self-dominion.

3   Go forward, meet the foe, be brave,
      thy thunder-bolt can't be resisted;
    Indra, manliness is thy strength;
      drive out Vritra, win the waters,
        acclaiming self-dominion.

4   From the earth thou hast struck Vritra,
      thou hast struck him, Indra, from the sky;
    now let loose the life-sustaining
      waters with Maruts[5] to drive them,
        acclaiming self-dominion.

5   The wrathful Indra, encountering him
      struck with his thunder-bolt
    the malignant Vritra on the jaw,

From *Hymns from the Vedas*, trans. by Abinash Chandra Bose (London: Asia Publishing House, 1966). Reprinted by permission of Asia Publishing House.
  1. Soma was a plant juice which produced visions and hallucinatory effects. It was employed at the sacrifice.
  2. The dragon Vritra.
  3. I.e., from an inaccessible place.
  4. Or waters, clouds.
  5. The storm-gods who accompanied Indra into battle.

and impelled the waters to flow,
 acclaiming self-dominion.

6 On the jaw he struck him with
 the hundred-edged thunder-bolt,
and rejoicing in the juice,[6] wished
 prosperity for his friends,
  acclaiming self-dominion.

7 Thunder-armed, Indra, caster of
 the stone, in thee lies matchless strength,
because thou slewest the artful beast
 with thy own superior art,
  acclaiming self-dominion.

8 Thy thunder-bolts were widely spread
 over the nine and ninety floods,
Great, O Indra, is thy valour,
 and strength is lodged within thy arms,
  acclaiming self-dominion.

9 A thousand pray to him together,
 and twenty sing the hymn of praise,
A hundred have glorified him;
 to Indra is the prayer raised,
  acclaiming self-dominion.

.   .   .   .

6. Soma juice.

The One in the Many (Rig Veda II. 1)

1 Thou, Agni, thou, through the days brightly shining,
 thou, sovereign Lord of men, art born pure,
born of the waters, and of the stone,
 and of the forest trees and of the herbs.

2 Thine, Agni, is the office of invoker, of purifier,
 priest and leader. Thou art kindler of the devout.
Thine is the function of praiser. Thou art preparer of the
  rites
 and supervisor, and thou the Lord of our homes.

3   Thou, Agni, art Indra, the hero of heroes,
       thou art Vishnu[1] of the wide stride, adorable,
    thou, Brahmanaspati,[2] art the Veda-knower, the wealth-
       finder;
    thou, the sustainer, unitest us with wisdom.

4   Thou, Agni, art King Varuna[3] who upholds the law,
       thou, as Mitra,[4] wonder-worker, art to be worshipped;
    thou art Aryaman,[5] Lord of the virtuous, delighting all,
       thou art liberal Amsa[6] in the assembly.

5   Thou as Tvastri,[7] givest great strength to the worshipper,
       thine the praises, thine the kinship with Mitra power;
    Thou with thy fleet horses bestowest noble steeds,
       thou, Lord of great wealth, art the power of heroes.

6   Thou, Agni, art Rudra,[8] the deity of great heaven,
       thou art the troop of Maruts,[9] thou Lord of nurture,
    thou goest with the red winds, blessing the household,
       as Pushan[10] thou savest worshippers by thy own will.

7   Thou, Agni, thou givest wealth to him who serves thee,
       thou God Savitri,[11] art the bestower of jewels,
    as Bhaga,[12] Lord of men, thou rulest over riches,
       thou protector at home of one who worships thee.

8   Thee Agni at home, the Lord of the people,
       the people propitiate as their gracious king,

1. The god Vishnu crossed the heavens with three steps, as the morning, noonday, and evening sun.
2. Or Brihaspati: the god of prayer, priest to the gods.
3. The god Varuna was pictured as a king in his palace surrounded by servants, not as a warlike deity like Indra.
4. (The Persian Mithra): a sun-god associated with Varuna.
5. The guardian deity of compacts and marriages.
6. One of the Adityas (twelve gods of light).
7. The craftsman-god.
8. A storm-god, feared as the bringer of destruction and disease.
9. Lesser storm-gods who accompanied Indra in battle.
10. A solar deity, the guardian of herdsmen, cattle, and roads.
11. A sun-god.
12. The god of wealth.

Thou, beautiful to look at, lordest it over all,
  thou who surpassest ten hundred, yea, a thousand.

9   Thee Agni as father men approach with worship,
      thee, bright-formed, they with good acts seek as brother;
  A son thou becomest to him who prays to thee,
      and thou, a good friend, protectest us from harm.

10   Thou, Agni, are Ribhu[13] near us, meet for homage,
      thou art Lord of nourishing power and riches,
  Thou shinest and burnest to make us thy gifts,
      thou, all pervading, directest the holy rite.

11   Thou, Agni, deva,[14] art Aditi[15] to the offerer of oblation,
      thou art the invoker, and Bharati[16] thriving by praise-
        songs;
  thou art Ila[17] of a hundred winters to the deft performer of
        rites,
      thou, Lord of wealth, art Vritra-slayer[18] and Sarasvati.[19]

12   Thou Agni, well cherished, art the best vital strength;
      in thy welcome and pleasant hues beauties abound;
  thou art the great power that takes us beyond evil,
      thou art wealth manifold, diffused on every side.

13   Thee, Agni, the Adityas[20] have made their medium,
      the radiant ones, have made thee, O sage, their own,
  thee the lovers of gifts seek in the sacrifices,
      through thee the devas partake of our offerings.

13. The Ribhus were three gnomes who worked in metal.
14. *Deva* is a general term for "god."
15. The mother of the gods.
16. A goddess personifying prayer, often mentioned together with Ila and
Sarasvati.
17. A goddess of prayer and worship.
18. Indra, who slew the dragon Vritra (see previous hymn).
19. A goddess who guarded the waters and bestowed fertility.
20. The twelve gods of light, children of the mother-goddess Aditi.

14 Through thee, Agni, all immortal devas, free from hate,
    partake of the offerings of oblation;
through thee mortals taste the enlivening flavour;
    thou art born pure, the spark of life in plants.

15 Thou art united with these; in thy majesty
    a deva of noble birth, thou surpassest them all;
through thy greatness the sacrificial food was here
    diffused in the heaven, on the earth, in both the worlds.

16 The noblemen, Agni, who to thy singers
    make gifts headed by kine and graced with horses,
lead them and us forward to greater bliss!
    Loud may we speak with heroes in the assembly.

The Divine Observer (Atharva Veda IV. 16)

1 The great Ruler of all these worlds,
    beholds as if from near at hand
the man who thinks he acts by stealth,
    The Devas know all this of him.

2 When one stands or walks or moves in secret,
    or goes to his lying down or uprising,
when two sitting together take secret counsel,
    King Varuna knows, being there the Third.

3 This earth belongs to Varuna, the King,
    and the heavens, whose ends are far apart.
Both the oceans are the loins of Varuna,
    and he is merged within the small water-drop.

4 If one will go away beyond the heavens,
    still he cannot escape King Varuna;
his envoys move about here from the heavens,
    and thousand-eyed, they look upon the earth.

5 King Varuna observes all that which lies
      between heaven and earth and beyond them;
   the twinklings of men's eyes have been counted by him;
      as a dicer the dice, he measures everything.

6 These fatal snares of thine, O Varuna,
      that stand stretched seven by seven and threefold,
   let all these catch up the man who tells a lie,
      but pass by one who speaks the truth.

7 With a hundred nooses bind him, Varuna,
      let him not who lies escape thee, looker on men!
   Let the mean fellow sit stretching his belly
      like a cask of which the bands have been cut.

8 Varuna is that which exists alongside,
      Varuna is that which exists crosswise,
   Varuna is of our own land, he is of
      foreign land. Varuna is divine, he is human.

Introduction to the Upanishads

Although all parts of the Vedas are classed as sacred, revealed scriptures (*shruti*), they represent various strata of religious development. The hymns—songs of praise to many gods and prayers for material benefits—compose the earliest portion, dating from the period of the Aryan invasions of India (*ca.* 1500-1000 B.C.) Attached to the hymns of each Veda are compositions later in date and very different in content, known respectively as Brahmanas, Aranyakas, and Upanishads. The Brahmanas—elaborate and often far-fetched analyses of the ritual of worship—originated between about 900 and 600 B.C., when the sacrificial religion of the Aryans had reached its highest point of development and influence. No doubt embodying the opinions of Brahmin priests, the Brahmanas seek to exalt the sacrifice, going so far as to assert that properly performed ritual is necessary to maintain the whole cosmic order. But the Aranyakas ("forest treatises") represent a reaction to this extreme point of view. Written probably by hermits who retired to the forest to meditate, they attempt to interpret the sacrifice in a symbolic rather than a literal sense. Finally, the Upanishads embody the earliest Indian attempts at abstract philosophical thought. Their point of departure is the speculation of the Brahmanas and Aranyakas, but they seek a profounder meaning behind the varied phenomena of the universe and re-interpret the Vedic traditions accordingly. The period of the earliest Upanishads overlaps with that of the later Brahmanas and Aranyakas; and frequently the final chapter of one of the earlier works becomes the first chapter of an Upanishad.

The number of recognized Upanishads is sometimes given as 108; however, there is no general agreement on this point. Certain Hindu sects produced compositions called Upanishads at a comparatively late date; but these are not universally regarded as belonging to the Vedas. Those which are recognized by all Hindus as holy writ (*shruti*) were produced between about 700 and 500 B.C., in direct continuation of the Brahmanas. These oldest Upanishads, numbering no more than fifteen or twenty, are the richest in content and most important historically. They constitute the basis for the later system of thought known as Vedanta ("end of the Veda"), which has dominated Indian philosophy down to the present day.

The Upanishads are by no means internally consistent compositions. Within a single Upanishad a variety of doctrines may be set forth, with little attempt at reconciliation. Parts of the Upanishads continue the attempts of the Brahmanas and Aranyakas to elucidate the sacrifice. But on the whole they regard sacrifice as an inferior road to salvation, and in a few instances even make mocking remarks about the priests. Without discarding the polytheism of the Vedic hymns, they relegate the gods to a secondary role. The theme which pervades the Upanishads, and which had the greatest influence on subsequent Indian philosophy, is the doctrine of the unity of Brahman and Atman.

In the Vedic hymns, the word *brahman* (neuter gender) denotes magical power. Thus the possessors of this power, the priests who officiated at the sacrifices, became known as *Brahmins* (masculine gender). But in the Upanishads *Brahman* has become the essence of the entire universe, the basic nature of all phenomena, that from which everything arises and to which all things return. What Brahman is can be suggested only in a roundabout way; it is beyond the power of words to describe. It is referred to largely in negative terms, as "not this, not that"—neither large nor small, neither here nor there, etc. It is sometimes defined as *sat-chit-ananda* (Sanskrit for "Being; intelligence; bliss"); but it lacks personal characteristics and cannot be called God.

Atman is the Self, or essence, of the individual person. The Upanishads assert that Atman is identical in nature with Brahman; and in fact, the two terms are sometimes used interchangeably. Liberation is defined as realization of the identity of Atman and Brahman. The recognition "that art thou," i.e., thou art Brahman, is not merely an intellectual conviction; it is an indescribable experience, mystic in nature. It is an enhanced state of consciousness, inexpressible in words, which ordinarily is preceded by a long period of preparatory discipline.

The authors of the Upanishads were almost certainly influenced by mysticism; the experience they describe is analogous to that of mystics the world over. In India, however, speculation concerning the one-ness of Brahman and Atman soon became associated with the notions of *karma* and transmigration. The mystic unity came to be considered superior to the mere residence in Heaven which might be won through good *karma*. From Heaven a soul was thought to return to earth when his *karma* was exhausted; but the mystic unity put an end to the production of *karma* (and the resultant rebirths) altogether. The oldest Upanishads, to be sure, give merely a suggestion of such ideas. But escape from transmigration—the succession of births and deaths—eventually became the major goal of most of the religions and philosophies of India.

FROM THE BRIHADARANYAKA UPANISHAD

Chapter II, Section 4

1 Now when Yajñavalkya was going to enter upon another state, he said: "Maitreyi, verily I am going away from this my house (into the forest). Forsooth, let me make a settlement between thee and that Katyayani (my other wife)."

2 Maitreyi said: "My Lord, if this whole earth, full of wealth, belonged to me, tell me, should I be immortal by it?"

From *The Upanishads*, trans. by F. Max Mueller, Vol. I of *The Sacred Books of the East* (Oxford: at the Clarendon Press, 1879-84).

"No," replied Yajñavalkya; "like the life of rich people will
be thy life. But there is no hope of immortality by wealth."

3   And Maitreyi said: "What should I do with that by which
I do not become immortal? What my Lord knoweth (of immortality), tell that to me."

4   Yajñavalkya replied: "Thou who art truly dear to me,
thou speakest dear words. Come, sit down, I will explain it to
thee, and mark well what I say."

5   And he said: "Verily, a husband is not dear, that you may
love the husband; but that you may love the Self, therefore a
husband is dear.

"Verily, a wife is not dear, that you may love the wife; but
that you may love the Self, therefore a wife is dear.

"Verily, sons are not dear, etc. . . .

"Verily, wealth is not dear, etc. . . .

"Verily, the Brahmin-class is not dear, etc. . . .

"Verily, the Kshatriya-class is not dear, etc. . . .

"Verily, the worlds are not dear, etc. . . .

13   . . . "For when there is as it were duality, then one sees
the other, one smells the other, one hears the other, one salutes
the other, one perceives the other, one knows the other; but when
the Self only is all this, how should he smell another, how
should he see another, how should he hear another, how should
he salute another, how should he perceive another, how should
he know another? How should he know Him by whom he
knows all this? How, O beloved, should he know (himself), the
Knower?"

Chapter III, Section 7

[One Uddalaka Aruni asks the sage Yajnavalkya about Brahman,
the inner controller.]

3   Yajñavalkya said : "He who dwells in the earth, and within
the earth, whom the earth does not know, whose body the earth
is, and who pulls (rules) the earth within, he is thy Self, the
puller (ruler) within, the immortal.

4   "He who dwells in the water, and within the water, whom
the water does not know, whose body the water is, and who

pulls (rules) the water within, he is thy Self, the puller (ruler) within, the immortal.

5 "He who dwells in the fire, and within the fire, whom the fire does not know, whose body the fire is, and who pulls (rules) the fire within, he is thy Self, the puller (ruler) within, the immortal.

6-22 "He who dwells in the sky, . . . the air . . . the heaven . . . the sun . . . space . . . the moon and stars . . . ether . . . darkness . . . light . . . all beings . . . speech . . . the eye . . . the ear . . . the mind . . . the skin . . . the under-standing. . . .

23 "He who dwells in the seed, and within the seed, whom the seed does not know, whose body the seed is, and who pulls (rules) the seed within, he is thy Self, the puller (ruler) within, the immortal; unseen, but seeing; unheard, but hearing; un-perceived, but perceiving; unknown, but knowing. There is no other seer but he, there is no other hearer but he, there is no other perceiver but he, there is no other knower but he. This is thy Self, the ruler within, the immortal. Everything else is of evil." After that Uddalaka Aruni held his peace.

Chapter III, Section 9

1 Then Vidagdha Shakalya asked him: "How many gods are there, O Yajñavalkya?" He replied with this very *Nivid*[1]: "As many as are mentioned in the Nivid of the hymn of praise addressed to the Vishve-devas,[2] viz. three and three hundred, three and three thousand."

"Yes," he said, and asked again: "How many gods are there really, O Yajñavalkya?"

"Thirty-three," he said.

"Yes," he said, and asked again: "How many gods are there really, O Yajñavalkya?"

"Six," he said.

"Yes," he said, and asked again: "How many gods are there really, O Yajñavalkya?"

1. A short invocation to the gods.
2. A group of gods.

"Three," he said.

"Yes," he said, and asked again: "How many gods are there really, O Yajñavalkya?"

"Two," he said.

"Yes," he said, and asked again: "How many gods are there really, O Yajñavalkya?"

"One and a half," he said.

"Yes," he said, and asked again: "How many gods are there really, O Yajñavalkya?"

"One," he said.

"Yes," he said, and asked: "Who are these three and three hundred, three and three thousand?"

2   Yajñavalkya replied: "They are only the various powers of them, in reality there are only thirty-three gods."

He asked: "Who are those thirty-three?"

Yajñavalkya replied: "The eight Vasus, the eleven Rudras, the twelve Adityas. They make thirty-one, and Indra and Prajapati make the thirty-three."

3   He asked: "Who are the Vasus."

Yajñavalkya replied: "Agni (fire), Prithivi (earth), Vayu (air), Antariksha (sky), Aditya (sun), Dyu (heaven), Chandramas (moon), the Nakshatras (stars), these are the Vasus, for in them all that dwells (in this world) rests; and therefore they are called Vasus."[3]

4   He asked: "Who are the Rudras?"

Yajñavalkya replied: "These ten vital breaths[4] and Atman, as the eleventh. When they depart from this mortal body, they make us cry (rodayanti), and because they make us cry, they are called Rudras."

5   He asked: "Who are the Adityas?"

Yajñavalkya replied: "The twelve months of the year, and they are Adityas, because they move along (yanti), taking up everything (adadanah). Because they move along, taking up everything, therefore they are called Adityas."

---

3. I.e., because they transform themselves into the bodies and organs of all beings.

4. The five powers of motor activity and the five sense perceptions.

6   He asked: "And who is Indra, and who is Prajapati?"

Yajñavalkya replied: "Indra is thunder, Prajapati is the sacrifice."

He asked: "And what is the thunder?"

Yajñavalkya replied: "The thunderbolt."

He asked: "And what is the sacrifice?"

Yajñavalkya replied: "The (sacrificial) animals."

7   He asked: "Who are the six?"

Yajñavalkya replied: "Agni (fire), Prithivi (earth), Vayu (air), Antariksha (sky), Aditya (sun), Dyu (heaven), they are the six, for they are all this, the six."

8   He asked: "Who are the three gods?"

Yajñavalkya replied: "These three worlds, for in them all these gods exist."

He asked: "Who are the two gods?"

Yajñavalkya replied: "Food and breath."

He asked: "Who is the one god and a half?"

Yajñavalkya replied: "He that blows."

9   Here they say: "How is it that he who blows like one only, should be called one and a half (*adhyardha*)?" And the answer is: "Because, when the wind was blowing, everything grew (*adhyardhnot*)."

He asked: "Who is the one god?"

Yajñavalkya replied: "Breath (*prana*), and he is Brahman, and they call him That."

.   .   .   .

FROM THE CHANDOGYA UPANISHAD

Chapter VI, Section 9

[Shvetaketu has returned home after completing his period of studentship, highly arrogant because he has studied all the Vedas. But he has not heard about Brahman; so his father proceeds to instruct him.]

From *The Upanishads*, trans. by F. Max Mueller, Vol. I of *The Sacred Books of the East* (Oxford: at the Clarendon Press, 1879-84).

1   "As the bees, my son, make honey by collecting the juices of distant trees, and reduce the juice into one form,

2   "And as these juices have no discrimination, so that they might say, I am the juice of this tree or that, in the same manner, my son, all these creatures, when they have become merged in the True (either in deep sleep or in death),[1] know not that they are merged in the True.

3   "Whatever these creatures are here, whether a lion, or a wolf, or a boar, or a worm, or a midge, or a gnat, or a mosquito, that they become again and again.

4   "Now that which is that subtile essence,[2] in it all that exists has its self. It is the True. It is the Self, and thou, O Shvetaketu, art it."

"Please, Sir, inform me still more," said the son.

"Be it so, my child," the father replied.

Section 10

1   "These rivers, my son, run, the eastern (like the Ganges) toward the east, the western (like the Sindhu) toward the west. They go from sea to sea (i.e. the clouds lift up the water from the sea to the sky, and send it back as rain to the sea). They become indeed sea. And as those rivers, when they are in the sea, do not know, I am this or that river,

2   "In the same manner, my son, all these creatures, when they have come back from the True, know not that they have come back from the True. Whatever these creatures are here, whether a lion, or a wolf, or a boar, or a worm, or a midge, or a gnat, or a mosquito, that they become again and again.

3   "That which is that subtile essence, in it all that exists has its self. It is the True. It is the Self, and thou, O Shvetaketu, art it."

"Please, Sir, inform me still more," said the son.

"Be it so, my child," the father replied.

---

1. According to the Upanishads, union with Brahman occurs naturally in deep sleep or in death; the wise man must seek to become conscious of this unity in his waking lifetime.

2. Brahman.

Section 11

1   "If some one were to strike at the root of this large tree here, it would bleed, but live. If he were to strike at its stem, it would bleed, but live. If he were to strike at its top, it would bleed, but live. Pervaded by the living Self that tree stands firm, drinking in its nourishment and rejoicing;

2   "But if the life (the living Self) leaves one of its branches, that branch withers; if it leaves a second, that branch withers; if it leaves a third, that branch withers. If it leaves the whole tree, the whole tree withers. In exactly the same manner, my son, know this." Thus he spoke:

3   "This (body) indeed withers and dies when the living Self has left it; the living Self dies not.

"That which is that subtile essence, in it all that exists has its self. It is the True. It is the Self, and thou, Shvetaketu, art it."

"Please, Sir, inform me still more," said the son.

"Be it so, my child," the father replied.

Section 12

1   "Fetch me from thence a fruit of the Nyagrodha[3] tree."

"Here is one, Sir."

"Break it."

"It is broken, Sir."

"What do you see there?"

"These seeds, almost infinitesimal."

"Break one of them."

"It is broken, Sir."

"What do you see there?"

"Not anything, Sir."

2   The father said: "My son, that subtile essence which you do not perceive there, of that very essence this great Nyagrodha tree exists.

3   "Believe it, my son. That which is the subtile essence, in it

3. Banyan.

all that exists has its self. It is the True. It is the Self, and thou, O Shvetaketu, art it."

"Please, Sir, inform me still more," said the son.

"Be it so, my child," the father replied.

Section 13

1 "Place this salt in water, and then wait on me in the morning."

The son did as he was commanded.

The father said to him: "Bring me the salt, which you placed in the water last night."

The son having looked for it, found it not, for, of course, it was melted.

2 The father said: "Taste it from the surface of the water. How is it?"

The son replied: "It is salt."

"Taste it from the middle. How is it?"

The son replied: "It is salt."

"Taste it from the bottom. How is it?"

The son replied: "It is salt."

The father said: "Throw it away and then wait on me."

He did so; but salt exists for ever.

Then the father said: "Here also, in this body, forsooth, you do not perceive the True (*Sat*), my son; but there indeed it is.

3 "That which is the subtle essence, in it all that exists has its self. It is the True. It is the Self, and thou, O Shvetaketu, art it."

"Please, Sir, inform me still more," said the son.

"Be it so, my child," the father replied.

Chapter VIII Section 1

[The following passage seeks to elucidate the nature of Atman (the Self).]

1 Om.[4] There is this city of Brahman (the body), and in it the palace, the small lotus (of the heart), and in it that small

4. This sacred syllable was believed to contain the entire essence of the Vedas.

ether.[5] Now what exists within that small ether, that is to be sought for, that is to be understood.

2　　And if they should say to him: "Now with regard to that city of Brahman, and the palace in it, i.e. the small lotus of the heart, and the small ether within the heart, what is there within it that deserves to be sought for, or that is to be understood?"

3　　Then he should say: "As large as this ether (all space) is, so large is that ether within the heart. Both heaven and earth are contained within it, both fire and air, both sun and moon, both lightning and stars; and whatever there is of him (the Self) here in the world, and whatever is not (i.e. whatever has been or will be), all that is contained within it."

4　　And if they should say to him: "If everything that exists is contained in that city of Brahman, all beings and all desires (whatever can be imagined or desired), then what is left of it, when old age reaches it and scatters it, or when it falls to pieces?"

5　　Then he should say: "By the old age of the body, that (the ether, or Brahman within it) does not age; by the death of the body, that (the ether, or Brahman within it) is not killed. That (the Brahman) is the true Brahma-city (not the body). In it all desires are contained. It is the Self, free from sin, free from old age, from death and grief, from hunger and thirst, which desires nothing but what it ought to desire, and imagines nothing but what it ought to imagine. Now as here on earth people follow as they are commanded, and depend on the object which they are attached to, be it a country or a piece of land,

6　　"And as here on earth, whatever has been acquired by exertion, perishes, so perishes whatever is acquired for the next world by sacrifices and other good actions performed on earth. Those who depart from hence without having discovered the Self and those true desires, for them there is no freedom in all the worlds. But those who depart from hence, after having discovered the Self and those true desires, for them there is freedom in all the worlds."[6]

5. Ether (being invisible and all-pervading) is a symbol of Brahman.
6. Through knowing the Self, one knows everything and is not affected by earthly limitations.

Introduction to the Yoga Sutra

All the major religious systems of India depend upon some form of the discipline called Yoga, which is a technique of asceticism and meditation. The word Yoga signifies the binding of the mind and the emotions; it is etymologically related to the English "yoke." There are many forms of Yoga; but the classical type is that expounded by Patanjali in his *Yoga Sutra*, the earliest systematic treatise on the subject. The date of the *Yoga Sutra* cannot be established with even approximate certainty—the second century B.C. and the third or even the fifth century A.D. have been suggested—but the precise date of composition is of little importance. This little volume, consisting of fewer than two hundred aphorisms, is the fruit and summary of centuries of Yoga practice. Brief to the point of unintelligibility, it is a reminder and overview of the system for those already acquainted with it rather than an explanation for the uninitiated. Yoga cannot be learned from a book; it requires a teacher, or *guru*.

The physical exercises of Yoga have as their objective mental self-discipline—restraining the turbulence which is ordinarily characteristic of consciousness. Unification of the mind-forces must precede unification with God or Brahman. The activity of the senses and of the subconscious mind (the "latencies" in Yogic terminology) constantly introduces into consciousness objects which have the effect of preventing concentration. The purpose of Yoga is to subject the senses and the subconscious mind to the domination of the will.

The path to final enlightenment, or *samadhi*, has eight stages. The first two, *yama* and *niyama*, are moral disciplines prerequisite to the stages which follow. The technique of Yoga in the true sense begins with *asana*, stable and agreeable posture by which physical effort is reduced to the minimum. The object is to eliminate all bodily hindrances to concentration. *Pranayama*, the fourth stage, is breath control. Normally a person's breathing is irregular and unrhythmic; *pranayama* aims to make it effortlessly rhythmic, as in sleep. Mastery of this breath-technique enables the Yogi to penetrate into states of consciousness proper to sleep. Step five, *pratyahara,* means "retraction of the senses," the freeing of sense activity from the power of external objects. By controlling his sense activity, the Yogi ceases to be distracted by objects or memories.

The last three stages of Yoga represent experiences closely linked, attainable only after the previous exercises have been mastered. *Dharana* is concentration on a single point to the exclusion of all others. *Dhyana* is penetration into the essence of objects, coherence of thought, and a state of complete lucidity. The final goal is *samadhi,* signifying union, totality, and complete concentration of the spirit. *Samadhi* is an indescribable experience. It is the contemplative state in which the meditator and the object of meditation are no longer distinct, and the object is known in its true essence, without the intermediary of thought.

Popular belief has always linked Yoga with magic and occultism; and unquestionably the adept Yogin is capable of feats beyond the ordinary ken of mortals. But the ability to perform apparent miracles is by no means equivalent to the spiritual release (*moksha*) sought by philosophers and saints. Yoga technique may be learned solely for the sake of acquiring super-human powers. It is not necessarily associated with any religion, though it is adaptable to the goals of many. Classical Yoga, however, affirms the existence of a god, Ishvara (Iswara), who is not a creator or judge, but merely a sort of super-Yogin who can aid in the process of deliverance. Ishvara is a soul who has been liberated throughout eternity. The Yogi may take him as an object of concentration; but *samadhi* is attainable without him.

FROM THE YOGA SUTRA OF PATANJALI

Chapter II

29 *Yama, Niyama, Asana, Pranayama, Pratyahara, Dharana, Dhyana, Samadhi,* are the limbs of Yoga.

30 Non-killing, truthfulness, non-stealing, continence, and non-receiving [of gifts], are called *Yama.*

31 These, unbroken by time, place, purpose, and caste, are (universal) great vows.

32 Internal and external purification, contentment, mortifi-

From Patanjali's *Yoga Aphorisms,* trans. by Swami Vivekananda in *Vedanta Philosophy, Lectures on Raja Yoga* (New York: Baker & Taylor, 1899).

cation [of the body], study, and worship of God, are the *Niyamas*.

33 To obstruct thoughts which are inimical to Yoga contrary thoughts will be brought.[1]

34 The obstructions to Yoga are killing, etc., whether committed, caused, or approved; either through avarice, or anger, or ignorance; whether slight, middling, or great, and result in innumerable ignorances and miseries. This is (the method of) thinking the contrary.

35 Non-killing being established, in his [the Yogi's] presence all enmities cease (in others).

36 By the establishment of truthfulness the Yogi gets the power of attaining for himself and others the fruits of work without the works.

37 By the establishment of non-stealing all wealth comes to the Yogi.

38 By the establishment of continence energy is gained.[2]

39 When he [the Yogi] is fixed in non-receiving he gets the memory of past life.

40 Internal and external cleanliness being established, arises disgust for one's own body, and non-intercourse with other bodies.

41 There also arises purification of the *Sattva*,[3] cheerfulness of the mind, concentration, conquest of the organs, and fitness for the realisation of the Self.

42 From contentment comes superlative happiness.

43 The result of mortification is bringing powers to the organs and the body, by destroying the impurity.

44 By repetition of the *Mantra* [prayer formula] comes the realisation of the intended deity.

45 By sacrificing all to Iswara comes *Samadhi*.

46 Posture [*Asana*] is that which is firm and pleasant.

---

1. I.e., a thought can be neutralized if one thinks its opposite.

2. According to Yoga theory, each action renounced represents a corresponding gain in power.

3. According to the theory of Sankhya and Yoga, matter is composed of three *gunas: sattva* (tranquillity); *tamas* (dullness, inertia); and *rajas* (action, passion). In the Yogi, *sattva* is predominant.

47 By slight effort and meditating on the unlimited (posture becomes firm and pleasant).

48 Seat being conquered, the dualities do not obstruct.

49 Controlling the motion of the exhalation and the inhalation [*Pranayama*] follows after this.

50 Its modifications are either external or internal, or motionless,[4] regulated by place, time, and number, either long or short.

51 The fourth [sort of *Pranayama*] is restraining the *Prana*[5] by directing it either to the external or internal objects.

52 From that, the covering to the light of the *Chitta* [mind] is attenuated.[6]

53 The mind becomes fit for *Dharana*.[7]

54 The drawing in of the organs [*Pratyahara*] is by their giving up their own objects and taking the form of the mind-stuff.

Chapter III

1 *Dharana* is holding the mind on to some particular object.

2 An unbroken flow of knowledge in that object is *Dhyana*.[8]

3 When that, giving up all forms, reflects only the meaning, it is *Samadhi*.

4 (These) three (when practised) in regard to one object is *Samyana*.

5 By the conquest of that [*Samyana*] comes light of knowledge.

6 That should be employed in stages.[9]

7 These three [*Dharana, Dhyana, Samadhi*] are nearer [to the ultimate, "seedless" *Samadhi*] than those that precede.

8 But even they are external to the seedless (*Samadhi*).

9 By the suppression of the disturbed modifications of the

4. I.e., in-breathing, out-breathing, and holding the breath in the lungs.

5. *Prana* means "breath" in the sense of the total energy of the body.

6. Mind is composed of *sattva* particles which are covered by *rajas* and *tamas*. Through *pranayama* this covering is removed.

7. I.e., after the covering of the *chitta* is removed.

8. While *dharana* is the reception of sensations only from a particular object, in *dhyana* the mind succeeds in keeping itself in a state of concentration for a long period.

9. I.e., one should not attempt to go too fast.

mind, and by the rise of modifications of control, the mind is said to attain the controlling modifications—following the controlling powers of the mind.[10]

10 Its flow [the flow of controlling modifications] becomes steady by habit.

11 Taking in all sorts of objects, and concentrating upon one object, these two powers [the disturbed modifications and the modifications of control] being destroyed and manifested respectively, the *Chitta* [mind] gets the modification called *Samadhi*.

10. Attainment of the controlling modifications marks the first state of *samadhi*; but in the real *samadhi* the modifications themselves have ceased to exist.

Introduction to the Yoga of Action

The notion of salvation through action is undoubtedly the single idea most responsible for the immense popularity of the *Bhagavad Gita* in India. The traditional Indian holy man was an ascetic hermit or wanderer, uninvolved in the usual concerns of the world. Through avoidance of action he prevented unnecessary accumulation of *karma*, and thus made possible his final liberation from rebirth. But to people engaged in the ordinary work of the world—who also wished for salvation—action was unavoidable.

The doctrine of action without attachment to its fruits admirably filled the needs of such people. The *Gita*, to be sure, does not discard the old ideal of renouncing action, but proclaims instead that renunciation can be achieved *through* action. Not only is action permissible; it is actually a positive duty, provided that the actor is indifferent to the results of his deeds, does not expect any personal advantage from them, and dedicates the fruits to God. This teaching fits in perfectly with the traditional class order; for it not only

All passages from the *Bhagavad Gita* are from *Srimad Bhagavad Gita, or The Blessed Lord's Song*, trans. by Swami Paramananda (Boston: The Vedanta Center, 1913).

asserts the duty of each person to fulfill the obligations attached to his status in life, but makes such fulfillment serve as a means to salvation.

Renunciation of the fruits of action, however, demands equanimity and inner tranquillity. The aspirant must concentrate his mind and resist the attachments and impulses of the senses. Such calmness can be achieved even in the midst of turmoil. Thus Krishna recommends it to Arjuna, whose position requires that he engage in fratricidal warfare.

FROM THE BHAGAVAD GITA*

Chapter II

THE YOGA OF ACTION

39 . . . Listen now, O son of Pritha,[1] regarding Yoga, by knowing which thou shalt be freed from the bonds of Karma (cause and effect).

40 In this (Yoga) there is neither waste of effort nor possibility of evil results.[2] Even a little practice of this (Yoga) delivers one from great fear.

41 O son of Kuru,[3] in this (Yoga), the well-resolved mind is single and one-pointed; but the purposes of the irresolute mind are many-branched and endless.

42 O son of Pritha, those who delight in the flowery speech of the unwise and are satisfied with the mere letter of the Vedas (Scriptures) saying: "There is naught else";

43 And those who are full of desires for self-gratification, regarding heaven as their highest goal,[4] and are engaged in many intricate Scriptural rites just to secure pleasure and power as the result of their deeds for their future incarnations;

* For Introduction to the *Bhagavad Gita*, see above, pp. 85-87.
  1. Pritha was Arjuna's mother.
  2. In contrast to other religious practices, which if performed incorrectly or left uncompleted may bring evil consequences.
  3. Kuru was the common ancestor of both the Kauravas and the Pandavas.
  4. Heaven is a temporary goal. The soul remains in heaven only until its store of merit is exhausted, after which it must return to earth.

44 Whose discrimination is stolen away by the love of power and pleasure and who are thus deeply attached therein, (for such people) it is impossible to obtain either firm conviction (in purpose) or God-consciousness.[5]

45 The Vedas deal with the three Gunas.[6] O Arjuna, be thou free from these three Gunas; free from the pairs of opposites (cold and heat, pleasure and pain); ever steadfast, be thou free from (thoughts of) acquiring or keeping and self-possessed.

46 To the Brahmin, the knower of Truth, all the Vedas are of as little use as a small water-tank is during the time of a flood, when water is everywhere.

47 To work alone thou hast the right, but never to the fruits thereof. Be thou neither actuated by the fruits of action, nor be thou attached to inaction.

Arjuna said:

54 O Keshava,[7] what are the signs of the man of steady wisdom, one who has attained God-consciousness? How does the man of steady wisdom speak? How does he sit? How does he walk?

The Blessed Lord said:

55 O Partha,[8] when a man is satisfied in the Self by Self alone and has completely cast out all desires from the mind, then he is said to be of steady wisdom.

56 He whose mind is not agitated in calamities and who has no longing for pleasure, free from attachment, fear and anger, he indeed is said to be a saint[9] of steady wisdom.

57 He who is free from all attachment and neither rejoices on

5. *Samadhi*, union of the individual with God.
6. The *gunas* are the three constituents of matter: *rajas* (passion, restlessness) is the active principle; *tamas* (darkness, dullness) the passive principle; *sattva* (tranquillity, enlightenment) is the principle of equilibrium. Every material object was supposed to be a combination of these three principles in varying proportions.
7. Krishna, slayer of the dragon Keshi.
8. Son of Pritha (Arjuna's mother).
9. *Muni*, a man devoted to meditation and contemplation.

receiving good nor is vexed on receiving evil, his wisdom is well-established.

58 When he completely withdraws his senses from sense-objects as the tortoise withdraws its limbs, then his wisdom becomes well-established.

59 The embodied,[10] through the practice of abstinence (i.e. not giving food to the senses), can deaden the feelings of the senses, but longing still lingers in the heart; all longings drop off when he has seen the Supreme.[11]

60 O son of Kunti,[12] dangerous are the senses, they even carry away forcibly the mind of a discriminative man who is striving for perfection.

61 The man of steady wisdom, having subdued them all (senses), becomes fixed in Me, the Supreme. His wisdom is well-established whose senses are under control.

. . . .

Chapter III

The Blessed Lord said:

3 O sinless one, in this world twofold is the path already described by me. The path of wisdom is for the meditative[13] and the path of work is for the active.[14]

4 A man does not attain to freedom from action by non-performance of action, nor does he attain to perfection merely by giving up action.[15]

5 No one can ever rest even for an instant without performing action, for all are impelled by the Gunas[16] (qualities), born of Prakriti (Nature), to act incessantly.

6 He who, restraining the organs of action, sits holding

10. The embodied soul.
11. The Supreme Lord, Krishna.
12. Kunti was another name for Arjuna's mother.
13. I.e., for those who renounce the world without having passed through the householder stage of life.
14. I.e., for those who engage in the activity of the world.
15. I.e., before a man is spiritually fit to renounce the world, mere abstention from action brings no results, and (as in the following verse) is impossible anyway.
16. See note 6 above.

thoughts of sense-objects in his mind, that self-deluded one is called a hypocrite.[17]

7   But, O Arjuna, he who, controlling the senses by the mind, follows without attachment the path of action with his organs of action, he is esteemed.

8   Do thou therefore perform right and obligatory actions,[18] for action is superior to inaction. Without work, even the bare maintenance of thy body would not be possible.

19   Therefore, being unattached,[19] perform thy duties (the work that ought to be done) unceasingly; for through the performance of action, unattached, man attains the highest.

20   Verily, by work alone, Janaka[20] and other (great souls) attained perfection. Also just from the point of view of benefiting mankind, thou shouldst perform action.

21   Whatsoever a superior (man) does, that alone inferior men do. Whatever example he sets by his actions, that the people (masses) follow.

22   O Partha, there is nothing for Me to accomplish; nothing there is in the three worlds unattained or to be attained by Me, and yet I continue in action.

23   For if I do not work unceasingly, O Partha, men would follow my path (example) in every way.

24   If I did not work, these worlds would perish.[21] I should cause the confusion of castes, and also the destruction of all beings.

25   O descendant of Bharata, as the ignorant (who are attached to results) work, so also (with the same fervor) the wise should act, devoid of attachment, being desirous to help mankind.

26   One should not unsettle the understanding of the ignorant who are attached to action; the man of wisdom, by steadily

17. I.e., renunciation is not mere abstention from physical action; it is control of the sense organs and the mind and the absence of any desire for activity.
18. I.e., actions in accordance with one's *dharma*.
19. Unattached to the results of action.
20. Janaka was a sage-king frequently mentioned in the Upanishads (and the father of Sita in the *Ramayana*).
21. From the lack of moral example.

performing actions, should engage (the ignorant) in all right action.

27 All actions are performed by the Gunas, born of Prakriti (Nature).[22] One whose understanding is deluded by egoism alone thinks: "I am the doer."

28 But, O mighty-armed, the Seer of Truth, understanding the divisions of Guna and Karma (qualities, senses and actions), and knowing that it is only the senses which run after sense-objects, does not become deluded therein.

29 A man of perfect wisdom should not unsettle the people of small and imperfect understanding, who are deluded by the qualities born of Nature and are attached to the function of the Gunas (senses).

30 Surrendering all action to Me[23] and fixing the mind on the Self, devoid of hope[24] and egoism,[25] and free from the fever (of grief), fight, O Arjuna!

· · · · · · · · · · · · · · · ·

Chapter IV

The Blessed Lord said:

5 O Arjuna, both you and I have gone through many births. I know them all, but thou knowest them not, O Parantapa.[26]

6 Though I am unborn and of unchangeable nature, and though I am Lord of all beings, yet by ruling over my Prakriti (Nature) I come into being by my own Maya (mysterious power).

7 O Bharata,[27] whenever there is decline of virtue and predominance of vice, then I embody Myself.[28]

22. This is an idea of the Sankhya philosophy, according to which the three bodily qualities (*gunas*) perform all actions while the Self looks on without participating. (Note that mind, perception, etc., are regarded as qualities of matter, not as constituents of the Self.)

23. I.e., acting at the direction of Krishna.

24. Hope for results.

25. Egoism is the erroneous belief that the qualities associated with the "I" constitute one's true nature.

26. Epithet meaning "destroyer of foes."

27. Bharata was one of the ancestors of the Pandavas and Kauravas; Krishna uses it as a complimentary form of address.

28. I.e., he voluntarily assumes corporeal form. The bodies of ordinary mortals are the involuntary and unavoidable result of actions in previous lives.

8   For the protection of the good and for the destruction of evil-doers and for the reestablishment of Dharma (virtue and religion) I am born from age to age.

9   He who thus understands truly My Divine birth and action is not born again on leaving his body, O Arjuna, but he attains unto Me.[29]

10   Freed from attachment, fear and anger, being absorbed in Me and taking refuge in Me, purified by the fire of wisdom, many have attained My Being.

16   Even wise men are bewildered regarding what is action and what is inaction. Therefore I shall teach thee that action, by knowing which thou shalt be freed from all evil.[30]

17   For verily the nature of right action should be understood, also that of unlawful action and of inaction. The nature of Karma (action) is indeed very difficult to understand.

18   He who sees inaction in action[31] and action in inaction,[32] he is intelligent among men; he is a man of established wisdom and a true performer of all actions.

19   Him the sages call wise whose undertakings are devoid of desire for results and of plans, whose actions are burned by the fire of wisdom.[33]

20   Having abandoned attachment for the fruits of action, ever content and dependent on none, though engaged in action, yet he does nothing.

21   Being freed from longing, with self under control, and giving up all sense of possession (ownership), he is not tainted by sin[34] merely by performing bodily action.

22   Content with whatever comes without effort, undisturbed by the pairs of opposites (pleasure and pain, heat and cold),

29. I.e., attains a (mystic) union with the deity, in contrast to the rewards promised by the Vedas.
30. I.e., freed from the round of birth and death.
31. I.e., who recognizes that beyond the obvious bodily activity there exists an actionless Self.
32. The body, mind, and senses are continually active, whether they appear to be so or not.
33. Wisdom is compared to a fire which consumes the *karma* of both good and evil deeds.
34. *Karma.* This includes even good actions, which by producing the *karma* which leads to rebirth are an obstacle to ultimate liberation.

free from envy, even-minded in success and failure, though acting (he) is not bound.[35]

23 One whose attachment is gone, who is liberated, whose mind is well-established in wisdom, who works for sacrifice alone, his whole Karma melts away.

33 O Parantapa (Arjuna), wisdom-sacrifice is far superior to the sacrifice performed with material objects.[36] The entire realm of action, O Partha, ends in wisdom.

34 Learn this by reverence, by enquiry and by humble service. Those men of wisdom, who have realized the Truth, will teach thee supreme wisdom.

36 Even if thou art the most sinful of the sinful, thou shalt cross over (the ocean of) sin by the bark of wisdom.

37 As kindled fire reduces fuel to ashes, O Arjuna, so does the wisdom fire reduce all actions (Karma) to ashes.[37]

38 Nothing indeed in this world purifies like wisdom. He who is perfected by Yoga,[38] finds it in time within himself by himself.

39 The man of (unflinching) faith, who has mastered his senses, attains wisdom. Having gained wisdom, immediately he attains to supreme peace.[39]

40 The ignorant, the faithless and one of doubting mind perishes. There is neither this world nor the next nor any happiness for the doubting self.

41 O Dhananjaya,[40] one who has renounced actions by Yoga and has cut asunder doubt by wisdom and who is self-possessed, actions bind him not.

42 Therefore, cutting asunder with the sword of wisdom this doubt of Self, born of ignorance, lying in the heart, take refuge in Yoga and arise, O Bharata!

---

35. Bound by *samsara*, the succession of births and deaths in the world.
36. The word *yajna* (sacrifice) refers to religious ceremonies or worship in general, as well as sacrifice in the strict sense.
37. I.e., it renders them incapable of producing rebirth.
38. The selfless performance of duty.
39. I.e., worldly events are no longer capable of affecting him.
40. Epithet meaning "subduer of foes."

Introduction to the Yoga of Meditation

The following passages from the *Bhagavad Gita* recommend a path to salvation which obviously is suited only to a life of quietude and withdrawal from the world. This is the technical discipline known as Yoga, the sort taught by Patanjali,* which, in order to distinguish it from the other types, we may term the Yoga of Meditation. It prescribes posture and breathing exercises, concentration of the mind, and the subjugation of the passions which finally leads to *samadhi*.

FROM THE BHAGAVAD GITA*

THE YOGA OF MEDITATION

Chapter VI

The Blessed Lord said:

5 Let a man raise himself by his Self,[1] let him never lower himself; for he alone is the friend of himself and he alone is the enemy of himself.

6 He who has conquered himself by the Self, he is the friend of himself; but he whose self is unconquered, his self acts as his own enemy like an external foe.

7 The Supreme Self of the self-subjugated and serene-minded, is ever undisturbed in heat and cold, pleasure and pain, as well as in honor and dishonor.

8 He who is satisfied with wisdom and direct vision of Truth, who has conquered the senses and is ever undisturbed, to whom a lump of earth, a stone and gold are the same, that Yogi is said to be a Yukta (a saint of established wisdom).

* For the *Yoga Sutra* of Patanjali, see above, pp. 197-202.

1. I.e., let him raise that self identified with the body and the senses (the ego) by means of his true Self, the Atman.

9   He is esteemed who looks with equal regard upon well-wishers, friends, enemies, neutrals, a mediator, the hateful, relatives, upon the righteous and the unrighteous.

10   A Yogi[2] should constantly practise concentration of the heart, remaining in seclusion alone, subduing his body and mind and being free from longing and possession (sense of ownership).

11   In a cleanly spot having established his seat firmly, neither too high nor too low, with a cloth, skin and Kusha grass, placed one on the other;

12   Being seated there, making the mind one-pointed and subduing the activities of mind and senses, let him practise Yoga for self-purification.

13   Let him hold his body, head and neck erect and motionless, fixing the gaze on the tip of his nose, not looking around.[3]

14   Being serene-hearted and fearless, ever steadfast in the vow of Brahmacharya[4] and controlling the mind, let him sit steadfastly absorbed in thoughts of Me, regarding Me as his supreme goal.

15   Thus ever keeping himself steadfast, the Yogi of subdued mind attains eternal peace and freedom, which abide in Me.

16   But, O Arjuna, (the practice of) Yoga is not for him who eats too much or who does not eat at all, nor for him who sleeps too much or keeps awake (in excess).

17   He who is moderate in eating and recreation, moderate in his efforts in work, moderate in sleep and wakefulness, (his practice of) Yoga becomes the destroyer of all misery.

18   When the mind, completely subdued, rests in Self alone, free from longing for all objects of desire, then he is said to be a Yukta (steadfast in Self-knowledge).

19   As a lamp placed in a windless spot does not flicker, the same simile is used to define a Yogi of subdued mind, practising union with the Self.

20   In that state, when the mind is completely subdued by the

2. One who practices the discipline of meditation.
3. This is a technique of concentration, preliminary to concentration on the Self.
4. Chastity and a virtuous life.

practice of Yoga and has attained serenity, in that state, seeing Self by the self, he is satisfied in the Self alone.

21 In that state, transcending the senses, he (the Yogi) feels that infinite bliss which is perceived by the purified understanding[5]; knowing that and being established therein, he never falls back from his real state (of Self-knowledge);

22 After having attained which, no other gain seems greater; being established wherein, he is not overwhelmed even by great sorrow.

23 Know that (state) of separation from the contact with pain as Yoga.[6] This Yoga should be practised with perseverance and undepressed heart.

24 Abandoning without reserve all the desires born of mental fancies, and restraining completely by the mind the entire group of the senses from all directions,

25 With understanding held by firmness, and mind established in the Self, let him (thus) by degrees attain tranquillity; let him not think of anything else.

26 Wheresoever the restless and unsteady mind may wander away, let him withdraw it from there and bring it under the control of the Self alone.

Arjuna said:

33 O Destroyer of Madhu[7] (Krishna), this Yoga, which has been declared by Thee as even-mindedness, I do not see (the possibility) of its lasting existence, owing to the restlessness of the mind.

34 O Krishna, the mind is restless, turbulent, strong and unyielding; I consider it as difficult to subdue as the wind.

The Blessed Lord said:

35 Doubtless, O mighty-armed, the mind is restless and difficult to control; but, O son of Kunti, through practice and dispassion (renunciation) it can be conquered.

5. I.e., purified from the influence of the senses.
6. In the state of concentration a Yogi does not feel pain.
7. The dragon.

36 Yoga is difficult to attain by him who is of uncontrolled
self: such is my conviction; but the self-subjugated can attain
it by following the right means.

Arjuna said:

37 O Krishna, he who, though possessed with faith,[8] yet lacks
in control and whose mind wanders away from Yoga, what end
does he meet, failing to reach perfection in Yoga?
38 O Mighty-armed (Krishna), does he not perish like a rent
cloud,[9] supportless, fallen from both (here and hereafter),[10]
deluded in the path of Brahman (Truth)?
39 O Krishna, this doubt of mine Thou oughtest to dispel, for
there is none but Thee who is able to destroy this doubt.

The Blessed Lord said:

40 O Partha, there is no destruction for him either here or
hereafter, for the well-doer (devotee), O Beloved, never comes
to an evil end.
41 One who is fallen from Yoga, after having attained the
regions of the righteous[11] and dwelling there for unlimited
time, reincarnates in the house of the pure and prosperous.
42 Or else he is born in the family of wise Yogis; but such a
birth is very rare to obtain in this world.
43 O descendant of Kuru, there (in that incarnation) he gains
the knowledge acquired in his previous incarnation, and he
strives again more (fervently) than before for perfection.
44 He is irresistibly led by the previous practice (of Yoga).
Even the enquirer of Yoga goes beyond the letter-Brahmin.[12]
45 But the Yogi, striving with perseverance, purified from all
sin, perfected through many births, reaches the supreme goal.

8. Faith in the efficacy of Yoga.
9. A patch of cloud which has detached itself from a large cloud, drifts,
and ultimately disappears.
10. Arjuna fears that someone who is unsuccessful at Yoga may not only
fail to attain the benefits of Yoga, but also be penalized for this failure by
being reborn in a lower status.
11. Heaven.
12. The Brahmin who performs rituals according to the letter of the Vedas.

46   The Yogi is superior to ascetics,[13] and superior to those who have attained wisdom through books; he is also superior to performers of action (according to the Scriptures). Therefore, O Arjuna! be thou a Yogi.

13. Those who merely mortify the body.

Introduction to the Yoga of Faith

For the person incapable of performing the severer Yogas of action and meditation, the *Bhagavad Gita* also provides a religion of faith. *Bhakti*—devotion to a personal god—was a prominent feature of many Hindu sects, who felt the need of a saviour-figure to serve as the object of devotion. The difficult concept of Brahman takes a secondary place in the *Gita*, though in a few instances *bhakti* is regarded as a preliminary step toward the absorption of the soul into Brahman. *Bhakti*-religion teaches the worshipper to place utter trust in God, to serve him devotedly, and submit without reserve to his will.

FROM THE BHAGAVAD GITA

THE YOGA OF FAITH

Chapter IX

The Blessed Lord said:

7   O son of Kunti, all beings, at the end of a cycle, go back to my Prakriti (Nature); again, at the beginning of a cycle, I send them forth.

8   Ruling over My Prakriti, I send forth again and again this vast multitude of beings, who are helplessly impelled by Nature.

9   O conqueror of wealth (Arjuna), these acts (of creation

and dissolution) do not bind Me,[1] sitting as one unconcerned and unattached to these acts.

10   O son of Kunti, with Me as the presiding Deity, Prakriti (Nature) sends forth the moving and the unmoving. For this reason the world wheels round and round.

11   Fools, unaware of My Supreme state, as the great Lord of beings, disregard Me dwelling in human form.[2]

12   They are of vain hopes, of vain deeds, of vain knowledge,[3] and senseless, possessed with the deluding nature of Rakshasas (unclean, passionate, and godless creatures) and Asuras (creatures of darkness and of ignorance).[4]

13   But, O son of Kunti, the great-souled ones, possessing the Divine Nature, knowing Me as Immutable and as the Source of beings, worship Me with single-minded devotion.

14   Ever singing My glory and striving with steadfast vows, bowing down to Me in devotion, (they) perpetually worship Me.

20   The knowers of the three Vedas, having worshipped Me[5] with sacrifice, drinking the Soma[6] and thus being purified from sin, pray for the goal of heaven; they, having reached the region of the ruler of the Devas,[7] enjoy in heaven the celestial pleasures of the Devas.

21   Having enjoyed that vast celestial world, they, at the exhaustion of the merit (of their good deeds), again enter into the mortal world; thus following the religion of the three Vedas, with the craving for objects of desire, they attain coming and going (birth and re-birth).

22   Those who worship Me and meditate on Me without any other thought, to these ever steadfast devotees I secure safety and supply all their needs (I carry their burden).

---

1. I.e., the Lord is not subject to the law of *karma*.

2. I.e., they regard him as an ordinary man.

3. Hopes and deeds which do not culminate in happiness; useless learning which brings no benefits.

4. Rakshas and Asuras are fiends and demons.

5. In the form of other deities who promise worldly rewards in exchange for sacrifice.

6. Soma was the intoxicating drink employed at the sacrifice.

7. The Devas, literally "shining ones," are gods who reside in heaven.

23 O son of Kunti, even those devotees who worship other gods with faith, they too worship Me, but contrary to the law.[8]

24 For I am alone the Enjoyer and Lord of all sacrifice,[9] but they do not know Me in truth, hence they return (fall into rebirth).

25 The worshippers of the gods go to the gods; to the ancestors go the ancestor-worshippers; the spirit-worshippers go to the spirits[10]; but My worshippers come unto Me.

26 He who, with devotion offereth to Me a leaf, a flower, a fruit and water, that love-offering I accept, made by the pure-hearted.

27 Whatever thou doest, whatever thou eatest, whatever thou offerest as oblation, whatever thou givest and the austerities thou performest, O son of Kunti, do that as an offering to Me.

28 Thus thou shalt be freed from the bonds of action that bears good and evil fruit; and thy soul, being steadfastly engaged in this devotion of renunciation, liberated thou shalt come unto Me.

29 Alike am I to all beings; hated or beloved there is none to Me. But those who worship Me with devotion, they are in Me and I am in them.

30 Even if the most wicked worships Me with undivided devotion, he should be regarded as good, for he is rightly resolved.

31 Very soon he becomes a righteous soul and attains to eternal peace. Know thou, O son of Kunti, that my devotee never perishes.

32 O Partha, even those who are of impure birth,—women, Vaishyas (merchant class) and Shudras (servant class),[11]—even they, by taking refuge in Me, attain to the Supreme Goal.

33 What need is there, then, to speak of the holy Brahmins and the royal Sages![12] Having come into this transitory and joyless world, do thou worship Me.

8. In a wrong way, because they do not seek final liberation.
9. Here Krishna declares himself to be the Self even of the gods; thus it is he who actually receives the sacrifice.
10. I.e., to the heavens of the gods, the ancestors, and the spirits, respectively.
11. These are classes for whom salvation is difficult according to the Vedic scheme. Women and Shudras were forbidden to study the Vedas at all.
12. For whom salvation is much more easily attainable.

34. Fill thy mind with Me, be thou My devotee, worship Me and bow down to Me; thus, steadfastly uniting thy heart with Me alone and regarding Me as thy Supreme Goal, thou shalt come unto Me.

Introduction to Buddhism

Gautama, the future Buddha ("Buddha" means "Enlightened One"), was born a prince of the Shakya tribe in the hill country bordering India and Nepal about 563 B.C. His father was the ruler of a small kingdom with its capital at Kapilavastu. Tradition has since surrounded the life of the Buddha with many supernatural elements. But there appears no reason to doubt the historical reality of this prince, who, touched by the suffering he saw around him, resolved to become a holy man. Gautama at first sought spiritual enlightenment in the traditional way—through severe ascetic practices. Ultimately he concluded that extreme austerities were useless, and henceforth practiced a "Middle Way" between self-indulgence and self-mortification. According to tradition, he reached enlightenment—Nirvana—under the Bo tree at Bodh Gaya, and shortly afterward founded the Buddhist monastic order with five disciples at the Deer Park at Sarnath, near Benares. Having spent the remaining forty-five years of his life as a teacher and leader of the Order, he died at the age of eighty (*ca.* 483 B.C.) at Kusinagara.

Perhaps inevitably, legend soon transformed Gautama Shakyamuni ("the sage of the Shakyas") from a simple human teacher into a divine figure, a spiritual principle (Tathagata). Especially the Mahayana—the later of the two main divisions of Buddhism—tended to regard him as a supernatural being who descends to earth from time to time in various human forms to preach the Law on behalf of the eternal Buddha-principle. But as he appears in the older scriptures, Gautama is a modest and unassuming man who claims neither divine origin for himself nor supernatural sanction for his teaching. Indeed, he decisively refused to discuss such subjects as the existence of God and the origin of the universe.

For some four hundred years the Buddhist tradition was transmitted by word of mouth without ever being put into writing. It is thus nearly impossible to tell which teachings go back to Gautama's lifetime and which arose several centuries afterward. Buddhists themselves divide their holy scriptures into *sutras*—words supposedly spoken by Gautama himself—and *shastras*—commentaries by known authors of later date—although many of the compositions called *sutras* evidently post-date the Buddha by half a millennium. At an unknown time, the Buddhist canon was arranged into the *Tripitaka* ("three baskets"): the *Vinaya Pitaka*, which lays down rules of conduct for monks; the *Sutta Pitaka*, dealing with the fundamentals of religious belief; and the *Abhidhamma Pitaka*, consisting of advanced treatises on doctrine. Much of the early canon originated in north India, and was written in the ancient Pali tongue—which was perhaps one of the popular north Indian dialects.* But the majority of the Buddhist scriptures now extant have been preserved in Ceylon (in Pali) or in Chinese or Tibetan translation. Even in their present form these writings bear distinct marks of their origin as oral tradition: they are extraordinarily repetitious and full of mnemonic devices such as numerical lists and recurring stanzas.

In contrast to Hinduism, which is firmly bound to a rigid class structure, Buddhism is a universal religion open to all believers on equal terms. Its refusal to recognize the divine authority of the Vedas places it outside the pale of Hindu orthodoxy. Nonetheless, throughout its history Buddhism has drawn substantially upon the general stock of contemporary Indian religious ideas. While denying the validity of inborn class distinctions, it accepts the ideas of *karma* and transmigration and the division of historical time into enormously long, recurring periods. Buddhist meditation depends heavily on the traditional techniques of Yoga. In India, Buddhists frequently retained their beliefs in the deities of the Vedic pantheon, even though denying the sacred status of the Vedas. The gods, to be sure, were subject to birth and death just like human beings, and certainly inferior in merit to the enlightened Buddhist; but they were nonetheless treated with affection and reverence. Buddhism never attempted to interfere with superstition or magical practices, which to certain of its adherents formed an important part of the faith.

* Scholars are not certain which of the Indian vernaculars may be identified with Pali (a word meaning simply "text" rather than any particular dialect). As a heresy, Buddhism never succeeded to any great extent in making use of Sanskrit, the classical language of India.

Although Buddhism has developed a complicated metaphysics, it is above all a practical spiritual discipline, the goal of which is liberation (in Sanskrit: Nirvana; in Pali: Nibbana). All Buddhist schools agree upon this goal and concur in the fundamental assumption that the world is evil. This view, to be sure, runs counter to the ordinary opinion of mankind; but Buddhists cite in support of it the undeniable fact that all phenomena are impermanent; that suffering or anxiety is unavoidable; and that no one can control his own destiny. Even apparently pleasant things either involve the suffering of others, or cause anxiety because we are afraid to lose them, and finally, are incapable of satisfying the deepest human longing. To eliminate suffering it is necessary to recognize its cause. The cause, according to Buddhists, is desire for and attachment to the things of this world—family, friends, possessions, pleasures. Desire is insatiable, for no one is ever satisfied; and attachment to people or things causes sorrow at their loss. To eliminate the cause of suffering is to eliminate the suffering itself; and Buddhism prescribes the means in the Noble Eightfold Path.

Early Buddhists regarded meditation, rather than good works, as the principal means of liberation. Buddhism, in fact, was a religion designed for monks—persons able and willing to devote all their time to the pursuit of enlightenment. The three aspects of meditation were defined as moral discipline, concentration, and wisdom. Moral discipline begins when the monk renounces all his worldly ties. He cultivates an attitude of detachment from his own sense of individuality. Buddhism teaches that there exists no soul, no ego, nothing than can be considered as "I." What appears to be an "I" is in fact the interplay of the five constituents of matter (the five *skandhas*)—physical body, feelings, perceptions, impulses, and acts of consciousness. All experiences are merely the interaction of impersonal forces which are constantly in flux, unrelated to any concrete center of consciousness.

Through concentration, the monk narrows his field of attention to a single point. The aim is to eliminate the usual confusion of impressions in the mind and produce a state of tranquillity. Similarly, he cultivates the four desirable emotions—friendliness, compassion, sympathetic joy, and even-mindedness—in order to reduce his sense of separation from other creatures. To induce concentration, he practices the eight *Dhyanas* (in Pali: *Jhanas*) of classical Yoga. The result is trance, which is short-lived; but the experience of it shatters common-sense faith in the ultimate reality of the everyday world. The goal of Buddhist striving is wisdom; and the

highest wisdom is Nirvana. Nirvana is contemplation of the ultimate, pure, unconditioned Truth. It can only be experienced; to the
mind it is unthinkable and incomprehensible. Through renouncing
all limited things and completely extinguishing the notion of self,
the perfected Buddhist automatically passes into Nirvana.

The three foundations of Buddhism are sometimes listed as the
Buddha himself, the doctrine (*dharma*), and the monastic Order
(*vinaya*).* The first Buddhists took as their highest ideal the *arhat*
(*arahant*)—the monk who had gained perfect enlightenment. Such
an ideal, obviously, was attainable only by a small minority of spiritually gifted persons who could arrange to renounce the world. Ordinary laymen, engaged in the normal tasks of society, felt the need for
a form of the faith in which they too might participate. Thus about
the time of Ashoka (third century B.C.), increasingly liberal tendencies began to develop within the Buddhist community. The new
direction (subsequently known as the Mahayana, or "Great Vehicle," in contrast to the Hinayana, or "Lesser Vehicle") was less
strict about monastic discipline, and more willing to concede that
householders, women, and spiritually less-talented monks might
gain Nirvana. The Mahayana did not reject the scriptures or the
goals of the Hinayana, but considered them insufficient and incom-
plete. The ideal of the *arhat*, who renounced the world to seek his
own enlightenment, gave way to that of the *bodhisattva*, who postponed his own Nirvana in order to aid others in reaching that goal.

Where the Hinayana stressed the effort and exertion of the individual monk, the Mahayana attached a much greater importance to
faith. The ordinary Buddhist layman could hardly be expected to
follow the rigorous discipline of the monk or understand the subtle-
ties of Buddhist metaphysics. He must be helped toward enlightenment. Thus the Mahayana produced a number of saviours—Buddhas or future Buddhas—whose function it was to guide the believer on the Path. It invented the doctrine of the transfer of merit,
whereby (in contravention of the law of *karma*) the surplus good
works of the saviour could be transferred to the believer; and it
taught that all beings are potentially of the same nature as Buddha. As a faith accessible to everyone, the Mahayana clearly had a
broader appeal than its predecessor. In the foreign lands to which
it penetrated, it virtually replaced the Hinayana, which survives
today only in Ceylon, Burma, Cambodia, and Thailand.

It is one of the ironies of history that Buddhism, which today is

* See "The Monastic Vows," below, pp. 284-85.

the dominant faith of much of East and Southeast Asia, has utterly disappeared from the land of its birth. The reasons for its decline—after centuries of extraordinary flourishing—can only be surmised. One factor, no doubt, was the so-called Hindu Renaissance—the development of reformed systems of belief which, unlike Buddhism, fully accepted the authority of the Vedas. Opposition from the powerful Brahmin priesthood certainly played a part; for Buddhism rejected the notion of caste, and with it the basis of Brahmin pre-eminence in Indian society. The decline of Buddhism probably began as early as the fifth or sixth centuries A.D. The final blow came from the Muslim invasions of the twelfth and thirteenth centuries, whereby Islam was established in large parts of northern India.

THE BUDDHA

Introduction to the Jatakas

The Jatakas are stories of diverse origin which purport to relate important events of the Buddha's life, both in his former incarnations and in his most recent earthly existence as Gautama Shakyamuni. Many of these tales undoubtedly were current as oral folk literature before being transformed into Jatakas. A number of them show decided affinities with the purely secular fables of the *Panchatantra*. The Jatakas are included in the Buddhist canon as a section of the *Khuddaka Nikaya*, which is the fifth principal division of the *Sutta Pitaka*.

The following selections were translated from Pali, the language of the Buddhist canon preserved in Ceylon. Proper names thus show certain variations in spelling from their better-known Sanskrit forms.

The following selections from the *Jatakas* are from *Buddhism in Translations*, translated from the Pali by Henry Clarke Warren (Cambridge, Mass.: Harvard University Press, 1896), pp. 38-53, 55-64, 67-71, 75-83.

FROM THE JATAKAS
OF THE KHUDDAKA NIKAYA

The Birth of the Buddha

Now while the Future Buddha was still dwelling in the city of the Tusita gods[1] the "Buddha-Uproar," as it is called, took place. For there are three uproars which take place in the world,—the Cyclic-Uproar, the Buddha-Uproar, and the Universal-Monarch-Uproar. They occur as follows:—

When it is known that after the lapse of a hundred thousand years the cycle is to be renewed, the gods called Loka-byuhas, inhabitants of a heaven of sensual pleasure, wander about through the world, with hair let down and flying in the wind, weeping and wiping away their tears with their hands, and with their clothes red and in great disorder. And thus they make announcement:—

"Sirs, after the lapse of a hundred thousand years, the cycle is to be renewed; this world will be destroyed; also the mighty ocean will dry up; and this broad earth, and Sineru,[2] the monarch of the mountains, will be burnt up and destroyed,—up to the Brahma heavens[3] will the destruction of the world extend. Therefore, sirs, cultivate friendliness; cultivate compassion, joy, and indifference; wait on your mothers; wait on your fathers; and honor your elders among your kinsfolk."

This is called the Cyclic-Uproar.

Again, when it is known that after a lapse of a thousand years an omniscient Buddha is to arise in the world, the guardian angels of the world wander about, proclaiming:

"Sirs, after the lapse of a thousand years a Buddha will arise in the world."

---

1. "The heaven of the satisfied gods."
2. The legendary mountain supposedly situated at the center of the (flat) earth, surrounded by other high peaks where the gods dwelt.
3. The heavens presided over by the high god Brahma.

This is called the Buddha-Uproar.

And lastly, when they realize that after the lapse of a hundred years a Universal Monarch[4] is to arise, the terrestrial deities wander about, proclaiming:—

"Sirs, after the lapse of a hundred years a Universal Monarch is to arise in the world."

This is called the Universal-Monarch-Uproar. And these three are mighty uproars.

When of these three Uproars they hear the sound of the Buddha-Uproar, the gods of all ten thousand worlds come together into one place, and having ascertained what particular being is to be The Buddha, they approach him, and beseech him to become one. But it is not till after omens have appeared that they beseech him.

At that time, therefore, having all come together in one world, . . . they approached the Future Buddha in the Tusita heaven, and besought him, saying,—

"Sir, it was not to acquire the glory of a Sakka,[5] or of a Mara,[6] or of a Brahma, or of a Universal Monarch, that you fulfilled the Ten Perfections; but it was to gain omniscience in order to save the world, that you fulfilled them. Sir, the time and fit season for your Buddhaship has now arrived."

But the Great Being, before assenting to their wish, made what is called the five great observations. He observed, namely, the time, the continent, the country, the family, and the mother and her span of life.

In the first of these observations he asked himself whether it was the right time or no. Now it is not the right time when the length of men's lives is more than a hundred thousand years. And why is it not the right time? Because mortals then forget about birth, old age, and death. And if The Buddhas, who always include in their teachings the Three Characteristics, were to attempt at such a time to discourse concerning transitoriness,

4. A Universal Monarch (*Chakravartin*) who would conquer all of India and rule prosperously and righteously was supposed to appear from time to time in the cosmic cycle.

5. King of the gods.

6. Ruler of the highest heaven of sensual pleasure; the Buddhist equivalent of the devil.

misery, and the lack of substantive reality, men would not think it worth while listening to them, nor would they give them credence. Thus there would be no conversions made; and if there were no conversions, the dispensation would not conduce to salvation. This, therefore, is not the right time.

Also it is not the right time when men's lives are less than a hundred years. And why is it not the right time? Because mortals are then exceedingly corrupt; and an exhortation given to the exceedingly corrupt makes no impression, but, like a mark drawn with a stick on the surface of the water, it immediately disappears. This, therefore, also is not the right time.

But when the length of men's lives is between a hundred years and a hundred thousand years, then is it the right time. Now at that time men's lives were a hundred years; accordingly the Great Being observed that it was the right time for his birth.

Next he made the observation concerning the continent. Looking over the four continents with their attendant isles, he reflected: "In three of the continents the Buddhas are never born; only in the continent of India are they born." Thus he decided on the continent.

Next he made the observation concerning the place. "The continent of India is large," thought he, "being ten thousand leagues around. In which of its countries are The Buddhas born?" Thus he decided on the Middle Country. . . .[7]

Then he made the observation concerning the family. "The Buddhas," thought he, "are never born into a family of the peasant caste, or of the servile caste; but into one of the warrior caste, or of the Brahman caste, whichever at the time is the higher in public estimation. The warrior caste is now the higher in public estimation. I will be born into a warrior family, and king Suddhodana shall be my father." Thus he decided on the family.

Then he made the observation concerning the mother. "The mother of a Buddha," thought he, " is never a wanton, nor a drunkard, but is one who has fulfilled the perfections through a hundred thousand cycles, and has kept the five precepts un-

7. A small region of north India around the city of Kapilavatthu (Kapilavastu).

broken from the day of her birth. Now this queen Maha-Maya
is such a one; and she shall be my mother."—"But what shall
be her span of life?"[8] continued he. And he perceived that it
was to be ten months[9] and seven days.

Having thus made the five great observations, he kindly
made the gods the required promise, saying,—

"Sirs, you are right. The time has come for my Buddhaship."

Then surrounded by the gods of the Tusita heaven, and dis-
missing all the other gods, he entered the Nandana Grove of
the Tusita capital,—for in each of the heavens there is a Nandana Grove. And here the gods said, "Attain in your next existence your high destiny," and kept reminding him that he had
already paved the way to it by his accumulated merit. Now it
was while he was thus dwelling, surrounded by these deities,
and continually reminded of his accumulated merit, that he
died, and was conceived in the womb of queen Maha-Maya. . . .

.   .   .   .

From the time the Future Buddha was thus conceived, four
angels with swords in their hands kept guard, to ward off all
harm from both the Future Buddha and the Future Buddha's
mother. No lustful thought sprang up in the mind of the Future
Buddha's mother; having reached the pinnacle of good fortune
and of glory, she felt comfortable and well, and experienced no
exhaustion of body. And within her womb she could distinguish
the Future Buddha, like a white thread passed through a transparent jewel. And whereas a womb that has been occupied by a
Future Buddha is like the shrine of a temple, and can never be
occupied or used again, therefore it was that the mother of the
Future Buddha died when he was seven days old, and was reborn in the Tusita heaven.

Now other women sometimes fall short of and sometimes run
over the term of ten lunar months, and then bring forth either
sitting or lying down; but not so the mother of a Future Buddha.
She carries the Future Buddha in her womb for just ten months,
and then brings forth while standing up. This is a characteristic
of the mother of a Future Buddha. So also queen Maha-Maya

8. I.e., how long will she live after conceiving me?
9. Ten lunar months.

carried the Future Buddha in her womb, as it were oil in a vessel, for ten months; and being then far gone with child, she grew desirous of going home to her relatives, and said to king Suddhodana,—

"Sire, I should like to visit my kinsfolk in their city Deva-daha."

"So be it," said the king; and from Kapilavatthu to the city of Devadaha he had the road made even, and garnished it with plantain-trees set in pots, and with banners, and streamers; and, seating the queen in a golden palanquin borne by a thousand of his courtiers, he sent her away in great pomp.

Now between the two cities, and belonging to the inhabitants of both, there was a pleasure-grove of sal-trees, called Lumbini Grove. And at this particular time this grove was one mass of flowers from the ground to the topmost branches, while amongst the branches and flowers hummed swarms of bees of the five different colors, and flocks of various kinds of birds flew about warbling sweetly. Throughout the whole of Lumbini Grove the scene resembled the Cittalata Grove in Indra's paradise,[10] or the magnificently decorated banqueting pavilion of some potent king.

When the queen beheld it she became desirous of disporting herself therein, and the courtiers therefore took her into it. And going to the foot of the monarch sal-tree of the grove, she wished to take hold of one of its branches. And the sal-tree branch, like the tip of a well-steamed reed, bent itself down within reach of the queen's hand. Then she reached out her hand, and seized hold of the branch, and immediately her pains came upon her. Thereupon the people hung a curtain about her, and retired. So her delivery took place while she was standing up, and keeping fast hold of the sal-tree branch.

At that very moment came four pure-minded Maha-Brahma angels bearing a golden net; and, receiving the Future Buddha on this golden net, they placed him before his mother and said,—

"Rejoice, O queen! A mighty son has been born to you."

. . . .

10. The heaven of the god Indra.

Now on the fifth day they bathed the Future Buddha's head, saying, "We will perform the rite of choosing a name for him." And they prepared the royal palace by anointing it with four kinds of perfumes, and by scattering Dalbergia blossoms and other flowers, five sorts in all. And making some porridge of whole rice-grains boiled in milk, they invited one hundred and eight Brahmans, men who had mastered the three Vedas. And having seated these Brahmans in the royal palace, and fed them with delicate food, and showed them every attention, they asked them to observe the marks and characteristics of the Future Buddha's person, and to prophesy his fortune.

Among the hundred and eight, . . . eight Brahmans were the fortune-tellers, being the same who had interpreted the dream of the night of the conception.[11] Seven of these raised two fingers each, and gave a double interpretation, saying, "If a man possessing such marks and characteristics continue in the household life, he becomes a Universal Monarch; if he retire from the world, he becomes a Buddha." And then they set forth all the glory of a Universal Monarch.

But the youngest of them all, a youth whose clan-name was Kondañña, after examining the splendid set of marks and characteristics on the person of the Future Buddha, raised only one finger, and gave but a single interpretation, saying, "There is here naught to make him stay in the household life. He will most undoubtedly become a Buddha, and remove the veil of ignorance and folly from the world." For this Kondañña was one who had made an earnest wish under former Buddhas, and was now in his last existence. Therefore it was that he outstripped the other seven in knowledge, and saw but one future; inasmuch as a person possessed of such marks and characteristics would never stay in the household life, but would undoubtedly become a Buddha. So he raised only one finger, and gave that interpretation. . . .

Then said the king, "What shall my son see to make him retire from the world?"

11. The dream of Queen Maha-Maya, which the Brahmans interpreted to mean that she would give birth either to a Universal Monarch or to a Buddha.

"The four signs."

"What four?"

"A decrepit old man, a diseased man, a dead man, and a monk."

"From this time forth," said the king, "let no such persons be allowed to come near my son. It will never do for my son to become a Buddha. What I would wish to see is my son exercising sovereign rule and authority over the four great continents and the two thousand attendant isles, and walking through the heavens surrounded by a retinue thirty-six leagues in circumference." And when he had so spoken he placed guards for a distance of a quarter of a league in each of the four directions, in order that none of these four kinds of men might come within sight of his son.

. . . .

The Great Retirement

. . . In due course, the Future Buddha attained to the age of sixteen years. And the king built three palaces for the Future Buddha, suited to the three seasons,[1]—one of nine stories, another of seven stories, and another of five stories. And he provided him with forty thousand dancing girls. And the Future Buddha, with his gayly dressed dancers, was like a god surrounded by hosts of houris[2]; and attended by musical instruments that sounded of themselves, and in the enjoyment of great magnificence, he lived, as the seasons changed, in each of these three palaces. And the mother of Rahula[3] was his principal queen.

. . . .

Now on a certain day the Future Buddha wished to go to the park, and told his charioteer to make ready the chariot. Accordingly the man brought out a sumptuous and elegant chariot, and adorning it richly, he harnessed to it four state-horses of the Sindhava breed, as white as the petals of the white lotus,

1. The entire year, which by one Indian system of reckoning was divided into three seasons.
2. Beautiful and seductive women.
3. Gautama's son, who will later become his disciple.

and announced to the Future Buddha that everything was ready. And the Future Buddha mounted the chariot, which was like to a palace of the gods, and proceeded towards the park.

"The time for the enlightenment of prince Siddhattha draw- eth nigh," thought the gods; "we must show him a sign:" and they changed one of their number into a decrepit old man, bro- ken-toothed, gray-haired, crooked and bent of body, leaning on a staff, and trembling, and showed him to the Future Buddha, but so that only he and the charioteer saw him.

Then said the Future Buddha to the charioteer, in the manner related in the Mahapadana,[4]—

"Friend, pray, who is this man? Even his hair is not like that of other men." And when he heard the answer, he said, "Shame on birth, since to every one that is born old age must come." And agitated in heart, he thereupon returned and ascended his palace.

"Why has my son returned so quickly?" asked the king.

"Sire, he has seen an old man," was the reply; "and because he has seen an old man, he is about to retire from the world."

"Do you want to kill me, that you say such things? Quickly get ready some plays to be performed before my son. If we can but get him to enjoying pleasure, he will cease to think of re- tiring from the world." Then the king extended the guard to half a league in each direction.

Again, on a certain day, as the Future Buddha was going to the park, he saw a diseased man whom the gods had fashioned; and having again made inquiry, he returned, agitated in heart, and ascended his palace.

And the king made the same inquiry and gave the same or- ders as before; and again extending the guard, placed them for three quarters of a league around.

And again on a certain day, as the Future Buddha was going to the park, he saw a dead man whom the gods had fashioned; and having again made inquiry, he returned, agitated in heart, and ascended his palace.

And the king made the same inquiry and gave the same or-

4. A Buddhist text.

ders as before; and again extending the guard, placed them for a league around.

And again on a certain day, as the Future Buddha was going to the park, he saw a monk, carefully and decently clad, whom the gods had fashioned; and he asked his charioteer, "Pray, who is this man?"

Now although there was no Buddha in the world, and the charioteer had no knowledge of either monks or their good qualities, yet by the power of the gods he was inspired to say, "Sire, this is one who has retired from the world;" and he thereupon proceeded to sound the praises of retirement from the world. The thought of retiring from the world was a pleasing one to the Future Buddha, and this day he went on until he came to the park. The repeaters of the Digha,[5] however, say that he went to the park after having seen all the Four Signs on one and the same day.

. . . .

And the Future Buddha entered his palace in great splendor, and lay on his couch of state. . . .

To him that magnificent apartment, as splendid as the palace of Sakka, began to seem like a cemetery filled with dead bodies impaled and left to rot; and the three modes of existence appeared like houses all ablaze. And breathing forth the solemn utterance, "How oppressive and stifling is it all!" his mind turned ardently to retiring from the world. "It behooves me to go forth on the Great Retirement this very day," said he; and he arose from his couch, and coming near the door, called out,—

"Who's there?"

"Master, it is I, Channa," replied the courtier who had been sleeping with his head on the threshold.[6]

"I wish to go forth on the Great Retirement to-day. Saddle a horse for me."

"Yes, sire." And taking saddle and bridle with him, the cour-

5. The *Digha Nikaya*, one of the five major divisions of the *Sutta Pitaka*.
6. The threshold is exposed even when the door is shut. In India, to allow for ventilation, doors are frequently constructed with a gap of two feet or so between the bottom of the door and the threshold.

tier started for the stable. There, by the light of lamps fed with sweet-smelling oils, he perceived the mighty steed Kanthaka in his pleasant quarters, under a canopy of cloth beautified with a pattern of jasmine flowers. "This is the one for me to saddle to-day," thought he; and he saddled Kanthaka. . . .

Now the Future Buddha, after he had sent Channa on his errand, thought to himself, "I will take just one look at my son;" and rising from the couch on which he was sitting, he went to the suite of apartments occupied by the mother of Rahula, and opened the door of her chamber. Within the chamber was burning a lamp fed with sweet-smelling oil, and the mother of Rahula lay sleeping on a couch strewn deep with jasmine and other flowers, her hand resting on the head of her son. When the Future Buddha reached the threshold, he paused, and gazed at the two from where he stood.

"If I were to raise my wife's hand from off the child's head, and take him up, she would awake, and thus prevent my departure. I will first become a Buddha, and then come back and see my son." So saying, he descended from the palace. . . .

When the Future Buddha had thus descended from the palace, he came near to his horse, and said,—

"My dear Kanthaka, save me now this one night; and then, when thanks to you I have become a Buddha, I will save the world of gods and men." And thereupon he vaulted upon Kanthaka's back. . . .

The Future Buddha rode on the mighty back of the mighty steed, made Channa hold on by the tail, and so arrived at midnight at the great gate of the city.

Now the king, in order that the Future Buddha should not at any time go out of the city without his knowledge, had caused each of the two leaves of the gate to be made so heavy as to need a thousand men to move it. . . . But the divinity that inhabited the gate opened it for them.

At this moment came Mara,[7] with the intention of persuading the Future Buddha to turn back; and standing in the air, he said,—

7. Mara stands for the pleasures of the senses, and is thus the Buddha's natural enemy.

"Sir, go not forth! For on the seventh day from now the wheel of empire will appear to you, and you shall rule over the four great continents and their two thousand attendant isles. Sir, turn back!"

"Who are you?"

"I am Vasavatti."

"Mara, I knew that the wheel of empire was on the point of appearing to me; but I do not wish for sovereignty. I am about to cause the ten thousand worlds to thunder with my becoming a Buddha."

"I shall catch you," thought Mara, "the very first time you have a lustful, malicious, or unkind thought." And, like an ever-present shadow, he followed after, ever on the watch for some slip.

Thus the Future Buddha, casting away with indifference a universal sovereignty already in his grasp,—spewing it out as if it were but phlegm,—departed from the city in great splendor on the full-moon day of the month Asalhi,[8] when the moon was in Libra. . . .

8. About July 1st.

The Great Struggle

Now the Future Buddha, having thus retired from the world,— in that place there was a mango-grove named Anupiya, and here he first spent a week in the joy of having retired from the world,—in one day went on foot to Rajagaha, a distance of thirty leagues, and entering the city, he begged for food from house to house, without passing any by. . . .

Now the Great Being, after collecting a number of scraps, sufficient, as he judged, for his sustenance, left the city by the same gate he had entered, and sitting down with his face to the east, in the shade of Pandava rock, he attempted to eat his meal. But his stomach turned, and he felt as if his inwards were on the point of coming out by his mouth. Thereupon, in the midst of his distress at that repulsive food,—for in that existence he had never before so much as seen such fare,—he began to admonish himself, saying, "Siddhattha, although you were born into a family having plenty to eat and drink, into a station in life where you lived on fragrant third season's rice[1] with various sauces of the finest flavors, yet when you saw a monk clad in garments taken from the rubbish heap, you exclaimed, 'Oh, when shall I be like him, and eat food which I have begged? Will that time ever come?' And then you retired from the world. And now that you have your wish, and have renounced all, what, pray, is this you are doing?" When he had thus admonished himself, his disgust subsided, and he ate his meal. . . .

Then the Future Buddha . . . proceeded on his way; and coming to Alara Kalama and Uddaka, the disciple of Rama,[2] he acquired from them the eight stages of meditation.[3] But becoming convinced that they did not lead to enlightenment, he ceased to practise them. And being desirous of making the Great Struggle, so as to show the world of gods and men his fortitude and heroism, he went to Uruvela, and saying, "Truly, delightful is this spot," he there took up his abode, and began the Great Struggle. . . .

And the Future Buddha, thinking, "I will carry austerity to the uttermost," tried various plans, such as living on one sesamum seed or on one grain of rice a day, and even ceased taking nourishment altogether, and moreover rebuffed the gods when they came and attempted to infuse nourishment through the pores of his skin. By this lack of nourishment his body became emaciated to the last degree, and lost its golden color, and became black, and his thirty-two physical characteristics as a great being became obscured. Now, one day, as he was deep in a trance of suppressed breathing, he was attacked by violent pains, and fell senseless to the ground, at one end of his walking-place.

And certain of the deities said, "The monk Gotama is dead;" but others said, "This is a practice of the saints." . . .

Now the six years which the Great Being thus spent in austerities were like time spent in endeavoring to tie the air into

1. Supposedly the tastiest kind.
2. Rama was regarded as an incarnation of the god Vishnu.
3. As prescribed, for example, in the *Yoga Sutra* of Patanjali (see above, pp. 198-201).

knots. And coming to the decision, "These austerities are not the way to enlightenment," he went begging through villages and market-towns for ordinary material food, and lived upon it. And his thirty-two physical characteristics as a great being again appeared, and the color of his body became like unto gold.

. . . .

The Attainment of Buddhaship

Now [one] night the Future Buddha had five great dreams, and on considering their meaning reached the conclusion, "Without doubt I shall become a Buddha this very day." And when night was over, and he had cared for his person, he came early in the morning to that tree, to await the hour to go begging. And when he sat down he illumined the whole tree with his radiance. . . .

Then the Future Buddha took his noonday rest on the banks of the river, in a grove of sal-trees in full bloom. And at nightfall, at the time the flowers droop on their stalks, he rose up, like a lion when he bestirs himself, and went towards the Bo-tree, along a road which the gods had decked, and which was eight usabhas wide. . . .

Then the Future Buddha turned his back to the trunk of the Bo-tree and faced the east. And making the mighty resolution, "Let my skin, and sinews, and bones become dry, and welcome! and let all the flesh and blood in my body dry up! but never from this seat will I stir, until I have attained the supreme and absolute wisdom!" he sat himself down cross-legged in an unconquerable position, from which not even the descent of a hundred thunder-bolts at once could have dislodged him.

At this point the god Mara, exclaiming, "Prince Siddhattha is desirous of passing beyond my control, but I will never allow it!" went and announced the news to his army, and sounding the Mara war-cry, drew out for battle. Now Mara's army extended in front of him for twelve leagues, and to the right and to the left for twelve leagues, and in the rear as far as to the confines of the world, and it was nine leagues high. And when it shouted, it made an earthquake-like roaring and rumbling over a space of a thousand leagues. And the god Mara, mounting his elephant, which was a hundred and fifty leagues high, and had the name "Girded-with-mountains," caused a thousand arms to appear on his body, and with these he grasped a variety of weapons. Also in the remainder of that army, no two persons carried the same weapon; and diverse also in their appearances and countenances, the host swept on like a flood to overwhelm the Great Being.

. . . But as Mara's army gradually drew near to the throne of wisdom, not one of these great gods was able to stand his ground, but each fled straight before him. . . . Not a single deity was able to stand his ground, and the Great Being was left sitting alone.

Then said Mara to his followers,—

"My friends, Siddhattha, the son of Suddhodana, is far greater than any other man, and we shall never be able to fight him in front. We will attack him from behind. . . ."

Thereupon the god Mara caused a whirlwind, thinking, "By this will I drive away Siddhattha." Straightway the east wind and all the other different winds began to blow; but although these winds could have torn their way through mountain-peaks half a league, or two leagues, or three leagues high, or have uprooted forest-shrubs and trees, or have reduced to powder and scattered in all directions, villages and towns, yet when they reached the Future Buddha, such was the energy of the Great Being's merit, they lost all power and were not able to cause so much as a fluttering of the edge of his priestly robe.

Then he caused a great rain-storm, saying, "With water will I overwhelm and drown him." And through his mighty power, clouds of a hundred strata, and clouds of a thousand strata arose, and also the other different kinds. And these rained down, until the earth became gullied by the torrents of water which fell, and until the floods had risen over the tops of every forest-tree. But on coming to the Great Being, this mighty inundation was not able to wet his priestly robes as much as a dewdrop would have done.

Then he caused a shower of rocks, in which immense mountain-peaks flew smoking and flaming through the sky. But on reaching the Future Buddha they became celestial bouquets of flowers. . . .

Then he caused a shower of weapons, . . . a shower of live coals, . . . a shower of hot ashes, . . . a shower of sand, . . . a shower of mud, . . . a darkness. . . . And the darkness became fourfold, and very dense. But on reaching the Future Buddha it disappeared like darkness before the light of the sun.

Mara, being thus unable with these nine storms of wind, rain, rocks, weapons, live coals, hot ashes, sand, mud, and darkness, to drive away the Future Buddha, gave command to his followers, "Look ye now! Why stand ye still? Seize, kill, drive away this prince!" And, arming himself with a discus, and seated upon the shoulders of the elephant "Girded-with-mountains," he drew near the Future Buddha, and said,—

"Siddhattha, arise from this seat! It does not belong to you, but to me."

When the Great Being heard this he said,—

"Mara, you have not fulfilled the Ten Perfections in any of their three grades; nor have you made the five great donations[1]; nor have you striven for knowledge, nor for the welfare of the world, nor for enlightenment. This seat does not belong to you, but to me."

Unable to restrain his fury, the enraged Mara now hurled his discus. But the Great Being reflected on the Ten Perfections, and the discus changed into a canopy of flowers, and remained suspended over his head. Yet they say that this keen-edged discus, when at other times Mara hurled it in anger, would cut through solid stone pillars as if they had been the tips of bamboo shoots. But on this occasion it became a canopy of flowers. Then the followers of Mara began hurling immense mountain-crags, saying, "This will make him get up from his seat and flee." But the Great Being kept his thoughts on the Ten Perfections, and the crags also became wreaths of flowers, and then fell to the ground. . . .

. . . Now the hundred-and-fifty-league-high elephant "Girded-with-mountains" fell upon his knees before the Great Being.

1. The donations of treasure, child, wife, royal rule, and life and limb.

And the followers of Mara fled away in all directions. No two went the same way, but leaving their head-ornaments and their cloaks behind, they fled straight before them.

Then the hosts of the gods, when they saw the army of Mara flee, cried out, "Mara is defeated! Prince Siddhattha has conquered! Let us go celebrate the victory!" And the snakes egging on the snakes, the birds the birds, the deities the deities, and the Brahma-angels the Brahma-angels, they came with perfumes, garlands, and other offerings in their hands to the Great Being on the throne of wisdom. . .

And the remaining deities, also, throughout the ten thousand worlds, made offerings of garlands, perfumes, and ointments, and in many a hymn extolled him.

It was before the sun had set that the Great Being thus vanquished the army of Mara. And then, while the Bo-tree in homage rained red, coral-like sprigs upon his priestly robes, he acquired in the first watch of the night the knowledge of previous existences; in the middle watch of the night, the divine eye; and in the last watch of the night, his intellect fathomed Dependent Origination.[2]

Now while he was musing on the twelve terms of Dependent Origination, forwards and backwards, round and back again, the ten thousand worlds quaked twelve times, as far as to their ocean boundaries. And when the Great Being, at the dawning of the day, had thus made the ten thousand worlds thunder with his attainment of omniscience, all these worlds became most gloriously adorned. . . . The system of ten thousand worlds was like a bouquet of flowers sent whirling through the air, or like a thick carpet of flowers; in the intermundane spaces the eight-thousand-league-long hells, which not even the light of seven suns had formerly been able to illumine, were now flooded with radiance; the eighty-four-thousand-league-deep ocean became sweet to the taste; the rivers checked their flowing; the blind from birth received their sight; the deaf from birth their hearing; the cripples from birth the use of their limbs; and the bonds and fetters of captives broke and fell off.

When thus he had attained to omniscience, and was the cen-

2. See "Discussion of Dependent Origination" below, pp. 246-49.

tre of such unparalleled glory and homage, and so many prodigies were happening about him, he breathed forth that solemn utterance which has never been omitted by any of The Buddhas:—

"Through birth and rebirth's endless round,
Seeking in vain, I hastened on,
To find who framed this edifice.
What misery!—birth incessantly!

"O builder! I've discovered thee!
This fabric thou shalt ne'er rebuild!
Thy rafters all are broken now,
And pointed roof demolished lies!
This mind has demolition reached,
And seen the last of all desire!"

The period of time, therefore, from the existence in the Tusita Heaven to this attainment of omniscience on the throne of wisdom, constitutes the Intermediate Epoch.

FROM THE DIGHA NIKAYA
The Death of the Buddha

1   Now the Blessed One addressed the venerable Ananda,[1] and said: "It may be, Ananda, that in some of you the thought may arise, 'The word of the Master is ended, we have no teacher more!' But it is not thus, Ananda, that you should regard it. The truths and the rules of the order which I have set forth and laid down for you all, let them, after I am gone, be the Teacher to you."

[The *Digha Nikaya* is the first of the five chief divisions of the *Sutta Pitaka*. This selection is taken from the "Maha-Parinibbana Sutta" ("Book of the Great Decease").]
From *Buddhist Suttas*, trans. from the Pali by T. W. Rhys Davids, Vol. XI of *The Sacred Books of the East* (Oxford: At the Clarendon Press, 1881), pp. 112-31.
  1. The Buddha's cousin, and one of his most prominent disciples.

5   Then the Blessed One addressed the brethren, and said:
"It may be, brethren, that there may be doubt or misgiving in
the mind of some brother as to the Buddha, or the truth, or the
path, or the way. Enquire, brethren, freely. Do not have to reproach yourselves afterwards with the thought, 'Our teacher
was face to face with us, and we could not bring ourselves to
enquire of the Blessed One when we were face to face with
him.' "

And when he had thus spoken the brethren were silent.

6   And again the second and the third time the Blessed One
addressed the brethren, and said: "It may be," etc.

And even the third time the brethren were silent.

8   And the venerable Ananda said to the Blessed One: "How
wonderful a thing is it, Lord, and how marvellous! Verily, I
believe that in this whole assembly of the brethren there is not
one brother who has any doubt or misgiving as to the Buddha,
or the truth, or the path, or the way!"

9   "It is out of the fulness of faith that thou hast spoken,
Ananda! But, Ananda, the Tathagata[2] knows for certain that
in this whole assembly of the brethren there is not one brother
who has any doubt or misgiving as to the Buddha, or the truth,
or the path, or the way! For even the most backward, Ananda,
of all these five hundred brethren has become converted, and
is no longer liable to be born in a state of suffering, and is assured of final salvation."

10   Then the Blessed One addressed the brethren, and said:
"Behold now, brethren, I exhort you, saying, 'Decay is inher-
ent in all component things! Work out your salvation with dili-
gence!' "

This was the last word of the Tathagata!

11   Then the Blessed One entered into the first stage of deep
meditation. And rising out of the first stage he passed into the
second. And rising out of the second he passed into the third.
And rising out of the third stage he passed into the fourth. And

---

2. The Buddha regarded as a spiritual principle.

rising out of the fourth stage of deep meditation he entered into the state of mind to which the infinity of space is alone present. And passing out of the mere consciousness of the infinity of space he entered into the state of mind to which the infinity of thought is alone present. And passing out of the mere consciousness of the infinity of thought he entered into a state of mind to which nothing at all was specially present. And passing out of the consciousness of no special object he fell into a state between consciousness and unconsciousness. And passing out of the state between consciousness and unconsciousness he fell into a state in which the consciousness both of sensations and of ideas had wholly passed away.

12   Then the venerable Ananda said to the venerable Anuruddha[3]: "O my Lord, O Anuruddha, the Blessed One is dead!"

"Nay! brother Ananda, the Blessed One is not dead. He has entered into that state in which both sensations and ideas have ceased to be!"

13   Then the Blessed One passing out of the state in which both sensations and ideas have ceased to be, entered into the state between consciousness and unconsciousness . . . [then] into the state of mind to which nothing at all is specially present . . . into the state of mind to which the infinity of thought is alone present . . . into the state of mind to which the infinity of space is alone present . . . into the fourth stage of deep meditation . . . into the third . . . into the second . . . into the first. And passing out of the first stage of deep meditation he entered into the second . . . into the third . . . into the fourth. And passing out of the last stage of deep meditation he immediately expired.

14   When the Blessed One died there arose, at the moment of his passing out of existence, a mighty earthquake, terrible and awe-inspiring: and the thunders of heaven burst forth.

16   When the Blessed One died, Sakka, the king of the gods, at the moment of his passing away from existence, uttered this stanza:

3. Another disciple.

"They're transient all, each being's parts and powers,
Growth is their nature, and decay.
They are produced, they are dissolved again:
And then is best, when they have sunk to rest!"

19 When the Blessed One died, of those of the brethren who were not yet free from the passions, some stretched out their arms and wept, and some fell headlong on the ground, rolling to and fro in anguish at the thought: "Too soon has the Blessed One died! Too soon has the Happy One passed away from existence! Too soon has the Light gone out in the world!"

But those of the brethren who were free from the passions (the Arahats) bore their grief collected and composed at the thought: "Impermanent are all component things! How is it possible that [they should not be dissolved]?"

33 Then the Mallas of Kusinara[4] said to the venerable Ananda: "What should be done, Lord, with the remains of the Tathagata?"

"As men treat the remains of a king of kings, so . . . should they treat the remains of a Tathagata. . . ."

34 Therefore the Mallas gave orders to their attendants, saying, "Gather together all the carded cotton wool of the Mallas!"

35 Then the Mallas of Kusinara wrapped the body of the Blessed One in a new cloth. And when that was done, they wrapped it in cotton wool. And when that was done, they wrapped it in a new cloth,—and so on till they had wrapped the body of the Blessed One in five hundred layers of both kinds. And then they placed the body in an oil vessel of iron, and covered that close up with another oil vessel of iron. And then they built a funeral pile of all kinds of perfumes, and upon it they placed the body of the Blessed One.

45 Then the venerable Maha Kassapa[5] went on . . . to the shrine of the Mallas, to the place where the funeral pile of the Blessed One was. And when he had come up to it, he arranged

4. The Malla people are often mentioned in Buddhist legend. Probably they were hill-men of the Mongolian type related to the Tibetans. The town of Kusinagara (Kusinara) was probably situated in Nepalese territory.
5. One of the Buddha's chief disciples.

his robe on one shoulder; and bowing down with clasped hands he thrice walked reverently round the pile; and then, uncovering the feet, he bowed down in reverence at the feet of the Blessed One.

46 And those five hundred brethren arranged their robes on one shoulder; and bowing down with clasped hands, they thrice walked reverently round the pile, and then bowed down in reverence at the feet of the Blessed One.

47 And when the homage of the venerable Maha Kassapa and of those five hundred brethren was ended, the funeral pile of the Blessed One caught fire of itself.

49 And when the body of the Blessed One had been burnt up, there came down streams of water from the sky and extinguished the funeral pile of the Blessed One; and there burst forth streams of water from the storehouse of the waters (beneath the earth), and extinguished the funeral pile of the Blessed One. The Mallas of Kusinara also brought water scented with all kinds of perfumes, and extinguished the funeral pile of the Blessed One.

50 Then the Mallas of Kusinara surrounded the bones of the Blessed One in their council hall with a lattice work of spears, and with a rampart of bows; and there for seven days they paid honour and reverence and respect and homage to them with dance and song and music, and with garlands and perfumes.

. . . .

THE DHARMA

Introduction to the Four Noble Truths

The Four Noble Truths are the very foundation of Buddhist doctrine. All the various schools of Buddhism—whatever else may distinguish them—accept the validity of these statements about the universality, cause, and elimination of misery.

These four Truths reveal an astonishing rationality at the very heart of the Buddhist religion. They do not merely assert that the world is evil or appeal to a vague feeling that this is so: they document the fact in agonizing detail. Once the omnipresence of evil is established, they proceed—like a researcher seeking the cause of a disease—to discover its cause. The origin of evil they find to lie in the fact of desire for the things of worldly existence. The cause being known, the rest is a matter of method: the Noble Eightfold Path, which leads to the cessation of desire.

The following exposition of the Four Noble Truths is from Sutta 22 of the *Digha Nikaya*.

FROM THE DIGHA NIKAYA

The Four Noble Truths

THE EXPOSITION OF MISERY

And how, O priests,[1] does a priest live, as respects the elements of being, observant of the elements of being in the four noble truths?

Whenever, O priest, a priest knows the truth concerning misery, knows the truth concerning the origin of misery, knows the truth concerning the cessation of misery, knows the truth concerning the path leading to the cessation of misery.

And what, O priests, is the noble truth of misery?

Birth is misery; old age is misery; disease is misery; death is misery; sorrow, lamentation, misery, grief, and despair are misery; to wish for what one cannot have is misery; in short, all the five attachment-groups are misery.[2]

. . . .

THE EXPOSITION OF THE ORIGIN OF MISERY

And what, O priests, is the noble truth of the origin of misery?

It is desire leading to rebirth, joining itself to pleasure and

From *Buddhism in Translations*, trans. by Henry Clarke Warren (Cambridge, Mass.: Harvard University Press, 1896), pp. 368-74.

1. Actually: monks.
2. Attachment to form, sensation, perception, predisposition, and consciousness.

passion, and finding delight in every existence,—desire, namely, for sensual pleasure, desire for permanent existence, desire for transitory existence.

But where, O priests, does this desire spring up and grow? where does it settle and take root?

Where anything is delightful and agreeable to men, there desire springs up and grows, there it settles and takes root.

And what is delightful and agreeable to men, where desire springs up and grows, where it settles and takes root?

The eye is delightful and agreeable to man; there desire springs up and grows, there it settles and takes root.

The ear . . . the nose . . . the tongue . . . the body . . . the mind is delightful and agreeable to men; there desire springs up and grows, there it settles and takes root.

Forms . . . sounds . . . odors . . . tastes . . . things tangible . . . ideas are delightful, etc. . . .

Eye-consciousness . . . ear-consciousness . . . nose-consciousness . . . tongue-consciousness . . . body-consciousness . . . mind-consciousness is delightful, etc. . . .

Contact of the eye . . . ear . . . nose . . . tongue . . . body . . . mind is delightful, etc. . . .

Sensation produced by contact of the eye . . . ear . . . nose . . . tongue . . . body . . . mind is delightful, etc. . . .

Perception of forms . . . sounds . . . odors . . . tastes . . . things tangible . . . ideas is delightful, etc. . . .

Thinking on forms . . . sounds . . . odors . . . tastes . . . things tangible . . . ideas is delightful, etc. . . .

Desire for forms . . . sounds . . . odors . . . tastes . . . things tangible . . . ideas is delightful, etc. . . .

Reasoning on forms . . . sounds . . . odors . . . tastes . . . things tangible . . . ideas is delightful, etc. . . .

Reflection on forms . . . sounds . . . odors . . . tastes . . . things tangible . . . ideas is delightful, etc. . . .

This, O priests, is called the noble truth of the origin of misery.

THE EXPOSITION OF THE CESSATION OF MISERY

And what, O priests, is the noble truth of the cessation of misery?

It is the complete fading out and cessation of this desire, a giving up, a loosing hold, a relinquishment, and a non-adhesion.

But where, O priests, does this desire wane and disappear? where is it broken up and destroyed?

Where anything is delightful and agreeable to men; there desire wanes and disappears, there it is broken up and destroyed.

And what is delightful and agreeable to men, where desire wanes and disappears, where it is broken up and destroyed?

The eye is delightful and agreeable to men; there desire wanes and disappears, there it is broken up and destroyed.

[Similarly respecting the other organs of sense, the six objects of sense, the six sense-consciousnesses, the six contacts, the six sensations, the six perceptions, the six thinkings, the six desires, the six reasonings, and the six reflections.]

This, O priests, is called the noble truth of the cessation of misery.

THE EXPOSITION OF THE PATH LEADING TO THE
CESSATION OF MISERY

And what, O priests, is the noble truth of the path leading to the cessation of misery?

It is this noble eightfold path, to wit, right belief, right resolve, right speech, right behavior, right occupation, right effort, right contemplation, right concentration.

And what, O priests, is right belief?

The knowledge of misery, O priests, the knowledge of the origin of misery, the knowledge of the cessation of misery, and the knowledge of the path leading to the cessation of misery, this, O priests, is called "right belief."

And what, O priests, is right resolve?

The resolve to renounce sensual pleasures, the resolve to have malice towards none, and the resolve to harm no living creature, this, O priests, is called "right resolve."

And what, O priests, is right speech?

To abstain from falsehood, to abstain from backbiting, to abstain from harsh language, and to abstain from frivolous talk, this, O priests, is called "right speech."

And what, O priests, is right behavior?

To abstain from destroying life, to abstain from taking that which is not given one, and to abstain from immorality, this, O priests, is called "right behavior."

And what, O priests, is right occupation?

Whenever, O priests, a noble disciple, quitting a wrong occupation, gets his livelihood by a right occupation, this, O priests, is called "right occupation."

And what, O priests, is right effort?

Whenever, O priests, a priest purposes, makes an effort, heroically endeavors, applies his mind, and exerts himself that evil and demeritorious qualities not yet arisen may not arise; . . . that evil and demeritorious qualities already arisen may be abandoned; . . . that meritorious qualities not yet arisen may arise; . . . exerts himself for the preservation, retention, growth, increase, development, and perfection of meritorious qualities already arisen, this, O priests, is called "right effort."

And what, O priests, is right contemplation?

Whenever, O priests, a priest lives, as respects the body, . . . as respects sensations, . . . as respects the mind, . . . as respects the elements of being, observant of the elements of being, strenuous, conscious, contemplative, and has rid himself of lust and grief, this, O priests, is called "right contemplation."

And what, O priests, is right concentration?

Whenever, O priests, a priest, having isolated himself from sensual pleasures, having isolated himself from demeritorious traits, and still exercising reasoning, still exercising reflection, enters upon the first trance which is produced by isolation and characterized by joy and happiness; when . . . he enters upon the second trance, which is an interior tranquilization and intentness of the thoughts, and is produced by concentration; when . . . he enters upon the third trance; when . . . he enters upon the fourth trance, which has neither misery nor happiness, but is contemplation as refined by indifference, this, O priests, is called "right concentration."

This, O priests, is called the noble truth of the path leading to the cessation of misery.

Introduction to Dependent Origination

The theory of Dependent Origination expresses the Buddhist conviction that everything in the universe is interconnected. Buddhist doctrine recognizes no such thing as an independent, self-sufficient entity; no permanent and unchanging center of existence, such as a soul. The whole world is constantly in flux. All life rests upon the continual and rapid succession—in conformance with natural laws —of a series of impermanent factors (*dharmas*).* It is these factors, rather than any eternal soul-substance, which constitute the personality and produce the various kinds of earthly existence.

The following discussion of Dependent Origination is from the "Maha-Nidana-Sutta" of the *Digha Nikaya*.

FROM THE DIGHA NIKAYA

Discussion of Dependent Origination

Thus have I heard.

On a certain occasion The Blessed One was dwelling among the Kurus[1] where was the Kuru-town named Kammasadhamma.

Then drew near the venerable Ananda to where The Blessed One was; and having drawn near and greeted The Blessed One, he sat down respectfully at one side. And seated respectfully at one side, the venerable Ananda spoke to the Blessed One as follows:

"O wonderful is it, Reverend Sir! O marvellous is it, Reverend Sir! How profound, Reverend Sir, is Dependent Origination, and of how profound an appearance! To me, nevertheless, it is as clear as clear can be."

From *Buddhism in Translations*, trans. by Henry Clarke Warren (Cambridge, Mass.: Harvard University Press, 1896), pp. 202-8.
* The *dharmas* are in turn classified into five *skandhas: rupa* (the physical body and senses); *vedana* (feeling); *sanjna* (the faculty of mental discrimination); *sanskara* (energy); and *vijnana* (consciousness). But not even consciousness—the *skandha* which most nearly resembles a soul—is self-sufficient; it depends upon the eye, ear, forms, etc.
1. A people of north central India.

"O Ananda, say not so! O Ananda, say not so! Profound, Ananda, is Dependent Origination, and profound of appearance. It is through not understanding this doctrine, Ananda, through not penetrating it, that thus mankind is like to an entangled warp, or to an ensnarled web, or to muñja-grass and pabbaja-grass, and fails to extricate itself from punishment, suffering, perdition, rebirth.

"Ananda, if it be asked, 'Do old age and death depend on anything?' the reply should be, 'They do.' And if it be asked, 'On what do old age and death depend?' the reply should be, 'Old age and death depend on birth.'

"Ananda, if it be asked, 'Does birth depend on anything?' the reply should be, . . . 'Birth depends on existence.'

"Ananda, if it be asked, 'Does existence depend on anything?' the reply should be, . . . 'Existence depends on attachment.'

"Ananda, if it be asked, 'Does attachment depend on anything?' the reply should be, . . . 'Attachment depends on desire.'

"Ananda, if it be asked, 'Does desire depend on anything?' the reply should be, . . . 'Desire depends on sensation.'

"Ananda, if it be asked, 'Does sensation depend on anything?' the reply should be, . . . 'Sensation depends on contact.'

"Ananda, if it be asked, 'Does contact depend on anything?' the reply should be, . . . 'Contact depends on name and form.'

"Ananda, if it be asked, 'Do name and form depend on anything?' the reply should be . . . 'Name and form depend on consciousness.'

"Ananda, if it be asked, 'Does consciousness depend on anything?' the reply should be, . . . 'Consciousness depends on name and form.'

. . . Thus does this entire aggregation of misery arise.

"I have said that on birth depend old age and death. This truth, Ananda, that on birth depend old age and death, is to be understood in this way. Suppose, Ananda, there were utterly and completely no birth at all for any one into any world, as, namely, for gods into the world of gods; . . . for demons into the world of demons; for men into the world of men; for quadrupeds into the world of quadrupeds; . . . pray, on the cessation of birth would there be any old age and death?"

"Nay, verily, Reverend Sir."

"Accordingly, Ananda, here we have in birth the cause, the occasion, the origin, and the dependence of old age and death.

". . . Suppose, Ananda, there were utterly and completely no existence at all for any one in any mode, as, namely, existence in the realm of sensual pleasure, existence in the realm of form, existence in the realm of formlessness; . . . pray, on the cessation of existence would there be any birth?"

"Nay, verily, Reverend Sir."

". . . Suppose, Ananda, there were utterly and completely no attachment at all of any one to anything, as, namely, the attachment of sensual pleasure, the attachment of heresy, the attachment of fanatical conduct, the attachment of the assertion of an Ego; . . . pray, on the cessation of attachment would there be any existence?"

"Nay, verily, Reverend Sir."

". . . Suppose, Ananda, there were utterly and completely no desire at all on the part of any one for anything, as, namely, desire for forms, desire for sounds, desire for odors, desire for tastes, desire for things tangible, desire for ideas; . . . pray, on the cessation of desire would there be any attachment?"

"Nay, verily, Reverend Sir."

". . . Suppose, Ananda, there were utterly and completely no sensation at all on the part of any one for anything, as, namely, sensation sprung from contact of the eye, . . . the ear, . . . the nose, . . . the tongue, . . . the body, . . . the mind; . . . pray, on the cessation of sensation would there be any desire?"

"Nay, verily, Reverend Sir."

". . . Suppose, Ananda, there were utterly and completely no contact at all of any organ with any object, as, namely, contact of the eye, contact of the ear, contact of the nose, contact of the tongue, contact of the body, contact of the mind; . . . pray, on the cessation of contact would there be any sensation?"

"Nay, verily, Reverend Sir. . . ."

"Suppose, Ananda, there were not these different traits, peculiarities, signs, and indications by which are made manifest the multitude of elements of being constituting name and the multitude of elements of being constituting form;—if there were not these different traits, peculiarities, signs, and indications, pray, would there be any contact?"

"Nay, verily, Reverend Sir. . . ."

"Suppose, Ananda, consciousness were to be severed from a child, either boy or girl, pray, would name and form attain to growth, increase, and development?"

"Nay, verily, Reverend Sir. . . ."

"Accordingly, Ananda, here we have in name and form the cause, the occasion, the origin, and the dependence of consciousness.

"Verily, Ananda, this name and form coupled with consciousness is all there is to be born, or to grow old, or to die, or to leave one existence, or to spring up in another. It is all that is meant by any affirmation, predication, or declaration we may make concerning anybody. It constitutes knowledge's field of action. And it is all that is reborn to appear in its present shape."

Introduction to Questions Which Tend Not to Edification

Although the schools of the Mahayana eventually evolved a sophisticated metaphysics, the first Buddhists were apparently not inclined to speculate about the nature of the universe. Their goal was the practical one of release from earthly suffering, not a theoretical understanding of the cosmos. Early Buddhist philosophy was thus largely restricted to matters directly pertaining to the Path.

An ancient and probably authentic tradition states that Gautama himself always refused to discuss the origin, nature, and final end of the universe. His doctrine has sometimes been interpreted as agnosticism; but this is almost certainly erroneous. Nowhere is he recorded as stating that the ultimate religious questions—the existence of God, life after death—are insoluble. His chief concern, however, was not to elaborate a theory, but to show suffering man-

From *Buddhism in Translations*, trans. by Henry Clarke Warren (Cambridge, Mass.: Harvard University Press, 1896), pp. 118-22.

kind the way to liberation from further re-births. As a practical matter, he probably regarded metaphysical speculation as useless or even an obstacle in the striving for *moksha*.

The following discussion is from Sutta 63 of the *Majjhima Nikaya*, the second division of the *Sutta Pitaka*.

FROM THE MAJJHIMA NIKAYA

Questions Which Tend Not to Edification

. . . the venerable Malunkyaputta[1] arose at eventide from his seclusion, and drew near to where The Blessed One was; and having drawn near and greeted The Blessed One, he sat down respectfully at one side. And seated respectfully at one side, the venerable Malunkyaputta spoke to The Blessed One as follows:—

"Reverend Sir, it happened to me, as I was just now in seclusion and plunged in meditation, that a consideration presented itself to my mind, as follows: "These theories which The Blessed One has left unelucidated, has set aside and rejected,— that the world is eternal, that the world is not eternal, . . . that the saint neither exists nor does not exist after death,— these The Blessed One does not elucidate to me. And the fact that The Blessed One does not elucidate them to me does not please me nor suit me. I will draw near to The Blessed One and inquire of him concerning this matter. If The Blessed One will elucidate to me, either that the world is eternal, or that the world is not eternal, . . . or that the saint neither exists nor does not exist after death, in that case will I lead the religious life under The Blessed One. If The Blessed One will not elucidate to me, either that the world is eternal, or that the world is not eternal, . . . or that the saint neither exists nor does not exist after death, in that case will I abandon religious training and return to the lower life of a layman. . . ."

"Pray Malunkyaputta, did I ever say to you, 'Come, Mal-

1. A holy man, later the Buddha's disciple.

unkyaputta, lead the religious life under me, and I will elucidate to you either that the world is eternal, or that the world is
not eternal, . . . or that the saint neither exists nor does not
exist after death'?"

"Nay, verily, Reverend Sir."

"Or did you ever say to me, 'Reverend Sir, I will lead the
religious life under The Blessed One, on condition that The
Blessed One elucidate to me either that the world is eternal, or
that the world is not eternal, . . . or that the saint neither
exists nor does not exist after death'?"

"Nay, verily, Reverend Sir. . . ."

"Malunkyaputta, any one who should say, 'I will not lead
the religious life under The Blessed One until The Blessed One
shall elucidate to me either that the world is eternal, or that
the world is not eternal, . . . or that the saint neither exists
nor does not exist after death;'—that person would die, Malunkyaputta, before the Tathagata had ever elucidated this to him.

"It is as if, Malunkyaputta, a man had been wounded by an
arrow thickly smeared with poison, and his friends and companions, his relatives and kinsfolk, were to procure for him a
physician or surgeon; and the sick man were to say, 'I will not
have this arrow taken out until I have learnt whether the man
who wounded me belonged to the warrior caste, or to the Brahman caste, or to the agricultural caste, or to the menial caste.'

"Or again he were to say, 'I will not have this arrow taken
out until I have learnt the name of the man who wounded me,
and to what clan he belongs. . . . [Or] whether [he] was tall,
or short, or of the middle height. . . . [Or] whether [he was]
black, or dusky, or of a yellow skin. . . . [Or] whether [he
was] from this or that village, or town, or city.'

"Or again he were to say, 'I will not have this arrow taken
out until I have learnt whether the bow which wounded me was
a capa, or a kodanda. . . . [Or] whether the bow-string . . .
was made from swallow-wort, or bamboo, or sinew, or maruva,
or from milk-weed. . . .'

"The religious life, Malunkyaputta, does not depend on the
dogma that the world is eternal; nor does the religious life,
Malunkyaputta, depend on the dogma that the world is not

eternal. Whether the dogma obtain, Malunkyaputta, that the world is eternal, or that the world is not eternal, there still remain birth, old age, death, sorrow, lamentation, misery, grief, and despair, for the extinction of which in the present life I am prescribing.

"The religious life, Malunkyaputta, does not depend on the dogma that the world is finite; . . . [or] that the soul and the body are identical; . . . [or] that the saint exists after death; . . . [or] that the saint both exists and does not exist after death. . . .

"Accordingly, Malunkyaputta, bear always in mind what it is that I have not elucidated, and what it is that I have elucidated . . . I have not elucidated, Malunkyaputta, that the world is eternal; . . . [or] that the world is not eternal; . . . [or] that the world is finite; . . . [or] that the world is infinite; . . . [or] that the soul and the body are identical; . . . [or] that the soul is one thing and the body another; . . . [or] that the saint exists after death; . . . [or] that the saint does not exist after death; . . . [or] that the saint both exists and does not exist after death. . . . And why, Malunkyaputta, have I not elucidated this? Because, Malunkyaputta, this profits not, nor has to do with the fundamentals of religion, nor tends to aversion, absence of passion, cessation, quiescence, the supernatural faculties, supreme wisdom, and Nirvana; therefore have I not elucidated it.

"And what, Malunkyaputta, have I elucidated? Misery, Malunkyaputta, have I elucidated; the origin of misery have I elucidated; the cessation of misery have I elucidated; and the path leading to the cessation of misery have I elucidated. And why, Malunkyaputta, have I elucidated this? Because, Malunkyaputta, this does profit, has to do with the fundamentals of religion, and tends to aversion, absence of passion, cessation, quiescence, knowledge, supreme wisdom, and Nirvana; therefore have I elucidated it. Accordingly, Malunkyaputta, bear always in mind what it is that I have not elucidated, and what it is that I have elucidated."

Thus spake The Blessed One; and, delighted, the venerable Malunkyaputta applauded the speech of The Blessed One.

Introduction to the Questions of King Milinda

Milinda [Menander] was an actual historical personage, the ruler of one of the Hellenistic successor states established in northwest India in the wake of Alexander the Great's invasion (327-25 B.C.). Reliable information about him is scanty, however. He reigned sometime in the middle of the second century B.C.; his kingdom included Bactria—then a rich and civilized region—Ghazni, Gandhara, and part of the Punjab. He was a successful conqueror and able ruler; but posterity chiefly remembers him for his interest in Buddhism.

The *Questions of King Milinda* is among the most famous of all Buddhist scriptures. Compiled probably in the first century A.D., it is a dialogue on doctrinal subjects between the king and the learned monk Nogasena. The work treats in considerable detail the standard Buddhist themes of impermanence, universal flux, and the absence of any concrete entities in the world.

FROM THE QUESTIONS OF KING MILINDA

I. Talk on Secular Matters

The King named Milinda approached Nagasena[1] at Sagala,[2]
In the incomparable city, like the Ganges the ocean.
To him, the eloquent, the torch-bearer, dispeller of darkness,
    the king, drawing near,
Asked many abstruse questions about correct or faulty con-
    clusions.
The solutions to the questions likewise were given over to pro-
    found meanings,

From *Milinda's Questions*, Vol. I, trans. from the Pali by I. B. Horner, Vol. XXII of *The Sacred Books of the Buddhists* (London: Luzac & Co., 1963). Reprinted by permission of the Pali Text Society.

1. Nagasena may perhaps also have been a historical personage, though this is quite uncertain.
2. Possibly the modern city of Sialkot in the Punjab.

Going to the heart, pleasing to the ear, wonderful, astounding,
Plunging into Further-Dhamma and Vinaya, deliberating the
    net of the Suttas,[3]
Nagasena's talk was varied with similes and in the method.
Aspiring to knowledge herein while gladdening the mind,
Hearken to the abstruse questions, dissipating occasions for
    doubt.

According to what has been heard: There was a city called
Sagala, a centre of all kinds of merchandise for the Greek
Bactrians,[4] graced with rivers and mountain-slopes, having delightful districts and regions, possessed of parks, pleasure-
grounds, woods, lakes and lotus-pools—a lovely scene of rivers,
mountain-slopes and woods, it was laid out by knowledgeable
men. Enemies and adversaries had been destroyed, it was without oppression; diverse, varied and strong were its watchtowers
and ramparts, its splendid and noble arches curving over the
city-gates; the palace was surrounded by a deep moat and pale
encircling walls; well laid out were its carriage-roads, cross-
roads, squares and the places where three or four roads met, the
bazaar shops were filled inside with innumerable varieties of
well-displayed goods; it was richly adorned with a hundred
varieties of halls where gifts (were given); it was splendid
with hundreds of thousands of magnificent dwellings like crests
of snowy mountains; it was filled with elephants, horses, chariots and pedestrians, with groups of handsome men and women;
it was crowded with ordinary people, warriors, nobles, brahmans, merchants and workers; resounding with a variety of
salutations to ascetics and brahmans, it was the resort of skilled
men knowing a great variety (of things). It had diverse and
varied shops for cloths: Benares muslin, Kotumbara stuffs[5] and
so on. It was sweet-smelling with the great variety of shops for
flowers and perfumes, well and tastefully displayed. It was
filled with an abundance of alluring jewels. Its shops, well

3. The three divisions of the Buddhist canon are: *Abhidhamma* (*Further
Dhamma*) *Pitaka*, *Vinaya Pitaka*, *Sutta Pitaka*.
4. The Indian term is *Yonaka* or *Yavana*, i.e., Ionian.
5. The cities of Benares and Kotumbara were noted for their fine cloth.

displayed and facing (all) directions, were frequented by crowds of elegant merchants. Full of . . . silver, bronze and stone-ware, it was the abode of shining treasure. The warehouses were full of an abundance of riches and corn and wealth; there were many foods and drinks, a great variety of solid and soft foods, sweets, beverages and savouries as in Uttarakuru.[6] Its harvests were heavy as in Alakamanda, the city of devas.[7]

. . . .

Now one day King Milinda issued forth from the town as he wished to see his endless armed forces in their fourfold array.[8] When he had had the army mustered outside the town the king, who was fond of discussion and eager for conversation with natural philosophers,[9] sophists and others of the sort, looked at the sun and addressed his ministers, saying: "Much of the day still remains; what should we do if we returned to the town now? Is there any learned ascetic or brahman or leader of a company, leader of a group or teacher of a group who, perhaps claiming to be an arahant, a perfect buddha, could converse with me and dispel my doubts?"

. . . .

Now at that time the venerable Nagasena was surrounded by a group of ascetics. He was the leader of an Order, the leader of a group, the teacher of a group. He was well known, famous, highly esteemed by the manyfolk; wise, experienced, clever, abstruse, learned, intelligent, disciplined, confident; he was one who had heard much, he was versed in the three Pitakas, a master of knowledge,[10] grown in discretion, he was one to whom the tradition had been handed down, grown in analytical insight, expert in the nine divisions of the scriptures in the Teacher's Dispensation; he was one that had attained to the perfections[11]; he was skilled in the penetration of the teaching on the

6. Uttarakuru is often mentioned in Buddhist literature as a mythical region where food was always plentiful.
7. Alakamanda, "the city of gods," was the capital of Uttarakuru.
8. Elephants, horses, chariots, and infantry.
9. Lokayatas (materialists).
10. I.e., a master of the Vedas.
11. Exceptional perfections of conduct.

substance of Dhamma (found) in the word of the Conqueror[12]; he was prompt in answering a variety of questions, a speaker on a variety (of topics), of lovely enunciation; he was hard to equal, hard to overcome, hard to excel, hard to oppose, hard to check; he was imperturbable as the sea,[13] immovable as the king of mountains; getting rid of conflict, dispelling darkness, bringing light, he was a mighty talker, confounding the followers (of teachers) of other groups, crushing the followers of other sects; he was revered, venerated, reverenced, esteemed and honoured by monks, nuns, men and women lay-devotees, kings and kings' great ministers; and, the recipient of the requisites of robe-material, almsfood, lodgings and medicines for the sick, he had attained the highest gain and the highest fame. . . . Then Devamantiya[14] spoke thus to King Milinda: "Do you wait, sire; wait, sire. There is the Elder named Nagasena, sire, who is wise, experienced, clever, disciplined and confident; he is one who has heard much, a speaker on a variety (of topics), prompt in speaking what is lovely; and he has attained to perfection in the analytical insights of meanings, of Dhamma, of language and of perspicuity (in expression and knowledge). He is now staying in the Sankheyya Parivena. Do you go, sire, and ask questions of the venerable Nagasena. He is capable of conversing with you so as to dispel your doubts. . . ."

Now at that time the venerable Nagasena had been ordained more recently than the forty thousand (monks) of that company of monks who were in front of him, but was senior to the forty thousand (monks) of that company of monks who were behind him. Then King Milinda, closely observing that whole Order of monks—those in front and those behind and those in the middle—from a distance saw the venerable Nagasena sitting in the midst of that Order of monks like a maned lion devoid of fear and dread, devoid of terror, devoid of fear and trepidation. It was by this means that when he saw him he knew: "The one who is there is Nagasena." Then King Milinda

12. Buddha.
13. The sea is indifferent as to whether clean or soiled things are thrown into it.
14. Possibly an Indian rendering of the Greek name "Demetrius."

spoke thus to Devamantiya: "This one, Devamantiya, is the venerable Nagasena."

"Yes, sire, this is Nagasena; it is happy that you, sire, recognized Nagasena." The King was pleased in consequence and thought: "I recognized Nagasena without his being pointed out to me." But when King Milinda saw the venerable Nagasena he was greatly afraid, greatly agitated and his hair stood on end. So it is said.

When the King saw Nagasena, endowed with right behaviour,
Tamed in the supreme taming, he spoke these words:
"Many are the speakers I have seen, many the discussions I have held,
But there was no fear like unto this, no terror as is mine today.
Undoubtedly there will be defeat for me today
And victory for Nagasena, since (my) mind is not composed."

II. Distinguishing Marks

Then King Milinda approached the venerable Nagasena; having approached, he exchanged greetings with the venerable Nagasena; and, having exchanged greetings of friendliness and courtesy, he sat down at a respectful distance. And the venerable Nagasena greeted him in return so that he gladdened the heart of King Milinda. Then King Milinda spoke thus to the venerable Nagasena:

"How is the revered one known? What is your name, revered sir?"

"Sire, I am known as Nagasena; fellow Brahma-farers[15] address me, sire, as Nagasena. But though (my) parents gave (me) the name of Nagasena or Surasena or Virasena or Sihasena, yet it is but a denotation, appellation, designation, a current usage, for Nagasena is only a name since no person[16] is got at here."

15. The Hindu god Brahma was regarded as a very devout Buddhist.
16. *Puggala:* self, individual, soul.

Then King Milinda spoke thus: "Good sirs, let the five hundred Bactrian Greeks and the eighty thousand monks hear me: This Nagasena speaks thus: 'Since no person is got at here.' Now, is it suitable to approve of that?" And King Milinda spoke thus to the venerable Nagasena: . . .

"If you say: 'Fellow Brahma-farers address me, sire, as Nagasena,' what here is Nagasena? Is it, revered sir, that the hairs of the head are Nagasena?"

"O no, sire."

"That the hairs of the body are Nagasena?"

"O no, sire."

"That the nails . . . the teeth, the skin, the flesh, the sinews, the bones, the marrow, the kidneys, the heart, the liver, the membranes, the spleen, the lungs, the intestines, the mesentery, the stomach, the excrement, the bile, the phlegm, the pus, the blood, the sweat, the fat, the tears, the serum, the saliva, the mucus, the synovic fluid, the urine, or the brain in the head are (any of them) Nagasena?"

"O no, sire."

"Is Nagasena material shape, revered sir?"

"O no, sire."

"Is Nagasena feeling . . . perception . . . the habitual tendencies? Is Nagasena consciousness?"

"O no, sire."

"But then, revered sir, is Nagasena material shape and feeling and perception and habitual tendencies and consciousness?"

"O no, sire."

"But then, revered sir, is there Nagasena apart from material shape, feeling, perception, the habitual tendencies and consciousness?"

"O no, sire."

"Though I, revered sir, am asking you repeatedly, I do not see this Nagasena. Nagasena is only a sound, revered sir. For who here is Nagasena? You, revered sir, are speaking an untruth, a lying word. There is no Nagasena."

Then the venerable Nagasena spoke thus to King Milinda: "You, sire, are a noble delicately nurtured, exceedingly delicately nurtured. If you, sire, go on foot at noon-time on the scorching ground and hot sand, trampling on sharp grit and pebbles and sand, your feet hurt you, your body wearies, your thought is impaired, and tactile consciousness arises accompanied by anguish. Now, did you come on foot or in a conveyance?"

"I, revered sir, did not come on foot, I came in a chariot."

"If you, sire, came by chariot, show me the chariot. Is the pole the chariot, sire?"

"O no, revered sir."

"Is the axle the chariot?"

"O no, revered sir."

"Are the wheels the chariot?"

"O no, revered sir."

"Is the body of the chariot the chariot . . . is the flag-staff of the chariot the chariot . . . is the yoke the chariot . . . are the reins the chariot . . . is the goad the chariot?"

"O no, revered sir."

"But then, sire, is the chariot the pole, the axle, the wheels, the body of the chariot, the flag-staff of the chariot, the yoke, the reins, the goad?"

"O no, revered sir."

"But then, sire, is there a chariot apart from the pole, the axle, the wheels, the body of the chariot, the flag-staff of the chariot, the yoke, the reins, the goad?"

"O no, revered sir."

"Though I, sire, am asking you repeatedly, I do not see the chariot. Chariot is only a sound, sire. For what here is the chariot? You, sire, are speaking an untruth, a lying word. There is no chariot. You, sire, are the chief rajah in the whole of India. Of whom are you afraid that you speak a lie? Let the five hundred worthy Bactrian Greeks and the eighty thousand monks listen to me: This King Milinda speaks thus: 'I have come by chariot.' But on being told: 'If you, sire, have come by chariot, show me the chariot,' he does not produce the chariot. Is it suitable to approve of that?"

When this had been said, the five hundred Bactrian Greeks, applauding the venerable Nagasena, spoke thus to King Milinda: "Now do you, sire speak if you can." Then King Milinda spoke thus to the venerable Nagasena:

"I, revered Nagasena, am not telling a lie, for it is because

of the pole, because of the axle, the wheels, the body of a chariot, the flag-staff of a chariot, the yoke, the reins, and because
of the goad that 'chariot' exists as a denotation, appellation,
designation, as a current usage, as a name."

"It is well; you, sire, understand a chariot. Even so is it for
me, sire, because of the hair of the head and because of the hair
of the body . . . and because of the brain in the head and
because of material shape and feeling and perception and the
habitual tendencies and consciousness that 'Nagasena' exists
as a denotation, appellation, designation, as a current usage,
merely as a name. But according to the highest meaning[17] the
person is not got at here. . . .

. . . .

The King said: "Revered Nagasena, will you converse with
me?"

"I will converse if you, sire, will converse in the speech of
the learned, but if you converse in the speech of kings I will
not converse."

"How, revered Nagasena, do the learned converse?"

"When the learned are conversing, sire, a turning over (of
a subject) is made and an unravelling is made and a refuta-
tion is made, and a redress is made and a specific point is made
and a specific point is made against it, and the learned are not
angry in consequence—it is thus, sire, that the learned converse."

"And how do kings converse, revered sir?"

"When kings are conversing, sire, they approve of some
matter and order a punishment for whoever disagrees with that
matter, saying: 'Inflict a punishment on him'—it is thus, sire,
that kings converse."

"I, revered sir, will converse in the speech of the learned,
not in the speech of kings. Let the revered one converse un-
reservedly as he converses with a monk or novice or lay-follower or with a monastery-attendant— let the revered one converse thus, let him be not afraid."

The Elder assented by saying: "It is well, sire."

. . . .

17. Philosophically speaking, in the highest sense.

Then Devamantiya and Anantakaya and Mankura approached the venerable Nagasena, and when they had approached, they spoke thus to him: "Revered sir, King Milinda speaks thus: ' Let him come with as many monks as he likes.' " And the venerable Nagasena dressed early in the morning and, taking his bowl and robe, entered Sagala with the eighty thousand monks. Then as Anantakaya was walking beside the venerable Nagasena he spoke thus to him: "Revered sir, that which I call 'Nagasena,' which here is Nagasena?"

"But who do you think 'Nagasena' is here?"

"Revered sir, whatever is the inner mobile principle, the life-principle[18] that enters and issues forth, I think that is 'Nagasena.' "

"But if this breath has issued forth and does not enter (again) or has entered but does not issue forth (again), could that man live?"

"O no, revered sir."

"But when those who are conch-blowers blow on a conch, does their breath enter (again)?"

"No, revered sir."

"Or when those who are blowers on bamboo-pipes blow on a bamboo-pipe, does their breath enter (again)?"

"O no, revered sir."

"Or when those who are horn-blowers blow on a horn, does their breath enter (again)?"

"No, revered sir."

"Then why do they not die?"

"I am not competent to converse on this assertion with you. It were good, revered sir, if you uttered the meaning."

"This is not the life-principle; in-breathing and out-breathing are bodily activities," and the Elder gave a talk on Abhidhamma.[19] Then Anantakaya declared his status as a lay-follower.

. . . .

The King said: "Revered Nagasena, is there anyone who, when dead, does not reconnect?"[20]

18. *Jiva*, or soul.
19. Advanced study of Buddhist law.
20. Reconnect with another name and form, i.e., take on a new body.

The Elder said: "Some reconnect, some do not reconnect."

"Who reconnects, who does not reconnect?"

"He who has defilements reconnects, sire, he who is without defilements does not reconnect."

"Will you yourself reconnect, revered sir?"

"If I should have attachment, sire, I will reconnect, but if I am without attachment I will not reconnect."

"You are dexterous, revered Nagasena."

The King said: "Revered Nagasena, does he who does not reconnect not reconnect because of attentive consideration?"[21]

"Sire, it is because of attentive consideration and it is because of wisdom and it is because of other skilled mental states."

"Revered sir, is attentive consideration the same as wisdom?"

"No, sire, consideration is one thing, wisdom another. Of these (two), sire, goats, sheep, cows, buffaloes, camels and donkeys have consideration, but they have not wisdom."

"You are dexterous, revered Nagasena."

The King said: "What is the distinguishing mark of consideration, what the distinguishing mark of wisdom, revered sir?"

"Examination is the distinguishing mark of consideration, sire, cutting off[22] is the distinguishing mark of wisdom."

"How does consideration have the distinguishing mark of examination, how does wisdom have the distinguishing mark of cutting off? Make a simile."

"Do you, sire, know about barley-reapers?"

"Yes, revered sir, I do."

"How, sire, do barley-reapers reap the barley?"

"Revered sir, grasping a handful of barley in the left hand and a sickle in the right, they cut it off with the sickle."

"As, sire, a barley-reaper grasps a handful of barley in the left hand and a sickle in the right and cuts it off with the sickle, even so, sire, does the earnest student of yoga, taking hold of the mind with consideration, cut off the defilements with wis-

21. I.e., ordered thinking and reasoning.
22. Cutting off of the defilements and attachments.

dom. It is thus, sire, that examination is the distinguishing mark of consideration, thus that cutting off is the distinguishing mark of wisdom."

"You are dexterous, revered Nagasena."

The King said: "Revered Nagasena, when you said: 'And because of other skilled mental states,'—which are these skilled mental states?"

"Moral habit, sire, faith, energy, mindfulness and concentration—these are those skilled mental states."

"Revered sir, what is the distinguishing mark of moral habit?"

"Moral habit, sire, has as its distinguishing mark that it is the basis of all skilled mental states. . . . In one who is based on moral habit, sire, none of these skilled mental states decreases."

"Make a simile."

"As, sire, whatever vegetable growth and animal growth comes to growth, increase and maturity all does so in dependence on the earth and based on the earth; even so, sire, does the earnest student of yoga, depending on moral habit and based on moral habit, develop the five controlling faculties: the controlling faculty of faith, of energy, of mindfulness, of concentration, of wisdom."

.   .   .   .

The King said: "Revered Nagasena, what is the root of past (samsaric)[23] time, what the root of future (samsaric) time, what the root of present (samsaric) time?"

"Of past (samsaric) time, sire, and of future (samsaric) time and of present (samsaric) time the root is ignorance; conditioned by ignorance are the karmic formations, conditioned by the karmic formations is consciousness, conditioned by consciousness is name-and-shape, conditioned by name-and-shape are the six (sensory) fields, conditioned by the six (sensory) fields is sensory impingement, conditioned by sensory impingement is feeling, conditioned by feeling is craving, conditioned

23. *Samsara* is the continual series of births and deaths.

by craving is grasping, conditioned by grasping is (karmic) becoming, conditioned by (karmic) becoming is birth, conditioned by birth there come into existence old age and dying, grief, sorrow, suffering, lamentation and despair. Thus the earliest point of this whole (samsaric) time cannot be shown."

"You are dexterous, revered Nagasena."

. . . .

The King said: "Revered Nagasena, are there any karmic formations that are produced?"

"Yes, sire, there are karmic formations that are produced."

"Which are they, revered sir?"

"Sire, when there is eye and when there are material shapes there is visual consciousness; when there is visual consciousness there is sensory impingement on the eye; when there is sensory impingement on the eye there is feeling; when there is feeling there is craving; when there is craving there is grasping; when there is grasping there is (continued) becoming; when there is (continued) becoming there is birth; when there is birth there come into existence old age and dying, grief, sorrow, suffering, lamentation and despair. Thus is the origination of this whole mass of anguish. But, sire, when there is not eye or material shapes there is no visual consciousness; when there is not visual consciousness there is no sensory impingement on the eye; when there is not sensory impingement on the eye there is no feeling; when there is not feeling there is no craving; when there is not craving there is no grasping; when there is not grasping there is no (continued) becoming; when there is not (continued) becoming there is no birth; when there is not birth there are no old age and dying nor grief, sorrow, suffering, lamentation or despair. Thus is the stopping of this whole mass of anguish."

"You are dexterous, revered Nagasena."

III. Questions for the Cutting off of Perplexity

. . . .

The King said: "Revered Nagasena, what is the reason that men are not all the same, some being short-lived, some long-lived, some weakly, others healthy, some ugly, others comely, some of few wishes, others of many wishes, some poor, others rich, some belonging to low families, others to high families, and some being weak in wisdom, others having wisdom?"

The Elder said: "But why, sire, are trees not all the same, some being acid, some salt, some bitter, some sharp, some astringent, others sweet?"

"I think, revered sir, that it is because of a difference in seeds."

"Even so, sire, it is because of a difference in kammas[24] that men are not all the same, some being short-lived, others long-lived, some weakly, others healthy, some ugly, others comely, some of few wishes, others of many wishes, some poor, others rich, some belonging to low families, others to high families, and some being weak in wisdom, others having wisdom. And this, sire, was also said by the Lord: 'Young man, beings have their own kamma, they are heirs to kamma, kamma is the matrix, kamma the kin, kamma the arbiter, kamma divides beings, that is to say into low and lofty.' "

"You are dexterous, revered Nagasena."

.   .   .   .

The King said: "Revered Nagasena, is stopping nibbana?"[25]

"Yes, sire, stopping is nibbana."

"How, revered sir, is stopping nibbana?"

"All those foolish average men, sire, who rejoice in the inner and outer sense-fields, approve of them and cleave to them— they are carried away by that stream, they are not utterly free from birth, old age and dying, from grief, sorrow, suffering, lamentation and despair, they are not, I say, utterly free from anguish. But, sire, the instructed disciple of the ariyans does not rejoice in the inner and outer sense-fields, does not approve of them or cleave to them. For him, not rejoicing in them, not approving of them or cleaving to them, craving is stopped; from the stopping of craving is the stopping of grasping; from the

24. Pali for *karma*.
25. Pali for *Nirvana*.

stopping of grasping is the stopping of (karmic) becoming; from the stopping of (karmic) becoming is the stopping of birth; from the stopping of birth, old age and dying, grief, sorrow, suffering, lamentation and despair are stopped. Thus is the stopping of this whole mass of anguish. In this way, sire, stopping is nibbana."

"You are dexterous, revered Nagasena."

The King said: "Revered Nagasena, does everyone obtain nibbana?"

"Not everyone, sire, obtains nibbana, but he obtains nibbana who, practising rightly, knows thoroughly the things that should be thoroughly known, comprehends the things that should be comprehended, gets rid of the things that should be got rid of, develops the things that should be developed, and realizes the things that should be realized."

"You are dexterous, revered Nagasena."

The King said: "Revered Nagasena, is there any being that passes over from this body to another body?"

"No, sire."

"If, revered Nagasena, there is no passing over from this body to another body, is not one freed from evil deeds?"

"Yes, sire, if one did not reconnect, one would be freed from evil deeds. But as, sire, one reconnects, therefore is one not utterly freed from evil deeds."

"Make a simile."

"Suppose, sire, some man were to steal another man's mangoes, would he deserve punishment?"

"Yes, revered sir, he would deserve punishment."

"But if those mangoes that he stole, sire, were not those that had been planted, why would he deserve punishment?"

"These mangoes, revered sir, exist because of (those others), therefore he would deserve punishment."

"In the same way, sire, it is through the deed one does with this name-and-shape, be it lovely or unlovely, that one reconnects (in) another name-and-shape and therefore is not utterly freed from evil deeds."

"You are dexterous, revered Nagasena. . . ."

The King said: "Revered Nagasena, a deed that is either skilled or unskilled has been done by this name-and-shape: where do these deeds remain?"

"Those deeds would follow it, sire, 'like a shadow that never leaves it.' "

"Is it possible to point to those deeds, revered sir, and say that they remain either here or there?"

"It is not possible, sire, to point to those deeds and say that they remain either here or there."

"Make a simile."

"What do you think about this, sire? Is it possible to point to the fruits of a tree that has not yet borne fruit and say that the fruits are either here or there?"

"On no, revered sir."

"In the same way, sire, so long as the (life-)continuity is not cut off, it is not possible to point to those deeds and say that they remain either here or there."

"You are dexterous, revered Nagasena. . . ."

The King said: "Revered Nagasena, is there the Buddha?"

"Yes, sire, there is the Lord."

"But is it possible, revered Nagasena, to point to the Buddha and say that he is either here or there?"

"Sire, the Lord has attained final nibbana in the element of nibbana that has no substrate remaining (for future birth). It is not possible to point to the Lord and say that he is either here or there."

"Make a simile."

"What do you think about this, sire? When the flame of a great burning mass of fire has gone out is it possible to point to that flame and say that it is either here or there?"

"O no, revered sir, that flame has stopped, it has disappeared."

"Even so, sire, the Lord has attained final nibbana in the element of nibbana that has no substrate remaining (for future birth); it is not possible to point to the Lord who has gone home and say that he is either here or there; but, sire, it is possible to point to the Lord by means of the body of Dhamma, for Dhamma, sire, was taught by the Lord."

"You are dexterous, revered Nagasena."

. . . .

Introduction to World Cycles

All ancient Indian cosmogonies were cyclic in character, dividing time into successive periods of rise and decline. Though Hindus, Jains, and Buddhists held variant notions of universal history, all agreed that the length of these periods was enormous. The basic unit of Hindu time-reckoning was the *kalpa* or "day of Brahma," consisting of 4320 million earthly years. The *kalpa* was in turn divided into 4000 *yugas* (ages), each beginning at a high point of human happiness, morality, longevity, and stature, but progressively declining. Various Hindu authors of the first several centuries A.D.—bemoaning the prevalence of heretical sects in India, the confusion of castes, and the rule of harsh and alien kings—supposed that the end of a *yuga* (i.e., the end of the world) was imminent.

Buddhists divided their basic cycle, the *maha-kalpa* ("great *kalpa*"), into four periods of immense (if often unspecified) length. In the first of these, mankind declines until everything in the universe is destroyed except the highest heaven. This is followed by a second period of quiescence. In the third period evolution begins again; a lower heaven and numerous earths take form. The first men now appear; they are originally godlike beings, but slowly degenerate and become human. The fourth period is again one of continuation, marked by a series of lesser cycles of rise and decline within the greater one. These lesser cycles are classed as "Buddha cycles" and "empty cycles"; the present one is a "Buddha cycle" in which four Buddhas (the latest being Gautama Shakyamuni) have already appeared on earth and the fifth (Maitreya) is yet to come.

The following passages describe the four periods (here called "immensities") within a *maha-kalpa*. The text is from the *Visuddhi-Magga*, a work of the early fifth century A.D. by Buddhaghosa, the great Buddhist editor and commentator.

FROM THE VISUDDHI-MAGGA
OF BUDDHAGHOSA

World Cycles

. . . Now the perishing and the existing of a world-cycle are after the following manner:

When a world-cycle perishes by fire,[1] there arises in the beginning a cycle-destroying great cloud, and a great rain falls throughout one hundred thousand times ten million worlds. The people are delighted and overjoyed, and bring forth seed of all kinds and sow; but when the crops have grown just large enough for cow-fodder, the clouds keep up a braying noise, but do not allow a drop to fall; all rain is utterly cut off. Concerning which the following has been said by The Blessed One:

"There comes a time, O priests, when, for many years, for many hundreds of years, for many thousands of years, for many hundreds of thousands of years, the god does not rain."

Those creatures who depend on rain die, and are reborn in the Brahma-world[2]; likewise the divinities who live on flowers and fruits. When thus a long time has elapsed, here and there the ponds of water dry up. Then, one by one, the fishes and turtles also die and are reborn in the Brahma-world; likewise the inhabitants of the hells. But some say the inhabitants of the hells perish with the appearing of the seventh sun. . . .

When now a long period has elapsed from the cessation of the rains, a second sun appears. Here is to be supplied in full what was said by The Blessed One in the Discourse on the Seven Suns, beginning with the words, "There comes, O priests, a time."

When this second sun has appeared, there is no distinction of day and night; each sun rises when the other sets, and an incessant heat beats upon the world. And whereas the ordinary

From *Buddhism in Translations*, trans. by Henry Clarke Warren (Cambridge, Mass.: Harvard University Press, 1896), pp. 321-30.

1. According to the text, the destruction may also occur by wind or water.
2. The heaven of the high god, Brahma.

sun is inhabited by its divinity, no such being is to be found in the cycle-destroying sun. When the ordinary sun shines, clouds and patches of mist fly about in the air. But when the cycle-destroying sun shines, the sky is free from mists and clouds, and as spotless as a mirror, and the water in all streams dries up, except in the case of the five great rivers. After the lapse of another long period, a third sun appears, and the great rivers dry up. After the lapse of another long period, a fourth sun appears, and the sources of the great rivers in the Himalaya Mountains dry up. . . . After the lapse of another long period, a fifth sun appears, and the mighty ocean gradually dries up, so that not enough water remains to moisten the tip of one's finger. After the lapse of another long period, a sixth sun appears, and the whole world becomes filled with smoke, and saturated with the greasiness of that smoke, and not only this world but a hundred thousand times ten million worlds. After the lapse of another long period, a seventh sun appears, and the whole world breaks into flames; and just as this one, so also a hundred thousand times ten million worlds. All the peaks of Mount Sineru,[3] even those which are hundreds of leagues in height, crumble and disappear in the sky. The flames of fire rise up and envelop the Heaven of the Four Great Kings. Having there burnt up all the mansions of gold, of jewels, and of precious stones, they envelop the Heaven of the Thirty-three. In the same manner they envelop all the heavens to which access is given by the first trance. Having thus burnt up three of the Brahma-heavens, they come to a stop on reaching the Heaven of the Radiant Gods. This fire does not go out as long as anything remains; but after everything has disappeared, it goes out, leaving no ashes, like a fire of clarified butter or sesamum oil. The upper regions of space become one with those below, and wholly dark.

Now after the lapse of another long period, a great cloud arises. And first it rains with a very fine rain, and then the rain pours down in streams which gradually increase from the

3. Mount Sineru (or Meru) was the legendary mountain supposedly located at the center of the earth. It was surrounded by other somewhat lower peaks on which the gods dwelt.

thickness of a water-lily stalk to that of a staff, of a club, of
the trunk of a palmyra-tree. And when this cloud has filled
every burnt place throughout a hundred thousand times ten
million worlds, it disappears. And then a wind arises, below and
on the sides of the water, and rolls it into one mass which is
round like a drop on the leaf of a lotus. But how can it press
such an immense volume of water into one mass? Because the
water offers openings here and there for the wind. After the
water has thus been massed together by the wind, it dwindles
away, and by degrees descends to a lower level. As the water
descends, the Brahma-heavens reappear in their places, and also
the four upper heavens of sensual pleasure. When it has descended to its original level on the surface of the earth, mighty
winds arise, and they hold the water helplessly in check, as if in
a covered vessel. This water is sweet, and as it wastes away, the
earth which arises out of it is full of sap, and has a beautiful
color, and a fine taste and smell, like the skimmings on the top
of thick rice-gruel.

Then beings, who have been living in the Heaven of the
Radiant Gods, leave that existence, either on account of having
completed their term of life, or on account of the exhaustion of
their merit, and are reborn here on earth. They shine with their
own light and wander through space. Thereupon, as described
in the Discourse on Primitive Ages, they taste that savory earth,
are overcome with desire, and fall to eating it ravenously. Then
they cease to shine with their own light, and find themselves in
darkness. When they perceive this darkness, they become
afraid. Thereupon, the sun's disk appears, full fifty leagues in
extent, banishing their fears and producing a sense of divine
presence. . . . After the sun has given light throughout the
day, it sets. . . . Thereupon, the disk of the moon appears,
forty-nine leagues in extent. . . . When thus the sun and the
moon have appeared, the constellations and the stars arise.
From that time on night and day succeed each other, and in
due course the months and half-months, seasons and years.
Moreover, on the same day with the sun and the moon, Mount
Sineru, the mountains which encircle the world, and the Himalaya Mountains reappear. These all appear simultaneously on

the day of the full moon of the month Phagguna.[4] And how? Just as when panick-seed porridge is cooking, suddenly bubbles appear and form little hummocks in some places, and leave other places as depressions, while others still are flat; even so the mountains correspond to the little hummocks, and the oceans to the depressions, and the continents to the flat places.

Now after these beings have begun to eat the savory earth, by degrees some become handsome and some ugly. Then the handsome despise the ugly, and as the result of this despising, the savoriness of the earth disappears, and the bitter pappataka plant grows up. In the same manner that also disappears, and the padalata plant grows up. In the same way that also disappears, and rice grows up without any need of cultivation, free from all husk and red granules, and exposing the sweet-scented naked rice-grain. Then pots appear for the rice, and they place the rice in the pots, and place these pots on the tops of stones. And flames of fire spring up of their own accord, and cook the rice, and it becomes rice-porridge resembling the jasmine flower, and needing the addition of no broth or condiments, but having any desired flavor. Now when these beings eat this material food, the excrements are formed within them, and in order that they may relieve themselves, openings appear in their bodies, and the virility of the man, and the femininity of the woman. Then the woman begins to meditate excessively on the man, and the man on the woman, and as a result of this excessive meditation, the fever of lust springs up, and they have carnal connection. And being tormented by the reproofs of the wise for their low conduct, they build houses for its concealment. And having begun to dwell in houses, after a while they follow the example of some lazy one among themselves, and store up food. From that time on the red granules and the husks envelop the rice-grains, and wherever a crop has been mown down, it does not spring up again. Then these beings come together, and groan aloud saying, "Alas! wickedness has sprung up among men; for surely we formerly were made of mind." The full account of this is to be supplied from the Discourse on Primitive Ages.

4. Late February and early March.

Then they institute boundary lines, and one steals another's share. After reviling the offender two or three times, the third time they beat him with their fists, with clods of earth, with sticks, etc. When thus stealing, reproof, lying, and violence have sprung up among them, they come together, and say, "What if now we elect some one of us, who shall get angry with him who merits anger, reprove him who merits reproof, and banish him who merits banishment. And we will give him in return a share of our rice." When, however, the people of this, our world-cycle came to this decision, our Blessed One, who was at the time a Future Buddha, was of all these beings the handsomest, the most pleasing of appearance, possessing the greatest influence and wisdom, and able to raise up and put down. Then they all came to him, and having gained his assent, they elected him their chief. . . . A Future Buddha always becomes chief in that position in life which is most highly esteemed by mankind. When thus the association of warriors had been formed, with the Future Buddha at its head, by degrees the Brahmans and the other castes arose.

Now from the cycle-destroying great cloud to the termination of the conflagration constitutes one immensity, and is called the period of destruction. And from the cycle-destroying conflagration to the salutary great rains filling one hundred thousand times ten million worlds is the second immensity, and is called the continuance of destruction. From the salutary great rains to the appearing of the sun and moon is the third immensity, and is called the period of renovation. From the appearing of the sun and moon to the cycle-destroying great cloud is the fourth immensity, and is called the continuance of renovation. These four immensities form one great world-cycle.

This, then, is the order of events in a world-cycle when it perishes by fire.

. . . .

Why does the world perish in these particular ways? It is on account of the special wickedness that may be at bottom. For it is in accordance with the wickedness preponderating that the world perishes. When passion preponderates, it perishes by fire;

when hatred, it perishes by water.—But some say that when hatred preponderates, it perishes by fire, and that when passion preponderates it perishes by water.—When infatuation preponderates, it perishes by wind.

Now the world, in perishing, perishes seven times in succession by fire, and the eighth time by water; and then again seven times by fire, and the eighth time by water. Thus the world perishes each eighth time by water, until it has perished seven times by water, and then seven more times by fire. Thus have sixty-three world-cycles elapsed. Then the perishing by water is omitted, and wind takes its turn in demolishing the world; and when the Completely Lustrous Gods have reached their full term of existence of sixty-four world-cycles, their heaven also is destroyed.

Now it is of such world-cycles that a priest[5] who can call to mind former existences and former world-cycles, can call to mind many destructions of a world-cycle, and many renovations of a world-cycle, and many destructions and renovations of a world-cycle.

[The proliferation of mythological beings and places—though far removed from the ethical teachings of Gautama the Buddha—is frequently encountered in Mahayana Buddhist texts. The following selection is from the *Mahavastu*, a Sanskrit work belonging to the *Vinaya Pitaka*.]

5. I.e., monk.

FROM THE MAHAVASTU

Maudgalyayana's Visits to Hell

The Enlightened One[1] himself looked on this world and the world beyond, on the coming and going of men, on the round of passing away and coming to be.

The Seer himself reflects upon and understands the peculiar

From *The Mahavastu*, Vol. I, trans. by J. J. Jones. Vol. XVI of *The Sacred Books of the Buddhists* (London: Luzac & Co., 1949), pp. 9-11. Reprinted by permission of the Pali Text Society.
1. Buddha.

fruition of acts which is bound up with the nature of man, and the place wherein they come to fruition.

Gotama, the Exalted One, the seer with clear insight into all things, has in his understanding named the eight hells, Sañjiva, Kalasutra, Sanghata, the two Rauravas, Mahavici, Tapana and Pratapana.

Thus are these eight hells named. Hard are they to traverse, being strewn with the consequences of terrible deeds. Each has its sixteen secondary hells.

They have four corners and four gates. They are divided up and well laid out in squares. They are a hundred *yojanas*[2] high, a hundred square.

They are encircled by a wall of iron, with a vault of iron above. The floor is of hot and glowing iron.

Habitations hard to dwell in are they, being everywhere expanses of iron boards, hair-raising, fearful, terrible, and full of woe.

All the fearful hells are filled with hundreds of flames, each of which spreads its glow abroad a hundred *yojanas*.

Here the many fearsome beings, the great sinners, burn a long time, even for hundreds of years.

With scourges of iron the ruthless warders of hell mercilessly beat those who have sinned.

These I shall tell of in well-ordered words. Give ear and attentively hear me as I speak.

In the Sañjiva hell beings hang with their feet up and their heads down, and are trimmed with axes and knives.

Carried away by frenzy of anger they fight among themselves, using their own sharp claws of iron.

Sharp knives also grow from their hands, and with them these utterly demented beings rend one another.

Though their bodies collapse under the cold wind that blows on them, yet all their limbs are afire as they reap the fruit of their past deeds.

Thus has the Master, the Tathagata, understanding its true nature, called this hell Sañjiva, a bourne of evil deeds.

2. A *yojana* is equivalent to about nine miles.

Released from Sañjiva they plunge into Kukkula. Foregathering there they are tortured for a long stretch of time.

There, in Kukkula, they run about in flames for many a *yojana*, and suffer great misery.

Released from Kukkula these broken men plunge into Kunapa, a vast expanse spreading far and wide.

There, asses, swarthy brutes, with mouths breathing fierce fire, rend their skin and devour and feed on their flesh and blood.

When they have passed out of Kunapa they catch sight of pleasant trees, and in quest of relief they make for the shelter of their verdant foliage.

But there, hawks and vultures and ravens, with beaks of iron drive them from under a green tree, and devour their torn and gory limbs.

And when they have been devoured until their bones alone are left, their skin and flesh and blood grow once more.

In their terror they run away, and deeming there was refuge where there was none, come all stricken to the terrible forest where the leaves are swords.

When they have escaped from the sword-leafed forest, wounded, racked, and steeped in blood, they go to the river Vaitarani.

There they dive into the river's hot and caustic water, which pierces all of their tortured limbs.

Then Yama's[3] myrmidons gaff them with hooks of iron, fling them on the river bank and give them pellets of iron to eat.

They give them molten red copper to drink, which passes through their inwards down to their lower parts.

Evil-doers, those who follow the wrong way and do not perform the right deed, go down into these hells.

Those who wholly eschew sinful deeds, those whose conduct is wholly virtuous do not pass to the bourne of ill.

Therefore the qualities of deeds are of two kinds, good and bad. Avoiding the bad, one should practise the good and fair.

. . . .

---

3. Yama is the god of the dead.

THE VINAYA

Introduction to the Inception of Discipline

Buddhaghosa was a great scholar of the early fifth century A.D., whose life's work was to preserve the traditions of Buddhist monasticism. Legend records that he was by origin a Brahmin from the region of Bodh Gaya in India, but after his conversion to Buddhism migrated to Ceylon. Ceylon at that time had been a Buddhist country for over six hundred years (ever since the days of Ashoka)* and the monks of the island were reputed to have preserved the original Buddhist faith in its purest form. The *Vinaya Pitaka*—containing regulations governing the monastic life—was especially revered; and over the centuries the monks had provided it with numerous exegetical commentaries.

Weaving together various of these interpretations, Buddhaghosa composed a commentary of his own on the *Vinaya Pitaka*. But whereas the Singhalese works—both written and oral—existed only in a local tongue unintelligible outside of the island, Buddhaghosa wrote in Pali, the language of the *Tripitaka*, which was understood by educated Buddhists throughout India. At the same time, he sought to establish beyond a doubt the authenticity of the Buddhist tradition as preserved in Ceylon. Thus he traced the history of the monastic order back to the time of its founders and noted the stages by which it had continued down to his own day.

Buddhaghosa upheld the orthodox Buddhist position that the entire Pali *Tripitaka* had been put together at the First Convocation, which reputedly was held in 483 B.C. just after the death of Buddha. But historically this claim is certainly false. Originally the Buddhists had no "scriptures" at all—just memories of Gautama's sayings. The compilation of the *Tripitaka* extended over a period of centuries; and no part of it as now extant antedates the time of Ashoka.

The following selection is from Buddhaghosa's introduction to his commentary on the Vinaya Pitaka. It dates from about 430 A.D.

* For Ashoka see above, pp. 101-12.

FROM THE INCEPTION OF DISCIPLINE
BY BUDDHAGHOSA

The First Great Convocation

When the Exalted One, the Lord of the world had passed away in the element of Nibbana which is devoid of any material substratum, at the hour of day-break on the full moon day of the month of Visakha[1] between the twin sala trees in the Upavattana sala-grove of the Mallas[2] in Kusinara, having discharged the functions of an Enlightened One, beginning with the turning of the Wheel of the Dhamma, down to the conversion of the wandering ascetic Subhadda,[3] the venerable Mahakassapa, the leading Elder among the 700,000 monks who had assembled at the passing away in perfect Nibbana of the Exalted One, recollecting after the lapse of seven days from the passing away in perfect Nibbana of the Exalted One, the words uttered by Subhadda[4] who had taken to the ascetic life in old age, namely, "Away with it friends, grieve not, lament not, we are well rid of the Great Recluse who was wont to tell us what was befitting and what was not and hence made our lives miserable; but now we will do whatever we please and not do what we please not"; kindled the enthusiasm among the Order of monks to bring about a rehearsal of the Dhamma and Vinaya and further reflected, "It may be that the occasion would arise for evil-minded monks to think that the Sacred-word is such that its Teacher is no more, to form factions and before long make the Good Teaching disappear for ever. As long as the Dhamma and Vinaya endure, so long will the Sacred-word be such that its Teacher has not passed into oblivion. And so has the Exalted

From *The Inception of Discipline and The Vinaya Nidana*, trans. by N. A. Jayawickrama, Vol. XXI of *The Sacred Books of the Buddhists* (London: Luzac & Co., 1962), pp. 3-14. Reprinted by permission of the Pali Text Society.

1. The end of April and beginning of May.
2. The Malla people were hill dwellers from the Nepalese border-region.
3. The last disciple converted by the Buddha before his final Nirvana.
4. Different from the earlier-mentioned Subhadda.

One said, 'O Ananda, the Dhamma and the Vinaya that I have declared to you and laid down before you (respectively) that itself will be your teacher after my demise.' It behoves me to rehearse the Dhamma and Vinaya so that the Dispensation would endure and remain for long. . . ."

Subsequently he said, "Let us, friends, rehearse the Dhamma and the Vinaya: in the past what was contrary to the Dhamma and the Vinaya prevailed, the Dhamma and the Vinaya were disregarded; those who held views contrary to the Dhamma and the Vinaya held sway while those who professed the Dhamma and the Vinaya were powerless." The monks rejoined, "If that be so, Sir, may the Elder select the monks (for the Convocation)."

The Elder rejected many hundreds and thousands of monks . . . and chose 499 . . . monks who alone were proficient with regard to the learning in all aspects of the Teachings in the entire Three Baskets, had attained mastery in analytical knowledge, were of no mean achievement, and for the greater part were classified by the Exalted One as an expert each in his field in the distinct spheres of the threefold knowledge. Regarding them it has been said, "Thereupon the venerable Mahakassapa selected five hundred Arahants less one."

Why did the Elder make the number fall short by one? To make room for the venerable Elder Ananda. It was not possible to hold the Convocation with or without that venerable one, for he was yet a Learner[5] with his (spiritual) task yet unaccomplished. Therefore it was not permissible to have him at the Convocation. Since there was no section whatsoever of the Teachings of the Lord of Ten Powers commencing with the discourses and mixed prose and verse utterances which he himself had not learned from the Exalted One, it was equally not possible to hold it without him. This being so, even though he was yet a Learner he would have to be selected by the Elder on account of the great service that might be rendered by him at the rehearsal of the Dhamma; but the reason for his not

5. A trainee on the path to Arhatship.

being selected was to absolve himself (Kassapa) of the blame of others. . . .

Thereupon the monks themselves begged of the Elder on Ananda's behalf; for it has been said: "The monks spoke thus to Venerable Mahakassapa, 'Yonder Venerable Ananda, Sir, even though he is yet a Learner, is incapable of going on a wrong course through desire, ill-will, fear, or delusion[6]; he has mastered much of the Dhamma and the Vinaya under the Exalted One. Therefore, Sir, may the Elder nominate Venerable Ananda as well.' " Thereupon Venerable Mahakassapa selected Venerable Ananda as well. There were thus 500 Elders including that venerable one who was selected on the express wish of the monks.

It then occurred to the Elder monks, "Where shall we rehearse the Dhamma and the Vinaya?" Thereupon it again occurred to them, "Food is plentiful at Rajagaha,[7] and lodgings are easy to obtain there. Well then, let us rehearse the Dhamma and the Vinaya spending the Rains-residence at Rajagaha, and let not other monks enter upon the Rains-residence there." Why did they think in this manner? (Their idea was:) "Perhaps some undesirable individual may come into the midst of the monks and disturb this gigantic undertaking of ours." Then the venerable Mahakassapa made an announcement followed by a formal Act of the Order. It should be understood as stated in the Section dealing with the Convocation.

A fortnight had elapsed since the time of the passing away of the Tathagata in perfect Nibbana when seven days were spent in sacred festivities[8] and a further seven days in paying homage to the relics and so on. And the Elder Mahakassapa, considering that one and a half months of the summer were yet remaining and that the day for entering upon the Rains-residence was fast drawing nigh, took with him half the number

6. These are the four wrong courses of action.
7. Capital of the state of Magadha.
8. To pay homage to the remains of the Buddha and perform the cremation ceremonies.

of the Order of monks saying, "Friends, we shall repair to Rajagaha," and went in one direction. The Elder Anuruddha took with him the other half and went by a different route. . . .

At that time there were eighteen great monasteries at Rajagaha. And all of them were soiled with the cast-off and accumulated rubbish. For, at the time of the passing away of the Exalted One in perfect Nibbana all the monks took each his bowl and robe and went away deserting the monasteries and cells. The Elders there, in order to honour the request of the Exalted One and to escape the adverse criticism of members of heretical schools, thought of repairing the dilapidations during the first month. For, should the heretics say, "The disciples of the Recluse Gotama looked after their monasteries while their Teacher was alive; now that he has passed away in perfect Nibbana, they have deserted them," it is said that they thought so to escape the blame from them.

And so it has been said: It then occurred to the Elder monks, "Friends, the Exalted One has praised the effecting of repairs to dilapidations. So let us, friends, during the first month, repair the dilapidations and assemble to rehearse the Dhamma and the Vinaya during the second month."

On the following day they went and stood at the palace gates. King Ajatasattu[9] came forth, saluted them and inquired from them why they had come and what they expected him to do. The Elders intimated their need of labour to effect the repairs to the dilapidations in the eighteen great monasteries. "Very well, Sirs," said the King and gave artisans. The Elders had all the monasteries repaired during the first month and informed the King, "Great King, the repairs to the monasteries are completed, we now wish to rehearse the Dhamma and Vinaya."

"Very well, Sirs, do so with full confidence. Mine is the wheel of command, let yours be the Wheel of the Dhamma. Command of me, Sirs, whatever you wish me to do."

"A place for the monks who make the rehearsal of the Dhamma to assemble, Great King."

9. An actual king of Magadha, reigned *ca.* 494-467 B.C.

"Where shall I build it, Sirs?"

"It is meet you erect it at the entrance to the Sattapanni Cave on the side of the mountain Vebhara,[10] Great King."

"So be it, Sirs," said King Ajatasattu and had a pavilion erected, resembling the handiwork of Vissakamma,[11] . . . and decorated it like the abode of Brahma,[12] . . . In that large pavilion he spread out 500 rugs which were permissible for use[13] for the 500 monks, prepared a seat for the president at the southern end facing the North and a seat for the preacher in the centre of the pavilion facing the East, a seat worthy even of the Buddha, the Exalted One; and placing there a fan inlaid with ivory he sent word to the Order of monks: "My task, Sirs, is done. . . ."

Thereupon, on the following day, the Elder monks, having finished their meal, arranged their bowls and robes and assembled in the convocation hall. . . .

The Elder Mahakassapa addressed the monks, "Friends, what shall we rehearse first, the Dhamma or the Vinaya?" The monks replied, "Sir, Mahakassapa, the Vinaya is the very life of the Dispensation of the Enlightened One: so long as the Vinaya endures, the Dispensation endures, therefore let us rehearse the Vinaya first."

"Placing whom in charge?"[14]

"The venerable Upali."

"Is not Ananda competent?"

"It is not that he is not competent, but the Perfectly Enlightened One, while he was living, considered the venerable Upali as the most pre-eminent in connexion with the learning of the Vinaya, saying, 'He, O monks, is the most pre-eminent among my disciples who are monks, in the retention of the

10. One of five main peaks on the range of mountains around the city of Rajagaha.
11. The divine architect, known as Tvashtr in the Vedas.
12. The high god of the Hindu pantheon.
13. According to the rules of the order.
14. From a very early date, the Vinaya seems to have taken precedence over the Dhamma, especially in the Theravada school of Hinayana Buddhism.

Vinaya, namely Upali.' Therefore let us rehearse the Vinaya in consultation with the Elder Upali." Thereupon the Elder (Mahakassapa) appointed himself for the purpose of questioning about the Vinaya, and the Elder Upali agreed to give explanations. . . .

Then the venerable Mahakassapa questioned the venerable Upali on the subject of the first Parajika,[15] the occasion, the person, the rule, the corollaries, and on what constitutes an offence and what does not. In the same way as of the first, then of the second, the third, and of the fourth Parajika he asked about the subject and so on and what did not constitute an offence. The Elder Upali explained whatever he was asked. . . .

Thus was made the compilation of the Vinaya Pitaka which consists of the Vibhanga of both categories, the Khandhaka and the Parivara. The Elder Mahakassapa questioned on everything and the Elder Upali explained. At the conclusion of the explanation of the questions the 500 Arahants rehearsed together in a group according to the exact way in which the compilation had been fixed. On the conclusion of the compilation of the Vinaya the Elder Upali placed aside the fan inlaid with ivory, descended from the preacher's seat, saluted the older monks, and sat in the seat assigned to him.

Having rehearsed the Vinaya, the venerable Mahakassapa, wishing to rehearse the Dhamma, asked the monks, "Whom shall we place in charge in rehearsing the Dhamma?" The monks replied, "Let us make the Elder Ananda to be in charge."

Thereupon the venerable Mahakassapa announced to the Order of monks, "Friends, may the members of the Order listen to me. If it is agreeable to the members of the Order, I shall question Ananda on the Dhamma." The venerable Ananda, too, announced to the Order of monks, "May it please the venerable members of the Order to listen to me. If it is agreeable to the members of the Order, I shall explain the Dhamma when ques-

15. The Parajikas, or "Defeats," are the four grave offenses which bring immediate expulsion from the Order, namely, sexual intercourse, theft, murder, and false claims to transcendental attainments.

tioned by the venerable Mahakassapa." Then the venerable Ananda rose from his seat, arranged his robe over one shoulder, saluted the Elder monks (i.e. those who were his seniors), and sat in the preacher's seat taking in his hand the fan inlaid with ivory. The Elder Mahakassapa questioned the venerable Ananda on the Dhamma. . . . And in the self-same manner he questioned him on all five Nikayas. . . .[16]

All this forms the word of the Buddha which should be known as uniform in sentiment, twofold as the Dhamma and the Vinaya, threefold according to the first, intermediate, and last words, and similarly as Pitakas (Baskets), fivefold according to the Nikayas (Collections), ninefold according to the Angas (Factors), and forming 84,000 divisions according to the Units of the Dhamma.

16. *Digha Nikaya, Majjhima Nikaya, Samyutta Nikaya, Anguttara Nikaya,* and *Khuddaka Nikaya* (the five divisions of the *Sutta Pitaka*).

Introduction to The Monastic Vows

The following vows, which supposedly originated with the Buddha himself, were (and still are) repeated by Buddhist novices at the ceremony marking their initiation into the Order. They were not meant as promises valid for life, but rather as sincere statements of intent which could be freely renounced at any time. The vows were renewed at frequent intervals, and sometimes expressly taken for a limited period only.

In contrast to their Christian counterparts, Buddhist monks took no vow of obedience. The Buddhist Order was essentially democratic; no central authority existed to enforce uniformity upon individual monasteries. Abbots were chosen through election by the local monks; and important decisions were reached only after consultation with an assembly of the entire monastery.

THE MONASTIC VOWS
The Three Refuges

I put my trust in Buddha.
I put my trust in the Law.[1]
I put my trust in the Priesthood.[2]
Again I put my trust in Buddha.
Again I put my trust in the Law.
Again I put my trust in the Priesthood.
Once more I put my trust in Buddha.
Once more I put my trust in the Law.
Once more I put my trust in the Priesthood.

The Ten Precepts or Laws of the Priesthood

Abstinence from destroying life;[3]
Abstinence from theft;
Abstinence from fornication and all uncleanness;
Abstinence from lying;
Abstinence from fermented liquor, spirits and strong drink which are a hindrance to merit;
Abstinence from eating at forbidden times;[4]
Abstinence from dancing, singing, and shows;[5]
Abstinence from adorning and beautifying the person by the use of garlands, perfumes and unguents;
Abstinence from using a high or a large couch or seat;
Abstinence from receiving gold and silver;[6]
    are the ten means (of leading a moral life).

From *Buddhism in Translations*, trans. by Henry Clarke Warren (Cambridge, Mass.: Harvard University Press, 1896), pp. 396-7.

1. The *dharma*.
2. The Order (Vinaya).
3. This vow was interpreted by some Buddhist communities to mean complete vegetarianism; but others allowed the eating of meat as long as the animal had not been slaughtered specifically for the monks' benefit.
4. Solid food was forbidden after noon, though sweet drinks were allowed at any hour.
5. This refers only to secular, not liturgical music.
6. Though complete poverty was enjoined for individual monks, the monastery itself was permitted to receive gifts for the use of its members.

[Begging was an important part of a monk's daily life. It emphasized the vow of poverty: monks were permitted to own only a robe, an alms-bowl, a needle, a razor, and a cloth for straining drinking water (to avoid killing any minute animals it might contain). Begging was also supposed to teach humility and the patient endurance of insults.

The following description of the ideal mendicant is from the *Samyutta Nikaya*, the third principal division of the *Sutta Pitaka*.]

FROM THE SAMYUTTA NIKAYA

The Mendicant Ideal

Thus have I heard.

On a certain occasion The Blessed One was dwelling at Savatthi in Jetavana monastery in Anathapindika's Park. And there The Blessed One addressed the priests:[1]

"Priests," said he.

"Lord," said the priests to The Blessed One in reply.

And The Blessed One spoke as follows:

"Take pattern by the moon, O priests, when ye go a-begging. Hold aloof, O priests, both in body and in mind, never weary your welcome, nor be impudent to your benefactors.

"Just as a man, O priests, would regard a dilapidated well, or a rugged mountain, or a river difficult to ford, and hold aloof both in body and in mind, in exactly the same way, O priests, take pattern by the moon when ye go a-begging, hold aloof both in body and in mind, never weary your welcome, nor be impudent to your benefactors. . . .

"What do you say to this, O priests? What sort of a priest is worthy to go a-begging?"

"Reverend Sir, our beliefs derive from The Blessed One, have The Blessed One for their guide and their authority. Pray, Reverend Sir, let the answer to this find expression in the mouth of The Blessed One. Anything the priests hear from The Blessed One will be kept in mind."

Then The Blessed One waved his hand in the air: "Just as

From *Buddhism in Translations,* trans. by Henry Clarke Warren (Cambridge, Mass.: Harvard University Press, 1896), pp. 417-19.

1. I.e., monks.

my hand, O priests, is not caught, nor seized, nor held fast by the air, in exactly the same way, O priests, when the mind of a priest who goes a-begging is not caught, nor seized, nor held fast, and when, willing that they should gain who wish for gain, and that they should acquire merit who wish to acquire merit, he is as delighted and pleased with the gains of others as with his own, such a priest, O priests, is worthy to go a-begging. . . .

"What do you say to this, O priests? What sort of a priest is an unworthy teacher of the Doctrine? And what sort of a priest is a worthy teacher of the Doctrine?" . . .

And The Blessed One spoke as follows:

"Any priest, O priests, who in teaching the Doctrine to others thinks as follows: 'O that they may hear from me the Doctrine! and be won over by what they hear, and manifest delight towards me,' such a priest, O priests, is an unworthy teacher of the Doctrine.

"Any priest, O priests, who in teaching the Doctrine to others thinks as follows: 'The Doctrine has been well taught by The Blessed One, avails even in the present life, is immediate in its results, is inviting and conducive to salvation, and may be mastered by any intelligent man for himself. O that they may hear from me the Doctrine, and be enlightened by what they hear, and as a result of their enlightenment begin to act accordingly!' and thus teaches the Doctrine to others because of that Doctrine's intrinsic goodness, and because of compassion, mercy, and kindness, such a priest, O priests, is a worthy teacher of the Doctrine.

[Buddhists regard the human body as an obstacle to spiritual progress. Therefore the monk practices yoga to reduce his physical needs to the absolute minimum necessary for life. Buddhist literature frequently portrays the body as thoroughly disgusting, in order to make the point that physical pleasures are transitory and ultimately worthless.

The following discourse from the *Digha Nikaya* is supposed to have been spoken by the Buddha himself.]

From *Buddhism in Translations*, trans. by Henry Clarke Warren (Cambridge, Mass.: Harvard University Press, 1896), pp. 354-61.

FROM THE DIGHA NIKAYA

The Contemplation of the Body

And how, O priests, does a priest live, as respects the body, observant of the body?

Whenever, O priests, a priest, retiring to the forest, or to the foot of a tree, or to an uninhabited spot, sits him down cross-legged with body erect and contemplative faculty intent, and contemplates his expirations, and contemplates his inspirations, and in making a long expiration thoroughly comprehends the long expiration he is making, and in making a long inspiration thoroughly comprehends the long inspiration he is making, and in making a short expiration thoroughly comprehends the short expiration he is making, and in making a short inspiration thoroughly comprehends the short inspiration he is making, and trains himself to be conscious of all his expirations, and trains himself to be conscious of all his inspirations, and trains himself to quiet his expirations, and trains himself to quiet his inspirations. . . .

Thus, O priests, does a priest live, as respects the body, observant of the body. . . .

But again, O priests, a priest considers this body upwards from the soles of the feet, and downwards from the crown of the head, enclosed by skin, and full of all manner of uncleanness, saying, "There is in this body hair of the head, hair of the body, nails, teeth, skin, flesh, sinew, bone, marrow of the bones, kidneys, heart, liver, pleura, spleen, lungs, intestines, mesentery, stomach, faeces, bile, phlegm, pus, blood, sweat, fat, tears, lymph, saliva, snot, synovial fluid, urine." Just as if, O priests, there were a double-mouthed vessel full of various sorts of grain, to wit, sali-rice, common paddy, beans, pulse, sesame, and husked rice; and some intelligent man were to open it and consider its contents, saying, "This is sali-rice, this is common paddy, these are beans, this is pulse, this is sesame, this is husked rice;" in exactly the same way, O priests, a priest considers this body upwards from the soles of the feet, and downwards from the crown of the head, enclosed by skin, and full of all manner of uncleanness, saying, "There is in this body hair of the head, hair of the body, nails, teeth, skin, [etc., as before]. . . .

But again, O priests, a priest, if perchance he sees in a cemetery a decaying body one day dead, or two days dead, or three days dead, swollen, black, and full of festering putridity, he compares his own body, saying, "Verily, my body also has this nature, this destiny, and is not exempt."

But again, O priests, a priest, if perchance he sees in a cemetery a decaying body being eaten by crows, or being eaten by eagles, or being eaten by vultures, or being eaten by dogs, or being eaten by jackals, or being eaten by various kinds of insects, he compares his own body, saying, "Verily, my body also has this nature, this destiny, and is not exempt."

.   .   .   .

[This poem in exaltation of the monk's life is from the *Sutta Nipata*—which is probably the most ancient part of the *Khuddaka Nikaya*.]

FROM THE KHUDDAKA NIKAYA

The Rhinoceros

Hurt naught that lives; do harm
to none; yearn not for sons
or friends; but live—as lives
th' rhinoceros—alone!

Alone! Companionships
breed fondness; fondness leads

From *Buddha's Teachings, Being the Sutta-Nipata*, trans. from the Pali by Lord Chalmers, Vol. 37 of the Harvard Oriental Series (Cambridge, Mass.: Harvard University Press, 1932). Reprinted by permission of Harvard University Press and Oxford University Press, London.

to Ills as consequence;
so mark where fondness ends!

Go forth alone! To live
for friends and comrades means
your own weal sacrificed;
—beware acquaintances!

Alone! A man absorbed
in wife and child is like
a tree with tangled boughs.
Copy the bamboo-shoot,
  —which grows up straight and free.

Alone! As wild things—free
to range the woodlands—browse
at pleasure where they will,
the sage seeks liberty.

Alone! For, fellows give
a man no peace,—in hall,
on walks, or tours for alms.
No liberty dwells there.

Alone! Though fellowship
bring mirth, and children joy,
beware the severance
affection's ties entail.

Alone! To all the world
—north, south, and east and west—
be kindly; take what comes;
brave perils manfully.

Alone! Grumbling is rife
with homeless Almsmen,[1] as

---

1. Monks.

in worldlings' homes.—Fret not
o'er sons of other men.

Alone! As trees shed leaves,
discard the layman's garb
and sever dauntlessly
all ties to house and home.

Alone! If fortune grant
a trusty, staunch, true friend,
with him brave dangers, cleave
to him,—with mindfulness.

If fortune grant thee no
such friend, then, like a king
who quits a conquered realm,
go forth and live—alone.